ICEWINE

ICEWINE

THE COMPLETE STORY

JOHN SCHREINER

Warwick Publishing
Toronto
www.warwickgp.com

Also by John Schreiner:
 The World of Canadian Wine
 The Wineries of British Columbia
 The British Columbia Wine Companion
 Chardonnay and Friends

Icewine: The Complete Story
Copyright ©2001 by John Schreiner

We acknowledge the financial support of the Government of Canada through the Book Publishing Industry Development Program for our publishing activities.

ISBN: 1-894622-13-8

Published by Warwick Publishing Inc.
161 Frederick Street
Toronto, Ontario M5A 4P3 Canada
www.warwickgp.com

Distributed in the United States by LPC Group
22 Broad Street, Milford, CT O6460 USA

Distributed in Canada by General Distribution Services Ltd.
325 Humber College Blvd., Toronto, ON M9W 7C3

Designer: Kimberley Young
Editor: Melinda Tate
Cover photo: Steven Elphick
Printed and bound in Canada

To my brother, Joseph, whose sweet tooth would have better qualified him than me to research this book; and to the memory of Walter Hainle, who gave me my first taste of icewine on an unforgettable morning in 1983.

Contents

Acknowledgments

While I take full responsibility for the contents of this book, I am immeasurably indebted to others for assistance.

In Austria, the Österreichische Weinmarketingservice GmbH opened doors and organized an itinerary of exemplary thoroughness. Individuals who provided help include Laurenz Moser, one of Austria's best wine ambassadors abroad.

In Germany, the Deutsches Weininstitut provided introductions and support. Ron Fiorelli of the German Wine Information Agency in Toronto provided additional support and information. I also received invaluable help from such individuals as Manfred Völpel, the director of winemaking for Deinhard AG; Dr. Monika Christmann, the director of enology at Geisenheim; and Nik Weis, who introduced me to the other young winemakers of Leiwen in the Mosel.

In Slovenia, my itinerary was organized on short notice but efficiently by Janez Vrečer, the director of the Slovenian Wine Producers Association, who also helped with the translation at some winery visits.

For helping me with the engaging challenge of getting responses from the insular wine producers of Switzerland, I was aided by Virginie Dayanir of Gültig GmbH (a cork supplier); by Dr. Werner Koblet, a retired director of the Swiss research institute at

Wädenswil; by John Sloan, a Canadian diplomat in London who has written a book on Swiss wines; by Tessie Huber, an enthusiastic wine writer in Switzerland; and Hans Juerg Ritter, a wine merchant.

In Canada, I have received encouragement and counsel from Donald Ziraldo, the co-founder of Inniskillin, and John Peller, the president of Andrés Wines, among many others.

I do not pretend that this book includes every single icewine producer in the world, for the number of producers continues to grow. However, this is a comprehensive portrait with a representative number of producers from each country.

In the translation of certain important documents and letters, I am indebted to Ingrid Lyon and Dr. Bernard Hoeter, two Vancouver friends who were generous with their help. Documents from the Czech Republic were turned into lucid English by Vera Klokocka, a Czech-born consulting winemaker in Quebec and the former owner of the Hillside Estate Winery in British Columbia. I am also indebted to winemakers and winery owners for answering my questions and for providing me with labels and photographs. Most of all, I am grateful to have had the opportunity to taste about 400 of the world's most extraordinary sweet wines during my research.

Preface

This book was prompted five years ago when Eric von Krosigk, a winemaker in British Columbia, suggested that someone should do a book on icewine. In searching English-language wine literature, I expected to find that a European wine writer had already explored the topic. I was surprised to find perhaps the only virgin ground left on an international wine style.

Now that the research is complete, I know why no one had written the book yet. While the first icewine is said to have been made about two hundred years ago in Germany, for a long time it was not a wine of commercial importance to most producers but rather a treasure made rarely, only for friends and prestige tastings. It was when the Canadian producers in the 1990s began making icewine in previously unthinkable volumes that consumers and the wine trade took notice.

Many producers in this book made no icewine before 1990. Now, most make it with some regularity, including a number who use artificial freezers in jurisdictions (United States, Australia, New Zealand) where regulation allows simulated icewines.

As if to prove that icewine has arrived, fraudulent sweet wines made from concentrates and packaged to look like icewine have shown up in important Asian markets. In Canada, a number of amateurs make their own with purchased icewine must. The less scrupulous amateurs make syrupy copies from commercial concentrates.

Most of the wineries discussed in this book make icewine by natural methods. It is widely accepted that natural icewines are more refined, with nuanced flavors, than those made with artificial freezing. The layered flavors develop as grapes remain on the vines late into the year, or even into the next year, until they can be frozen naturally at -8°C or lower, when they are picked and processed, still frozen. The juice yield is perhaps 15 to 20 per cent by volume of what those same grapes would have produced if picked earlier for table wine. The reduced volume is one explanation for the high price of icewine. Another is the loss of grapes left in vineyards until Christmas and not always well protected against hungry wild creatures, inclement weather, or even thieves.

The high cost of icewine limits its market. For every consumer who has actually tasted icewine, there are many more who would like to but are reluctant to spend the money. Those who enjoy icewine vicariously through the pages of this book should seize the opportunity to taste when icewine is offered, usually for a modest fee, in a winery's tasting room — unless the winery is serving icewine in absurdly small glasses. The sensory pleasure of icewine begins with the aromas, which are lost if served in tiny glasses. Georg Riedel, the Austrian master of wine glass design, for some years recommended a 13¾-ounce, tulip-bowled crystal glass for Eiswein and Sauternes. In 2000, Riedel in cooperation with Canada's Inniskillin Wines designed a new glass just for icewine, with a 10-ounce bowl capacity. There is minor controversy that this is still too large but there is no doubt that icewine needs to be served in wine glasses large enough to display the appearance and the aroma and to deliver the wine efficiently to the palate.

The issue of wine glasses leads to the other question always asked about icewine: with what food should it be served? Excessively rich or sweet desserts that upstage the wine are not recommended; rather, nothing more complicated should be matched with icewine than a fruit flan or a soft, savory blue cheese like Cambozolo. Many argue the wine should just be enjoyed on its

own. This view was held by H.W. Yoxall, an English wine lover. In
his 1972 book, *The Enjoyment of Wine,* he wrote,

> If you are lucky enough to drink beerenauslese,
> and still luckier to drink trockenbeerenauslese
> hocks and moselles, and even Eiswein ... I do not
> think they should be treated as table-wines. It is
> difficult to match food with them; indeed, food is
> apt to obscure their qualities. They should be
> drunk by themselves.[1]

As with any wine, there are collectors of icewine, encouraged
by the view that icewine can live indefinitely. The four hundred or
so icewines tasted while this book was in preparation included several in Germany and Austria that were more than 30 years old and
were still drinking well. It would seem this is the ideal wine to collect, or to lay away at a child's birth with the intention of opening
it when the child reaches majority.

The argument for icewine's longevity rests on its high sugar
content and its acidity, both of which are preservatives. However,
as icewine ages, it is likely to maderize, acquiring an amber color
and nutty flavors — a vinous antique that is still interesting but
which has lost its essential charm of fresh, piquant fruit. Wine
always ages more quickly in the small bottles in which most
icewines are packaged than it does in larger bottles.

"There is no need to say an icewine lasts 20 to 25 years," Klaus
Reif, a Canadian winemaker, contends. "Let's be realistic: it doesn't."

The most age-worthy of icewine varietals very likely is
Riesling, most notably those made in Germany by winemakers who
might dispute their colleague in Canada. Reif recommends drinking even Riesling by its twelfth birthday. The Vidal icewines, which
are widely produced in Ontario, have a lifespan of 10 years.

"After 10 years, you lose the fruit flavors in icewine," Reif
maintains. "I like icewines when they are three to four years old."
Reif would keep the old vintages just for display: "They become
classics, almost like historic cars."

But as categorical as Reif is, no one can be certain how long a well-made icewine can live because, as recently as 25 years ago, extremely few were made anywhere.

An effort has been made in this book to avoid unnecessary jargon and to place technical information in a self-explanatory context. However, there are a few pieces of information that should be set out in advance.

Generally, I used the local word for icewine — *Eiswein* (*Eisweine*, plural) in German-speaking regions, *Ledeno Vino* in Slovenia, and so on.

Wherever the text refers to a winery's production in numbers of bottles, that means half bottles containing 375 ml of wine unless otherwise stated. Icewine almost always is packaged in these bottles; occasionally in 200 ml or 500 ml bottles and almost never in bottles of 750 ml or larger. The small bottles are not as good as larger ones for long-term cellaring. However, the small bottle — along with its lesser price — is the more practical size for a market and for the average dinner party.

There also are the technical terms for the measurement of the sweetness of the juice fermented into icewine. In North American vineyards, the sweetness is measured in degrees Brix, with one degree Brix equaling 18 grams of natural sugar per liter. Must for icewine in most North American wineries ranges from 35° to 42° Brix. In Germany, the equivalent measurement is degrees Oechsle (named for Ferdinand Oechsle, a physicist who refined the scale in the 1830s). That measure has been used in the references to German wines; a quick if slightly inexact way for readers to convert Oechsle to Brix is to divide by four. Eiswein musts typically range between 120° Oechsle and 170° Oechsle.

There is yet another measure used in Austria called degrees KMW, or Klosterneuburger Mostwaage, because it was devised at the wine school and research center in the former Augustinian monastery of Klosterneuburg, west of Vienna. It roughly approximates the Brix scale. One degree KMW equals five degrees Oechsle. Eiswein musts in Austria range between 26° and 35° KMW.

PART I

Icewine's Beginnings

1

Icewine: The New Star of Dessert Wines

The most prized dessert wine in the world is the luxuriously silken Sauternes from Château d'Yquem in France. Before the first German Eiswein even was made, Thomas Jefferson, the connoisseur and future American president who collected only the best French wines when he was the ambassador there, specifically asked for 250 bottles of the 1784 vintage for his cellar.[1] In the twentieth century, one of the very best vintages from Yquem was the 1921.

"Two years ago, I had the opportunity of tasting a 1921 Eiswein from the Saar compared with the 1921 Yquem," Gerhard Grans, an Eiswein producer in the Mosel, recounted in a 1999 interview. "The Eiswein was much more fresh than the Yquem."

Dr. Dirk Richter, another Mosel producer, recounts that he gained his largest customer in the United States after a vertical tasting in the early 1980s in which five vintages of his Eisweine were matched against several vintages of Yquem. "These wines were all much fresher," he says of the German wines.

Across the Atlantic, where Canada's Inniskillin is the world's largest icewine producer, Donald Ziraldo, its co-founder, also brings subtle references to Yquem into his remarks about icewine. Yquem, along with Tokaj Aszú Eszencia, has been a benchmark for great sweet wines since well before Jefferson's day, leading the tradition of the exquisite late harvest wines that have been drunk at Europe's best tables for several centuries. Icewine, however, has emerged only in the last two decades, a distinctive new style of dessert wine made possible by simple technology and by the willingness of men like Grans and Ziraldo to take big risks in their vineyards.

Grans does not argue that the 1921 Eiswein (which was made by a state-owned winery) was better than the 1921 Yquem. They were, he says, quite different wines. Eiswein, or icewine in English, stands on its own. For many producers, it is the ultimate wine of the vintage.

Germany's Weingut Dr. Bürklin-Wolf long has been one of that country's superlative producers of dry Riesling. Yet between 1978 and 1999, Bürklin-Wolf made Eiswein eight times — for "prestige" according to Annette Siegrist of the winery's export department. "It is important for a German winery not only to have top quality dry wines but also to be successful in the dessert wine category."

By tradition and often by law, icewine is made from grapes that have been frozen while still on the vine. Although artificially frozen icewine is generally forbidden, it is allowed in countries where the major vineyard regions never have serious winter. The iconoclastic Randall Grahm, the largest American producer of artificially frozen icewine at his Bonny Doon winery in California, gently pokes fun at the Europeans. In 1994 he told writer Jerome Richard: "The Germans are going to be very unhappy when they realize that they needn't careen around those 45-degree slopes at five in the morning, freezing their clusters off, when a simple trip to a commercial freezer would accomplish basically the same effect."[2]

The assertion is dubious, although appealing sweet wines can be made with the help of the equivalent of the local morgue. These wines improve their appeal by selling typically for half the price of icewines, suggesting that the artificially frozen style occupies a value category of its own.

This technique of cryo-extraction, as it is called, is well known in Sauternes, where some producers began employing it in the mid-1980s to salvage rainy vintages. When vineyards of harvest-ready botrytized grapes suddenly are drenched, the grapes can be picked, placed immediately in a commercial freezer at about -5°C and crushed the following day. The mild freezing not only prevents the botrytis from turning into rot; it also concentrates the juice recovered at pressing, precisely as freezing concentrates icewine must. It is not the intent that cryo-extraction be used routinely when the harvest weather is fine but primarily when a harvest needs to be saved from inclement weather.[3]

Riesling is the premier variety for icewine, possessing a fine acidity that imparts a star-like sparkle to cleanly made icewines. Many producers prefer highly aromatic varieties, most notably Scheurebe and Muscat. The all-purpose white variety in Austria, Grüner Veltliner, brings its intriguing white pepper varietal character to Eisweine. In Slovenia and Austria, plump and juicy examples are made with Welschriesling.

Around the world, the varietal array for icewine runs the gamut from Chardonnay to Zweigelt. In North America, Vidal, a toughskinned variety notable for the voluptuous aroma and flavors of the wine, is very widely used. The Vidal berries have a superior ability to cling to the vines and resist rot a month or two beyond the normal end of harvest. The sharp frost — the minimum required typically is -8°C in Canada and much of Europe — freezes the water in the grapes while still leaving the natural sugar and fruit acids as a syrupy liquid. The grapes are pressed, still frozen, immediately after being picked and the syrup is then fermented into wines of intense aroma and taste.

The signature of a great icewine is the balancing tension between the sweetness and the acidity, with seductive tropical fruit flavors followed by a crisp, bracing finish which, when the wine is swallowed, is vividly refreshing. This brilliantly focused acidity distinguishes icewines from Sauternes and accounts for the freshness that Gerhard Grans found in the example from 1921.

While almost every wine region in the world produces dessert wines, naturally made icewine is limited to the vineyards in the northern hemisphere, beginning in Germany more than two hundred years ago. Icewine is made naturally now in Austria, Luxembourg, Croatia, Slovenia, the Czech Republic, Hungary, Romania, Switzerland, in the northern United States, and massively in Canada. The cold winters and the sturdy grape varieties in their vineyards enable the Canadians to produce between one million and two million bottles (375 milliliter bottles) a year, an overwhelming volume compared with Europe's output. Icewine for a European producer is a small-volume artisanal product made to gain prestige.

The world's first icewine, according to commonly accepted references in Germany,[4] was made in 1794 in the German wine region of Franconia, near the city of Würzburg. Europe's weather toward the end of the eighteenth century had been colder than normal as the northern hemisphere was experiencing what climatologists have called the Little Ice Age, a period of global cooling perhaps caused by sun spot activity that lasted from 1500 to about 1850.

France had an especially hard winter in 1788–89 and five years later, Europe remained gripped by abnormal weather. Franconian grape growers, desperate for adequate maturity in their grapes after a cool summer, still had their Riesling — a late-ripening grape at the best of times — on the vine when an unexpectedly hard frost occurred early in November. A producer whose identity is not recorded sought to salvage the vintage by pressing the frozen grapes. A similar anecdote is recounted in a 1969 volume, *The Wine Book,* by Alexander Dorozynski and Bibiane Bell, but with 1842 assigned as the date when it all began.

"Growers in Traben-Trarbach on the Moselle were grieved to see their grapes frozen hard in the vineyards by an untimely frost," the authors wrote. "They harvested the grapes nevertheless, but pressed them separately, for fear of spoiling the rest of the vintage. To their surprise, the resulting must, though sparse, was exceedingly sweet and pure ... ."[5]

To further cloud the genesis of Eiswein, there is a third reference in the 1852 edition of the *Yearbook of Fruit and Wine Producers of Germany,* a copy of which can be found in the library at Geisenheim.

> The cellarman Oppmann of the Royal Cellars in Würzburg reported about his experiences of the later harvested crops in 1835. During the harvest,

frost appeared beginning in mid-November so that the berries were frozen. Very good timing is crucial. If the berries warmed up too much, the watery parts which have been converted into ice would come back to the must as water, which results in strong frost aromas and does not do any good to the wine. Only a few centigrades of warming made it possible to press the berries and to obtain the ingredients of the berries only, leaving the watery parts as ice in the press. The result was a must with a high concentration of sugar and aromas, which did not have any frost aromas at all. The must was of very unique quality and hence was treated and stored separately. The quality was even far better than those of wines which have been harvested without being affected by frost, even if grown on better terroir. The remaining parts in the press, which only contained watery elements, are not of any further use either to make a Trester [distilled spirit] or any other drinkable product.[6]

(The Würzburg estate in Franconia, with a history dating from 1128, continues to make Eiswein. Its 1997 Würzburger Stein Rieslaner Eiswein won the trophy for the best German wine in the 1998 Japan Wine Challenge.)

Very likely, there were other opportunistic icewines made in years when winter came early but went unrecorded, blended into other dessert wines of the vintage. The accidental icewines would have been similar to the sweet late harvest wines already being made from grapes shriveled and concentrated by botrytis, the so-called noble rot, before being picked late in the year. German wine lore has it that the first botrytis-affected wine was made in 1775 at Schloss Johannisberg, the storied estate on the Rhine whose vineyard potential had been discovered a millennium earlier by Charlemagne.

The technique of making wine from berries affected by the noble rot fungus was certainly known earlier elsewhere. There are records of Yquem vintages as early as 1753 and of Tokaj wines two centuries before that. However, producers then were so at the mercy of nature that it was challenging to make such wines consistently each year. Schloss Johannisberg, in spite of its experience with noble rot wine, made no wine at all in 1816, leaving its Riesling grapes unharvested. The year before an erupting Indonesian volcano called Tambora threw so much ash into the atmosphere that 1816 was recorded in Europe as the year without summer, with snow and frost at midyear.

Almost no one would have set out deliberately to make an icewine each year until the 1960s; one German winewriter once calculated that there only were 10 Eiswein vintages between 1875 and 1962. It is apparent that very little Eiswein made it to market. In his *The Great Vintage Wine Book,* the British writer Michael Broadbent,[7] who is renowned for having tasted more than 70,000 wines in his distinguished career, began the notes in the book's German wine section with a 1653 vintage table wine from Rüdesheim; but a 1961 was the first Eiswein vintage on which he commented. The wine was a Mercer Königslay Klosterberg Spätlese Eiswein from the Mosel, made from grapes harvested on November 25, 1961. Broadbent was disappointed that the bouquet had been deadened by too much sulphur.[8]

Tastings of other Eisweine from later vintages seldom aroused much enthusiasm from Broadbent, an extravagant admirer of other German late harvest wines. He dismissed a 1962 Niersteiner Auflangen Eiswein Christwein as a "quite nicewein." After tasting a 1970 Eiswein from a Mosel producer, he groused: "These ice wines seem gimmicky to me. Give me a wine made from beautifully sun-ripened grapes any day."[9]

Broadbent was not alone in his lukewarm regard for icewines. Fellow British wine writer Hugh Johnson, in *Wine,* the 1966 book that launched his reputation, referred to icewines as "more as a curiosity — for the German wine-growers love showing off — than as a commercial proposition."[10]

The accuracy of that observation is evidenced by the Germans' custom, when they did make a rare icewine, of naming it for the day of the saint or religious festival on which the grapes were picked. A St. Nikolaus was one made from grapes picked on December 6, that saint's day; wines made from grapes picked on New Year's Eve were called St. Sylvester wine. Those made from Christmas Day grapes — Broadbent's "nicewein" was such an example — were called Christwein. Those made from grapes harvested on January 6, the feast of the three kings who first visited the child Jesus, were called Dreikönigswein (Three Kings Wine).

The humorless German wine law of 1971 sadly banished these names, but clever winemakers still find a way to echo tradition. Louis Guntrum of Nierstein, where winemaking history dates from 1648, harvested its 1996 Eiswein before dawn on Christmas that year, at a frigid temperature of -12°C and under the only Christmas-night full moon between 1856 and 2102. This truly rare wine, an Oppenheimer Herrenberg Silvaner, has been put in elegant crystal and marketed as Cristallo.

"One thing is for sure," asserts Austrian-born Karl Kaiser, a leading icewine maker and the other founder with Ziraldo of Canada's Inniskillin winery, "icewine was not that highly respected before 1983." The German wine law of 1971 did not assign a regulatory class of its own to Eiswein but left it an adjunct to other classes, as in Spätlese-Eiswein.

Eiswein achieved its own regulatory class in 1983, evidence that enough producers had begun to make it that the standards needed to be clarified. That was the first year, for example, that the Germans set -7°C (later -8°C) as the minimum temperature at which grapes could be picked for icewine. This was much more precise than an earlier rule that all icewine grapes had to be picked before 10 A.M., on the sensible presumption that the coldest part of the day is at or just after dawn, when, even today, most icewine grapes are picked.

Eiswein only received its own category long after German winemakers in the 1960s learned to make it systematically, protecting their winter-harvest grapes by netting them against birds or shielding them from rain with plastic sheets. The same simple technology was required elsewhere as well before icewine could be produced successfully. Kaiser learned that in 1983: he left grapes hanging unprotected in the vineyard for icewine, only to lose the entire harvest one afternoon to a voracious flock of starlings. Ever since, he has used nets.

Making icewine is fraught with risk. In the northern hemisphere, the normal harvest generally is complete by the end of October while the botrytis-affected grapes for Sauternes and other noble-rot wines are usually picked by the end of November. Icewine grapes are occasionally picked in November but more typically in December and sometimes as late as mid-February of the following year.

During that extended hang time, the grapes — even when protected — are vulnerable to birds and animals, to being knocked to the ground by wind storms, or to rotting after rain storms. If it does not rain, the healthy grapes slowly shrivel, reducing the ultimate yield of juice. This is one reason why botrytis, which is desirable for most other dessert wines, is unwanted in an icewine vineyard: the fungus does its work precisely by dehydrating individual grapes. It would suck the icewine grapes dry.

As it is, at least three-quarters of the normal volume of a grape is sacrificed when icewine is made instead of table wine. This accounts for the high price of icewine, particularly in Europe where it is a hand-crafted niche wine sold to collectors or the best restaurants. In Canada, some high-volume producers price it somewhat lower to reflect their economies of scale, perhaps to the detriment of those attempting to benchmark Yquem and its attendant prestige.

2

The Father of Eiswein

The leading German authority on Eiswein is Dr. Hans Georg Ambrosi, called the father of Eiswein by some of his peers. From 1966 until his retirement in 1990, he was the director of the Rheingau State Domaine — the Hessische Staatsweingüter — at Eltville, described by Hugh Johnson as "one of the greatest wine estates on earth."[1]

Ambrosi was born in Romania in 1925 into a family whose wine estates in Transylvania had been producing for several generations. Indeed, the Ambrosi estates continue to make wine but under other owners, for the Ambrosi family and most of the other Germans in this eight-century-old German-speaking enclave became refugees in western Europe after World War II.

Ambrosi enrolled at Geisenheim, the premier German wine university. He earned a doctorate in 1953 and spent the next two years as a teacher and scientist there. Skeptical that Germany would ever recover from war damage, he took a job in 1955 in South Africa at the University of Stellenbosch.

In 1966, his final year in South Africa, he made his first Eiswein. "That was more or less a joke," he said years later, recalling the episode in the sun-drenched garden of his comfortable retirement home not far from Kloster Eberbach, the 850-year-old former monastery on the Rhine that was the base of his many triumphs in wine.

At the time, there were many Germans living and working in the South African wine country, individuals who had gone there for much the same reason that Dr. Ambrosi did. In South Africa, his career blossomed and he became one of the viticultural leaders in the Cape.

In his final year there, a group of fellow Germans there, nostalgic for the dessert wines of the homeland, presented their winemaking friend with a truckload of Steen grapes — as Chenin Blanc is called in South Africa — and asked him to produce Eiswein. The grapes were frozen to -12°C overnight in a cold storage and were crushed the next day, with Ambrosi then fermenting the juice.

In Germany, making icewine artificially would have violated both tradition and the law. In South Africa, Dr. Ambrosi had neither to restrict him. The result fell short of the classic icewines made later under Ambrosi's direction, lacking acidity and thus being far too sweet. Yet his friends were pleased with the result, while he had learned lessons that were to prove useful almost immediately.

In 1966, at the urging of former colleagues at Geisenheim, Ambrosi applied for and got the job of director of the Staatsweingüter, one of the most prestigious posts in German wine and one of the most secure. As a state civil servant, Ambrosi was basically immune from being fired. That was a good thing. A strong-willed and volatile man, he got frequent letters of reprimand from his superiors in the public service who often were uncomfortable whenever their director once again had chosen to break new ground in winemaking.

Eiswein was one of these sensitive issues. When Ambrosi took over his new job and toured the extensive vineyards controlled by the Staatsweingüter, he found that the manager of one, the Assmannshäuser Höllenberg vineyard, had already made icewine in 1965 and was keen to continue doing so. Ambrosi needed no more encouragement to run with the idea.

Many other winemakers scoffed that icewine was simply not economic and that Ambrosi was only able to do it because his operation was subsidized by the state. He defused his critics by producing well-made icewines that commanded significant premiums at the winery's spring auctions. Ambrosi further deflated his opponents by publishing a detailed study showing how much more profitable icewine was than standard table wines from the same grapes.

Ambrosi had a grand stage on which to play out his ideas. Properly known as the Verwaltung der Staatsweingüter, this is one of Germany's largest wine estates, with about two hundred hectares of vines divided among six superb sites on the north bank of the Rhine, the most distinguished of which is the 31-hectare walled vineyard called Steinberg.

The vineyards were operated for centuries by monasteries; the former Cistercian monastery of Kloster Eberbach, founded in 1136 and beautifully renovated under Ambrosi, became the ceremonial headquarters. The vineyards were taken away from the monks in 1803 during the Napoleonic wars and were given to the Duke of Nassau. In 1866, ownership transferred to the King of Prussia and finally in 1946 to the state government of Hesse.

The Domaine's wines, as Hugh Johnson noted, "fetch high prices at auction, particularly the Eiswein, which it has made a specialty."[2] That was Dr. Ambrosi's doing. "Of course [German] ice wines have been made for decades — notably in 1875, 1880, 1890, 1902, 1908, 1912, 1949, 1950, 1961 and 1962 — but usually as an instantaneous exploitation of a freak frost," Stephen Brook wrote in a 1987 book on dessert wines. "Dr. Ambrosi set out to make Eiswein on a routine basis."[3]

The Rheingau had several centuries of tradition in the production of dessert wines and Ambrosi produced many noble rot wines when vineyards under his control were blessed with the proper conditions. However, he had other sites less likely to be so infected. Vines were set aside for Eiswein in those parts of vineyards where frost occurred first and where the grapes were healthy, untouched by noble rot — "the reverse of late harvest," he points out.

The consistent production of icewine was then highly unusual. Eiswein was an opportunistic rarity, made either when an early frost caught some winemakers with unharvested grapes or, as Hugh Johnson wrote, when "at the end of a merely average vintage, there are good-looking bunches of grapes left in the vine-yard which the grower is reluctant to pick; they give him the sporting chance of making an 'Eiswein'."[4] Ambrosi was able to give himself significantly better than a sporting chance; while he was in charge, he produced Eiswein at the domain every year but 1968. As many as three hundred pickers would be hired each year and the profits from the sale of the Eiswein easily covered the labor costs and then some.

Ambrosi and his managers selected low-lying patches of vine-yard most likely to get the hard frost needed for Eiswein. The man-ager at Assmannshausen had already concluded that grapes left hanging for months beyond the usual harvest date needed protec-tion from rain, wind and birds. His first effort at covering the vines with plastic sheets was unsatisfactory because the winds whipped the sheets away. After a few years of trial and error, Ambrosi and his vineyard managers refined the protection to draping the plastic sheeting along the grape zone only, a tunnel of plastic they called "hot pants." This pioneering technique has evolved considerably over the past 30 years as better netting materials have been devel-oped, but Ambrosi's basic concept remains sound.

Ambrosi mastered a range of technical issues, including han-dling the subtle but important balance between the wine's acidity and its residual sweetness. In 1977, a relatively unripe vintage, the icewine must had only 106° Oechsle (a German measurement that equates to about 24° Brix) and it was necessary to reduce the acidi-ty. (German wine law since 1982 requires a minimum must weight of 125° Oechsle.)

On occasion, circumstances enabled Ambrosi to make a block-buster. In the 1970 vintage, he harvested grapes at the estate's Hochheim vineyard just before dawn on January 6, 1971, at -13°C, to yield a must weight of 194° Oechsle and griping acidity of 16.2 grams per liter. This wine, of which 451 bottles were produced, established the Staatsweingüter's reputation for Eisweine which, previously, had been selling for less than its botrytized dessert wines. The wine, labeled Dreikönigs-Eiswein or Three Kings for the religious feast day on which it was picked, fetched a price of 206

Deutschmarks for a 700 ml bottle, then a record for Eiswein, at the May auction in Kloster Eberbach.[5] The Staatsweingüter soon began winning gold medals at international competitions for its Eiswein, now selling for more than its botrytized wines.

The style of the Ambrosi (and German) Eisweine is quite the opposite of botrytized dessert wines. While a trace of botrytis is possible, the usual practice is to make the wine with grapes that are as clean and healthy as possible, if only to avoid the dehydration that botrytis would cause in a prolonged hang time.

The desired object with icewine is to achieve fresh and vibrant flavors and aromas. The Riesling grape is excellent for this purpose because, even before the grapes are fully mature, the aromatic characters have developed, stepping out front brilliantly when concentrated by frost. Riesling also possesses a naturally high acidity which also is concentrated by freezing. In his initial years of making Eiswein, Dr. Ambrosi struggled with controlling this mouth-ripping acidity until he hit upon the technique of using the natural sugars to balance the acidity. This means extracting only the sweetest portion of the juice — that which comes first from the press — and stopping the process when the juice becomes somewhat diluted.

Ambrosi preferred, as do most winemakers, a relatively quick fermentation, followed by early bottling of the wine to preserve the freshness. "The big advantage of icewine is that you can drink it almost immediately," he says. "It can be sold already two months after you bottle it. Icewine should be clean, clean, clean — like summer wine, like terrace wine." And that is the paradox of well-made icewine: It is appealing early but, in Ambrosi's view, it can age easily for half a century.

What is the future of Eiswein? "Very good," Ambrosi insists, "and the bloody Germans don't understand that!" It irritates him that Geisenheim, which requires all of its graduates to write theses, does not provide courses and require theses in Eiswein production. "It is a niche product," responds Dr. Monika Christmann, the youthful director of enology at Geisenheim. "I don't know of any winery here that says they want to produce it every year."

Geisenheim, founded in 1872 and housed in a utilitarian collection of buildings at the edge of a medieval town beside the Rhine, operates a small commercial winery in which its research scientists and its students demonstrate their skill on a practical scale. Their success is measured in part through the institution's wine sales outlet. The wines on the price list published late in 1998 ranged from simple table wines to brandies. The most expensive was a 1994 Riesling Eiswein at DM150, or about $120, for a half-liter bottle. That was Dr. Christmann's first, and so far only, Eiswein, something of a rite of passage made in her first vintage as the head of winemaking there. "This is the highest perfection of making wine," she believes.

Feeling the need to prove she was up to the job at Geisenheim, Christmann took advantage of the healthy grapes at vintage in 1994 to set aside about four tonnes on the vine for Eiswein. Having put her reputation on the line, she waited and waited — for two months — until the required frost occurred that enabled her to harvest enough grapes to make about four hundred liters of wine. The resulting Eiswein, perfectly balanced with a honeyed aroma and a rich but not heavy palate, amply proved that she could scale the heights of winemaking.

"I said, 'That's it for the next 10 years,'" she admitted later. It is not that she is afraid of making another Eiswein vintage after her triumph in 1994. Unlike Ambrosi, she questions whether Eiswein is truly economic, given the risk that growers take, including the difficulty of finding pickers prepared to rise on Christmas morning and head for bitterly cold vineyards. It would be easier, she teases, to make a nice Eiswein artificially, through cryo-extraction. But she does not advocate that Germany ever take shortcuts in making Eiswein. "What makes them so special would be missing," she acknowledges.

The same heresy of cryo-extraction is raised by Dr. Dirk Richter, an Eiswein specialist in the Mosel, when he discusses how producers might reduce the risks inherent in making winter-harvest wines. "Why shouldn't I take the grapes at the end of October, bring them to the cold storage and let them freeze?" he asks rhetorically. "Which certainly might be done and then taken out when other people make proper Eiswein."

However, Richter doubts that the very best Eiswein can be

made artificially. "By hanging in the fresh air, with rain and with storms, the grapes get a totally different taste. There is much more mineral enrichment and the flavor is different. There is a difference, a noticeable difference."

A less earnest but equally emphatic rejection of freezer wine comes from Dr. Franz Werner Michel, the seventh-generation owner of Domdechant Werner'sches Weingut in Hochheim. "I prefer love *in vino* instead of *in vitro*. The result might be the same but not the pleasure." The matter is academic: Hans Ambrosi's South African "joke" is not permitted, neither in Germany nor in the other major areas of icewine production.

PART II

Eiswein in Germany and Austria

3
Eiswein Specialists

osel winemaker Dr. Dirk Richter, one of Germany's Eiswein specialists, strokes his neat beard reflectively and makes a confession about each Eiswein harvest. "It's a nerve-wracking time." Many events set this apart from his other winemaking: rising several times on dreary December nights to check the thermometer; preventing the wild boar from ravaging the vineyard; worrying that not all pickers will arrive as promised; agonizing that the grapes will deteriorate under freeze-thaw-freeze cycles.

Richter has a vivid recollection, supported by precise records, of the dates and the circumstances of every Eiswein vintage in the Mülheimer Helenenkloster vineyard since the first in 1961. There was, for example, the Christwein, or Christmas Day, Eiswein of 1986. As Richter and his father, Horst, went to church early on Christmas Eve, it was apparent that the temperature was dropping quickly. The acre of Riesling still on the vine would have to be picked very early the next morning, even if the friends and neighbors who had agreed to pick might still be celebrating from the evening before or would be busy with Christmas Day preparations.

The Richters rose at four in the morning, summoned the other pickers — in some cases, from all-night parties — and hurried to the little vineyard, where they harvested the grapes under improvised floodlights. "All the people came and helped," he says. "There was not a single exception." The very early start, Richter explains, was required to complete the harvest by eight in the morning so that the women among the crew could prepare elaborately festive Christmas luncheons.

Countless hundreds of German producers now make Eisweine regularly. As in North America, many only began doing so in the final two decades of the twentieth century with the emergence of markets for sweet wines at home and in Asia. The Weingut Max Ferd. Richter stands apart as an early producer and a consistent one, having grasped that fine Eisweine burnish a winery's reputation.

"It was possible to make it a riding horse for the estate, to give an identity for the estate," Richter explains. "When people think of Eiswein, our name is often involved. As we have done it always from the same vineyard, it is a bit of a collector's item."

Owned by the Richter family since 1680, this winery with its baroque estate house is one of the Mosel's most respected producers, with 14 hectares of vineyards located in some of the best sites in the valley. The Helenenkloster vineyard occupies a southwestern exposure on a hill overlooking Mülheim, a picturesque village just south of Bernkastel. Dating from the thirteenth century, the vineyard belonged to a nearby convent from which it derives its name. When the property was secularized, the Richter family acquired ownership in 1813.

Less than a hectare in size, it is one of the smallest single vineyards so designated under the German wine law of 1971. Richter believes that the sturdy stone wall on the western border of the vineyard has helped create the frost-retaining microclimate on the lower part of the slope that makes it suitable for Eiswein even in difficult years. In 1976 when, according to Richter, almost no other German producer was able to make Eiswein, some 330 liters were made from the Helenenkloster.

Richter's records of two dozen Eiswein vintages provide the unfailing correlation between early harvests and both the quantity and quality of the resulting Eiswein. Johannes Selbach, one of the owners of Weingut Selbach-Oster at Zeltingen, just north of Bernkastel, concurs: "The best Eisweine are always made in the year of the vintage." The grapes for both the 1995 and 1997 vintage were picked in January of the following year but Selbach did not bottle the Eiswein because he considered it lacking in grace and elegance. It is such attention to detail that has made Selbach-Oster and Max Ferd. Richter seasoned Eiswein specialists, members of a fellowship that includes such distinguished estates as the Hessische Staatsweingüter, Schloss Schönborn, and Schloss Johannisberg on the Rhine, all of them frequent producers since the 1960s.

The first recorded Eiswein vintage at Schloss Johannisberg was 1858, the next was 1890, and the third was 1950, illustrating that Eiswein formerly was an accident of nature and not, as is so common now, the result of deliberate planning backed up by technology, such as netting or plastic sheets to protect the grapes from rain, not generally available until the 1970s. The producers still need nature to deliver the hard frost when the grapes remain healthy, capable of wines unblemished by the off-flavors of deteriorating fruit.

"My ideal ingredient," Selbach says, "would be Spätlese to Auslese ripe grapes that are yellow, that have texture, that have acidity, that are juicy. This is my ideal to work with to make Eiswein. As soon as you get speckled grapes that are leaning toward botrytis, you lose acidity, you lose crunchiness. You lose texture, and with it, you lose delicacy and elegance in the wine."

The producers begin preparing in the spring by pruning the vines differently for Eiswein (more buds and canes remain on the vines) than for other table wines. The vines set aside for Eiswein are managed somewhat differently all year, with great care taken to keep the vineyard in the soundest and healthiest condition late into the year. Selbach attributes the swelling production of Eiswein in the 1980s not just to better technology but also to the more challenging quality standards mandated by the 1982 revision of the German wine law.

"In the 1960s and 1970s you could make an Eiswein from anything that froze deep enough," he says. "You could have unripe grapes and they froze and it was Eiswein Spätlese ... a lean wine with an Earl Grey–tea flavor which you could classify as interesting but not a flagship wine. In 1982 they changed the law that the grapes had to have a 110° Oechsle minimum [the sweetness required for a

Beerenauslese wine]. I think that was the birth of some of the greatest Eisweine because the standard was raised so high."

Schloss Johannisberg is famously associated with accidental discovery of botrytis-affected wine in 1775 and could have made — but did not — one of the first Eisweine. The estate has been producing wine for almost 1,200 years. It is said that the Emperor Charlemagne (768–814), who had a castle across the Rhine at Ingleheim, observed that the steeply inclined southern slopes of Johannisberg were the earliest to be clear of snow each spring. He ordered that the obviously warm slope be planted in vines. It is not known whether the emperor ever tasted a wine from this slope but his successor, Ludwig the Pious, recorded the production of six thousand liters of wine in 817.[1]

Benedictine monks established a monastery on the hill in 1100 and, 30 years later, a basilica dedicated to St. John the Baptist and thus the hill came to be called Johannisberg. The monks gradually acquired, usually as gifts, surrounding vineyard land. The property came under the control of the Prince-Abbot of Fulda in 1716.

Abbots, especially prince-abbots, were powerful and those in their employ waited for their instructions. The decision on when to begin the harvest was made by the abbot on the advice of his vineyard managers, who worked some considerable distance from the abbot's palace. In 1775 the courier from the Johannisberg vineyard seeking the bishop's permission to harvest took three weeks to complete what should have been a four-day round trip. During that delay, the grapes became affected with botrytis, a dehydrating fungus, and had shriveled by the time the courier returned with the instruction that the harvest could start. The estate did its best with those grapes — and its best was said to the first of the luscious German late harvest Rieslings, the wine having achieved a wonderful intensity of flavor from its unintended additional hang time.

There is documented support of this account, for the administrator at the Schloss, Johann Michael Engert, made a note in his cellarbook the following April that "I have never tasted such a wine before."[2] A few years later, Thomas Jefferson, the great American wine lover and a founder of the Republic, enthusiastically described Schloss Johannisberg's wines as "the best made on the Rhine without comparison."[3] The clerics did not have many years to savor this accidental creation for, in 1802, Schloss Johannisberg was secularized, becoming briefly the property of the Prince of Orange before ending up in Napoleon's hands.

After the Napoleonic Wars, it was taken over by the Austrian royal house which in turn gave it to their Chancellor, Clemens Wenzelaus L. Prince von Metternich-Winneberg as a reward for his sage diplomacy. He took control in the summer of 1816, a miserably cold year resulting from a dark blanket of volcanic ash in the upper atmosphere.

That autumn, like the Prince-Abbot, he also had a vintage decision to make. An unusually early frost settled on the normally sun-bathed slopes of Schloss Johannisberg before the harvest had begun. On learning that, the prince told the vineyard managers simply to abandon the harvest and make no wine at all. Undoubtedly, it would not have occurred to them that wine could be made from frozen grapes, and another generation passed before the first Eiswein was made there.

It was only in 1965, after three earlier accidental vintages over more than a century, that Schloss Johannisberg began making Eiswein more or less regularly, always from the same vineyard on a low-lying flat at the northern edge of its property, the only part of the Schloss's extensive holdings where the freeze is sufficiently deep in almost every year to yield Eiswein.

Two technologies empowered European Eiswein producers. One was the development by Willmes, a German manufacturer, of its high-pressure bladder press, which Dirk Richter says enabled the Richters in 1961 to begin producing Eiswein from the Helenenkloster vineyard. "For the first time it was possible to make Eiswein with that new pressing technique," he maintains.

Squeezing the essence from grapes that are nearly as hard as marbles requires considerable pressure. It can be done, and often still is, with sturdy basket presses, but the Willmes press works faster and is more efficient. Its tough internal bladder, as thick as an elephant's hide, is inflated rapidly to crush the grapes outward against a perforated drum, with the juice pouring through the perforations.

This design has been succeeded by bladder presses operating gently at lower pressures, desirable for quality table wines but less useful for Eiswein. When the 650-year-old Schloss Schönborn at Hattenheim replaced its presses in the mid-1990s, the old Willmes presses were purchased by an icewine producer in British Columbia, Gehringer Brothers.

"It was a really good idea for them," says Günther Thies, Schönborn's general director, a note of regret in his voice. While this producer, which only began making Eisweine in the 1960s, makes only about two hundred and fifty liters a year, Thies would still prefer to have the old but efficient Willmes press for the job. "You have to be very fast here, in our climatic conditions," he says, glancing out the window where the temperature-moderating Rhine flows mightily only a few hundred yards away.

The other empowering technology was the use either of nets or of perforated plastic sheets to protect the late-hanging grapes from birds or wind and rain damage. In Germany, the Hessische Staatsweingüter — the wine-producing estates on the Rhine owned by the state of Hesse — is credited as the first producer to begin using protective covering systematically. As a result, this winery has made Eiswein from one or other of its vineyards almost every year since 1965. Between six and ten hectares of vines are protected each vintage, making the Staatsweingüter one of Germany's most important producers of Eiswein, including not only classic examples from Riesling but also Eiswein from Pinot Blanc and Pinot Gris.

Since 1972, because its properties include one of the Rhine's best red wine vineyards at Assmannshausen, this producer also has been making Eiswein from Spätburgunder (Pinot Noir). These red-skinned grapes, highly visible in an otherwise barren winter vineyard, must be netted against birds.

Winter harvest grapes also lure ravenous packs of wild boars from the woodlands bordering many German vineyards. Richter is among those winemakers who deploy electric fences, the only effective deterrent to boar other than a good huntsman. No Eiswein was made in 1991 from the Helenenkloster after a pack of 17 boars stripped the vineyard clean in a single night.

"We will put a double electric fence around the vineyard," Johannes Selbach says of his Bernkastel Badstube vineyard where the vines are trained on individual posts and cannot be netted. "Why a double electric fence? Boars have very thick skins and are addicted gourmets. They will run through a single wire and it does not take them more than two minutes to devastate a vineyard.

"In 1996 when we made splendid Eiswein in Bernkastel, my friend who had a vineyard maybe a stone's throw away from ours, he had hung soap, 50 bars of soap, in and around the vineyard to deter the boars. It worked until the frost dropped very deeply and there was no moisture to carry the smell. The very night before the harvest — it was Christmas night — they ate his grapes."

The Selbach crew picked early Christmas morning from a vineyard full of healthy frozen grapes, unaware of what had happened just up the road. "We were celebrating how great the grapes were. I saw his group — he had 25 pickers — and he came up to us and looked into our bins and he was almost weeping. He got maybe five buckets of juice."

Electric fencing now has replaced the bars of soap. It also is common and somewhat effective to scatter human hair, collected from local barbershops, among vines because the scent deters the boars.

The vineyards set aside for Eiswein are nurtured through the season with that end in mind. "All of the treatment is done with the idea of very, very late grape-picking," Richter says. "The leaves tend to be greener much longer than anywhere else. By the end of October, we put nets around the grapes." From then until harvest, the vineyard is scoured regularly, even daily, to remove any unhealthy grapes, leaving only the cleanest fruit for the final Eiswein picking.

Because of the risks, some producers limit their exposure to loss by leaving a small quantity of grapes hanging for perhaps two or three weeks after the regular harvest is done, usually by the end of October. In occasional years, like 1998, the deep cold occurs by the third week of November and a good quantity of very fine Eiswein can be made. Selbach says that 1998, because of the good quantities that were produced, was one of the few vintages in which Eiswein was truly profitable. If nature does not deliver the cold weather by then, the cautious producers pick for late harvest wines. For the steely gamblers like Richter, it is Eiswein or bust.

"When you decide to go for Eiswein, then you have to make the complete mental write-off of your grapes in the vineyard," he says. "You may no longer think about the grapes. Once you decide to go for the Eiswein, you should forget about it. If you get a positive result, you can be happy, but you may not count on it."

One German producer in the vintage of 1996 dedicated itself exclusively to making Eiswein but did not continue this venture beyond that vintage. Most German and Austrian producers believe that such a narrow scope is both impractical (a producer needs more than one wine in its selection) and risky. The top producers set out to make wine in every category, with Eiswein as the ultimate achievement.

Johannes Selbach finds that the excitement of the vintage is so intense that he has never been aware of feeling cold while picking the grapes and he has never had difficulty getting pickers to help.

"Even our oldest help will be insulted if we don't call him or her to pick. It is the crowning achievement of our vintage. Even in 1996 when we picked on Christmas morning, December 25, everybody was there. Everybody! It's a special, special atmosphere. If it is perfect Eiswein weather, it is crisp and cold and you have the moon and the stars, and it is enchanting."

The 1996 harvest on the steep slopes of the Mosel, however, was less enchanting than most. "The weather turned on December 23 from rain to frost and snow," Selbach remembers. "On the 24th we had a solid blanket of ice covered with snow. You could not move a vehicle, let alone people, up and down the main vineyard access road."

The Selbach family pleaded with the mayor of Bernkastel for the community's snow plow and the mayor agreed to let volunteers plow the main vineyard access road on Christmas Eve. "We bribed them with good wine and cash on top. They made the road passable." The plowed route was then salted to make it less slippery. However, the Selbach tractor still had to negotiate treacherous slopes to haul loaded wagons of grapes from the Bernkastel vineyard five kilometers up the road to the winery in Zeltingen.

"We went centimeter by centimeter," Johannes recounts. "It took us two and a half hours to get the grapes in." And there was one casualty: Hans Selbach, the father of Johannes, who tore a shoulder muscle in a fall on the icy road.

The Eisweine at the Mülheimer Helenenkloster Vineyard

The table on the next pages, from the meticulous records kept by Dr. Dirk Richter at Weingut Max Ferd. Richter in the Mosel, reveals much about German Eiswein production. Firstly, it is difficult to make this wine each year because, unlike in Canada, the required hard frost does not occur with reliable regularity.

Secondly, like in Canada, the frost can occur any time from the beginning of November to the end of January and occasionally — but not in Richter's experience — as late as mid-February. In general, the largest quantities of Eiswein are made in early vintages before grapes have begun to dehydrate or drop to the ground, as happens in late vintages.

Thirdly, when freezing conditions last beyond one day, lower temperatures on subsequent days can yield more concentrated wines and thus two or more different wines in a single vintage.

Fourthly, there often is a ten to one ratio between the Oechsle reading (a measurement of the natural sugar) and the acidity. Experience has shown that this is the ideal relationship for a well-balanced Eiswein that is neither too sweet nor too tart.

Fifthly, the familiar late harvest classifications — Spätlese, Auslese, Beerenauslese, from less sweet to more sweet — were permitted on Eiswein labels before 1982 to signal to consumers how sweet the wine might be. Since 1982, the law requires that the minimum degree of natural sugar for Eiswein should be that of Beerenauslese. The Eisweine made at Richter in 1961, 1966, and 1970 were light compared to the generally riper later vintages.

Year	Harvest date	Class	Oechsle	Acidity (gms/liter)	Quantity made (liters)
1961	Nov. 23	Spätlese Eiswein	110	13.5	550
1966	Nov. 2	Spätlese Eiswein	116	11.6	1,600
1970	Dec. 23	Spätlese Eiswein	114	13	900
1971	Nov. 20	Auslese Eiswein	150	10.3	300
1973 (a)	Dec. 1	Auslese Eiswein	130	9.3	700
1973 (b)	Dec. 2	Beerenauslese Eiswein	170	11.5	550
1975 (a)	Nov. 23	Auslese Eiswein	115	9.5	650
1975 (b)	Nov. 24	Beerenauslese Eiswein	127	10.2	1,000
1976	Dec. 10	Auslese Eiswein	137	9.2	330
1979	Jan. 13, 1980	Spätlese Eiswein	127	8.6	180
1983	Nov. 15	Eiswein	164	13.1	1,350
1985	Dec. 31	Eiswein	128	13	750
1986	Dec. 25	Eiswein Christwein	145	14.6	300
1987	Dec. 9	Eiswein	122	16.4	550
1988	Nov. 22	Eiswein	160	11.3	780
1989	Nov. 26	Eiswein	140	13.2	680

1990	Dec. 8	Eiswein	130	13.7	300
1992	Dec. 30	Eiswein	149	11.4	400
1993	Nov. 24	Eiswein	130	12.9	500
1994	Jan. 5, 1995	Eiswein	150	10	120
1995	Nov. 6	Eiswein	120	12	1,000
1996	Dec. 20	Eiswein Christwein	138	16.5	150
1997	Jan. 28, 1998	Eiswein	166	9	100
1998	Nov. 21	Eiswein	168	15	510
1999	Jan. 25, 2000	Eiswein	130	10	300
2000	Dec. 23	Eiswein	140	10	300

4

A Parade of German Eiswein Producers

The world's first icewines occurred in German vineyards about two hundred years ago, the accidental consequence of unexpectedly sharp early frost. Only since 1965 have wineries begun making Eisweine systematically, increasingly so since 1985. For German winemakers, Eiswein crowns the quality pyramid alongside the noble botrytis-affected dessert wines. For some, it is the pinnacle: a wine that can be made only in the few years each decade when winter arrives early and, accordingly, is prized because it is rare and is priced appropriately.

It is hardly a surprise that most German Eisweine are made with the Riesling grape. This variety, which is believed to have descended from a wild vine indigenous to the Rhine valley, has been grown in the vineyards of Germany for more than a millennium. The grape is exceptionally versatile, capable of yielding distinguished wines in every style from bone dry to hugely sweet. When grown in the cool German vineyards, Riesling supports its fruity flavors with bracing acidity. The great German Eisweine — and many are great — are distinguished by piquant acidity which, on the palate, strains against the wine's natural sugar like a keenly taut violin string. This fine balance gives the Eiswein a cleansing freshness when young and the ability to age gracefully for a generation.

The Germans also employ a handful of other varieties for icewine, notably Scheurebe and Silvaner, both of which are able to hang on the vines better than Riesling in those years when the Eiswein freeze is late in arriving.

Badischer Winzerkeller Zum Kaiserstuhl 16, D-79206 Breisach

Established in 1952 and one of the largest producers in Germany, this is the central cellar for the cooperatives of Baden, with 10,000 grower members. The production was 30 million liters in 1999, a representative vintage. Because Baden is the warmest wine-growing area of Germany, the wines of Baden often are rich, full-bodied table wines. The Eisweine often also are higher in alcohol than others in Germany.

For all its size, the Badischer Winzerkeller, which made its first Eiswein in 1961, never produces Eisweine in quantity; in some vintages, the output has been as small as 50 liters.

The member cooperatives that deliver all their grapes to the central cellar are asked to nominate vineyards for Eiswein each autumn and these are inspected by Winzerkeller's own enologists. Growers whose vineyards are chosen for Eiswein are guaranteed a high price for the grapes, whether or not an Eiswein can be made. With a large number of growers to choose from, the Winzerkeller was able to produce Eiswein every year during the 1990s and, in favorable vintages, more than one. For example, in 1992 six Eisweine were made, from Gewürztraminer, Ruländer, and Pinot Noir.

Weingut Hans Barth Bergweg 20, D-65347 Hattenheim

The challenge of producing Eiswein in vineyards near the Rhine's warming influence is demonstrated by this winery, which made its first Eiswein in 1985 but not again until 1992. "We attempt it in every year but success does not come often," says Norbert Barth, the owner. He has had a good run recently, with consecutive vintages from 1995 through 1998 of Riesling in the Hattenheimer Schützenhaus vineyard. In 1998, for the first time, he also was able to produce 150 liters of Spätburgunder Weissherbst (Pinot Noir) Eiswein with a commendable 176° Oechsle and 14 grams of acidity.

Bischöfliche Weinguter Gervasiusstrasse 1, D-54203 Trier

This ecclesiastical estate, one of the largest Mosel producers, has a lengthy history of making good wines for the Bishop of Trier who has controlled the estate, or parts of it, since 1773. But it was two hundred years before the first Eiswein was made here, yet one more indication of how recent the Eiswein tradition is. The "Bishop's Winery" (to translate the name) encompasses three Church-owned properties that merged under single management in 1966.

The estate's 97 hectares of steeply sloped vineyards include sites in the narrow Saar or Ruwer Valleys where the winery tries to harvest enough Eiswein grapes each year for about a thousand liters. The favored Eiswein vineyard is the Nies'chen in the tiny Ruwer village of Kasel; the Eisweine always show an acidity that is piercing when young but a refreshing counterpoint to the sweetness as the wine ages. Very occasionally, the harvest is in the renowned Scharzhofberg in Wiltingen in the Saar. Ironically for a Church-owned winery, the Eiswein harvests in 1993 and again in 1996 occurred on Christmas Day, one of the greatest feast days of Christianity. But the harvest routine is no different here than at any other estate when the picking is on Christmas morning.

"Every time, it is a big party," confesses Gernot Kollmann, one of the former managers. "We start at five in the morning. We are done by seven. Then we drink hot wine and go back home for Christmas breakfast."

Weingut Ernst Bretz D-55234 Bechtolsheim

Ernst Bretz and his sons Horst and Harald operate this Rheinhessen estate which, they admit, is not "blessed with great classified vineyard names." However, the vineyards are far enough from the moderating influence of rivers to be "ideal" for Eiswein, which the Bretz family began making in 1978, initially with Riesling and Silvaner. Since 1992 the winery also has added a Spätburgunder Weissherbst Eiswein.

Weingut Georg Breuer Grabenstrasse 8, D-65385 Rüdesheim

One of Germany's top-rated producers, this estate was found- ed in 1880 and has been run for many years by the founder's sons, Bernhard and Heinrich Breuer, who more than doubled its vineyards to 26 hectares. Bernhard Breuer has been a leader in German wine as a founding director of the German Wine Academy, a forceful advocate for classifying German vineyards, and a co- author on wine with Dr. Hans Ambrosi, the "father" of German Eiswein production.

The first Breuer Eiswein was made in 1987. "We do not need it for the reputation," Bernhard Breuer says. "We also do not put our- selves under pressure to make Eiswein or botrytized wines, since our idea is to make the wines naturally as they grow and as they devel- op in the cellar. They usually end up as dry- fermented wines."

Dessert wines are only produced in those years when the vineyard conditions favor them. Breuer is very much a purist, refusing to cover the vines with a plastic wrap as protection against rain or birds.

"We consider the production of these wines to be a natural event which may or may not happen, The grapes should not in any way be shed of their natural environment to produce something they would not unless we interfered."

The winery only made Eiswein in the even years of the decade between 1990 and 2000. The acclaimed cask-matured Rüdesheimer Bischofsberg Eiswein is made with Riesling. The 1996, harvested on Christmas Day, was scored 93 by *Wine Spectator* magazine, while the 1994 (harvested January 6, 1995) was awarded 96 points by another magazine, *Wine Enthusiast*. The 1998 also was outstanding because an early harvest on November 23 provided winemaker Hermann Schmoranz with healthy grapes. Rare among German winemakers, Schmoranz has the opportunity to be familiar with Canadian icewine. His twin brother, Walter, is the general manager at the Pelee Island winery near Windsor, where icewine production began in 1983.

Weingut Reichsrat Von Buhl Weinstrasse 16, D-67146 Deidesheim

When Frank John, a skilled young winemaker, joined this Pfalz estate in 1994, the decision was made to produce wines in every one of the quality ranges mandated by the German wine law, from Kabinett to Eiswein. Born in 1960 and trained both as an agricultural engineer and as a microbiologist, John already had gained experience at Müller-Catoir and Heyl zu Herrnsheim, two of German's best wineries. At Von Buhl, John has met the high expectations, particularly with the winery's acclaimed sweet wines.

1998er Forster Ungeheuer Riesling Eiswein

"Eiswein doesn't happen by accident," says Nicole Rehehn, the winery's export manager. "You have to plan it." Beginning in spring, the winery applies a different management technique — from pruning to soil management and spraying — to the Riesling set aside for Eiswein in a microclimate in one of the most prestigious vineyards, the Forster Ungeheuer. In this way, winemaker John assures himself of grapes whose sugar levels are significantly higher than the required minimum but which retain a pronounced acidity.

"The acidity is really one of the most important characteristics of an Eiswein," Rehehn says. "German wines are unparalleled in the world for their austere acidity and their freshness. The acidity will be the most obvious difference between the Eisweins in Germany and in North America."

Weingut Dr. Bürklin-Wolf Weinstrasse 65, D-67157 Wachenheim

This is Germany's largest family-owned wine estate, with 110 hectares of vineyards, some of them owned since the sixteenth century. Because of the winery's tradition of harvesting late to capture the fullest maturity, its Rieslings are renowned for power and intensity. Bettina Bürklin, a Geisenheim graduate, is the twenty-second generation of the family in winemaking. In 1990, she and her husband, Christian von Guradze, took over the winery.

They have denominated their best vineyards as first and second growth based on an historic classification done in 1828 by the Bavarian tax collectors. Only wines from the two top quality levels are sold under the vineyard name. Both the Forster Pechstein and the Wachenheim Gerümpel, from which the winery often makes Eiswein, include first and second growth parcels.

The first Eiswein at Bürklin-Wolf was a 1978 Scheurebe harvested on December 6. Subsequent Eisweine, made either from Scheurebe or from Riesling, were produced only seven times, includ-

WEINGUT
Dr. Bürklin-Wolf

1991
Forster Pechstein
Riesling Eiswein

Qualitätswein mit Prädikat · A. P. Nr. 5 142 043 09 92
Erzeugerabfüllung · D-6706 Wachenheim

7,5% vol   Rheinpfalz   750 ml

ing the 1999 vintage and the average annual quantity is only two hundred liters.

Fürstlich Castell'sches Domänenamt Schlossplatz 5, D-97355 Castell

L iterally the "Prince of Castell's winery," this is an historic property. Some of the vineyards were defined as early as 1258 and the first cultivation of the Silvaner vine was documented in one of the vineyards in 1659.

The winery, large by German standards at 400,000 bottles a year, is only part of a range of businesses, from banking to forestry, in which this family has been engaged for almost one thousand years. Their commitment to wine goes beyond their own estate: in 1973, the prince formed the Castell Producers Association to help improve all of the wines made in the village.

The winery today is directed by his cousin, Wolfgang, the young Count of Castell-Castell. The first Eiswein was made in 1983, with seven subsequent vintages through to 1998 and seldom more than one hundred liters a year. The varieties employed usually are Silvaner or Rieslaner. The latter is a 1921 cross of Riesling and Silvaner developed at Würzburg. On one occasion the winery used Mariensteiner, another Würzburg variety developed in 1971 by crossing Silvaner and Rieslaner. It produced a successful Eiswein with what the winery termed "outstanding" fruitiness.

Weingut Dr. Dahlem Erben Rathoffstrasse 25, D-55276 Oppenheim

G eisenheim graduate Frank Dahlem is the fourteenth generation of his family to make wine at this estate, which, with 25 hectares of vineyard, is one of the largest in Oppenheim. The first Eiswein was made by his grandfather in the 1950s, the opportunistic result of an unexpected freeze in the vineyards. Now, Eiswein is made when conditions are favorable, occasionally with Ruländer but generally with Riesling from a top Dr. Dahlem vineyard such as Oppenheimer Sackträger. Annual production averages 2,000 liters.

Schlossgut Diel D-55452 Burg Layen

N estled against the ruins of Burg Layen, an ancient fortress not far from Bingen on the Rhine, this Nahe winery has been owned by the Diel family since 1802 and has been run since 1987 by Armin Diel. A forceful man, he is as renowned for his food and wine writing as for his innovative wines — such as an exceptional sparkling wine for the Millennium, a Riesling Sekt with an Eiswein dosage.

The first Eiswein made at Schlossgut Diel occurred opportunistically in 1966 when some Scheurebe grapes intended for a late harvest wine were caught on November 1 by an unexpectedly sharp freeze. It

was not until 1983 that another Eiswein was made, again from Scheurebe, one of a number of the "new" German grape varieties that had been planted by Diel's father under the encouragement of Dr. Helmut Becker, Geisenheim's prolific plant breeder. Armin Diel prefers the classic varieties and replaced the Becker varieties once Schlossgut Diel was under his management. He does admit some small regret in tossing Scheurebe, a grape useful for making voluptuous dessert wines. But since 1990 he has made Eiswein only from Riesling, in quantities ranging from two hundred to two thousand liters a year.

Diel's only disappointment was in 1997 when a planned harvest on December 17 was called off because the temperature stalled at -6°C, just a degree shy of the legal temperature for an Eiswein harvest. The netting had been removed from the vines in anticipation of picking but early morning snow and ice showers prevented replacing it. The grapes remained exposed to another six weeks of bad weather before a January 26, 1998, freeze enabled the harvest of what was left. Diel, whose 1992 Eiswein was twice scored 99 by Robert Parker, the influential American wine critic, was able to make a mere 20 liters of the 1997 and the quality was so disappointing that he declined to sell a bottle. "We should have picked the grapes in December and we would have had a great Auslese," Diel says now. "Things are as they are and you learn from your mistakes."

Weingut Dr. Deinhard Weinstrasse 10, D-67146 Deidesheim

This Pfalz winery, established in 1849 by a member of the great Koblenz Deinhard wine family, made its first Eiswein in 1989 and has made only occasional vintages since, in quantities of about 500 liters a time.

The winery is a Riesling specialist and its 1996 Ruppertsberger Reiterpfad Riesling Eiswein was very highly rated by the critics. It also has produced very concentrated Eiswein from Ehrenfelser. Unusually, it bottles many of these wines in full-size (750-milliliter) bottles.

Domdechant Werner'sches Weingut Rathausstrasse 30, D-65234 Hochheim

Riesling was documented in the vineyards at Hochheim on the Main river in the fifteenth century. In Queen Victoria's time, the wines were favored by the British court, where they were called Hock. The reputation of Riesling is guarded jealously by Dr. Franz Werner Michel. "My old family estate is just Riesling pure," he says.

In 1780 an ancestor, Dr. Franz Werner, acquired what is now a 12-

hectare estate. Werner was the Dean — *Domdechant* — of the Cathedral of Mainz, hence the name of the estate. Michel, who represents the seventh generation of the dean's family to manage the winery, believes that the estate began making Eiswein just after World War II. "My memory goes back to 1948 as the first vintage," he says. "In those days I was still in school. It was done from a desire to do something very special, Eiswein being the real specialty of cool climate viticulture."

In years when Hochheim gets the required frost, Michel makes two hundred to four hundred bottles of Eiswein, bottled in half-liter bottles because the wine lives longer in the larger containers. "Longevity is essential. Eiswein is to be sold by grandchildren." Even so, the winery's 1999 Hochheimer Kirchenstück Riesling Eiswein, delicately light with notes of tropical fruit, was in the bottle, elegant and approachable, by the spring after the vintage.

Weingut Hermann Dönnhoff Bahnhofstrasse 11, D-55585 Oberhausen

Helmut Dönnhoff, who runs a small but esteemed winery that has been in his family since 1750, is a friendly rival to Armin Diel in the production of Eiswein. In 1997 when Diel failed to make any Eiswein, Dönnhoff produced such a successful example from a vineyard called Oberhäuser Brücke that it scored 96, near perfection, in a guide co-written by Diel. "It was splendid," Diel says.

The microclimatic conditions of that vineyard were such that the grapes got the hard freeze that eluded Diel, only a few kilometers away. In more than one vintage, that vineyard has remained cold enough that Dönnhoff has been able to pick on three successive days, vinifying each lot separately. He was fortunate enough to get this trinity vintage in 1996 and again in 1998 and the wines made on the third day each year show extraordinary concentration of fruit. Dönnhoff's sure touch with Eiswein ranges over many vintages of the decade. He was named winemaker of the year in 1997 by the Koblenz Chamber of Commerce after a tasting in which Dönnhoff Eisweine took first, second and third.

The spa town of Bad Dürkheim's many attractions include the nearby ruin of Limburg Abbey and a bacchanalian wine festival every September known, incongruously, as the Sausage Fair. Also worth visiting is the Fitz-Ritter winery. Its classical mansion dates from 1785 and is set in a garden often described as one of the most beautiful on the German wine route. A point of pride is that a founder, Johann Fitz, led local winemakers in 1832 in a tax revolt.

Another point of pride is the Riesling Eiswein from the Dürkheimer Hochbenn vineyard, elegantly presented in slender frosted bottles. The winery only made its first Eiswein in 1992, a Silvaner, but switched to Riesling in subsequent years. The annual production averages 400 to 500 liters.

FITZ-RITTER
Weingut seit 1785

RIESLING
EISWEIN

Weingut Geheimer Rat Dr. v. Basserman-Jordan Kirchgasse 10, D-67142 Deidesheim

---

This winery, with a history of almost three hundred years in the Pfalz, only made its first Eiswein in 1996, a year which the winery's general manager, Gunther Hauck, describes as the best year for Eiswein in the decade. Riesling harvested in the estate's Forster Ungeheuer vineyard achieved a stunning 200° Oechsle. The intense sweetness, however, was balanced with what Hauck calls "enormous" acidity and the wine won critical praise. Encouraged by that, the winery made Eiswein in the following two vintages: the 1997 harvest occurred in February 1998 and the 1998 Eiswein grapes were picked in November 1998. The annual production averages about five hundred liters.

Weingut Geil Mittelstrasse 14, D-55278 Eimsheim

Thomas Geil, who took charge of the cellar here in 1993, is the seventh generation of his family to run this Rheinhessen estate since 1760, when the Geil family became the owners. Riesling Eiswein has been produced since 1977.

Wine critics give Thomas Geil credit for the rising quality of this estate's wines through better and more modern viticulture. It is evident that he has fresh ideas just from studying the labels for the Eiswein from the Eimsheimer Römerschanze vineyard. The labels of former times were traditionally German, with the blue and gold family crest colorfully prominent. Beginning with the 1993 vintage, Geil switched to a smart and clean label with no crest and with the family named embossed, cream-on-cream. Geil is in the forefront of German winemakers who are addressing the clutter of traditional labels.

Weingut Forstmeister Geltz-Zilliken Heckingstrasse 20, D-54439 Saarburg

The Saar River flows through an often dark, narrow and forested valley into the Mosel. In difficult Eiswein vintages like 1999, when frost came late to German vineyards, Saar winemakers are among the most successful Eiswein producers. Hans-Joachim Zilliken — whose ancestor Ferdinand Geltz was the state's director of the local forests — first made Eiswein in 1980. "My daughter was born in 1980 and I wanted to make something very special," he explains.

His 10-hectare Saarburger Rausch vineyard — one of the best sites in the Saar — yields classic Eiswein from Riesling, with the fruit and sweetness set against piquant acidity. Unusually for Eiswein, there may be a note of botrytis. "We prefer to make Eiswein with botrytized grapes," he says.

This Baden estate, which has been in Baron Hans Joachim von Gleichenstein's family since 1634, produced its first Eiswein in 1983, taking advantage of a crisp freeze of -9°C to produce a must with the commendable weight of 142° Oechsle. The grape variety used then, and in subsequent vintages, has been Weisser Burgunder, or Pinot Blanc. In a recent Eiswein vintage, 1995, the winery produced six hundred liters of wine, a portion of which was matured in stainless steel while another portion in new oak. The latter wine, with a light vanilla note from the barrel, is regarded as the winery's premium Eiswein and is priced accordingly.

Weingut Grans-Fassian Römerstrasse 28, D-54340 Leiwen

The young winemakers of Leiwen on the Mosel banded together in the 1980s to raise the quality of their community's wines. One of the leaders was Gerhard Grans, born in 1945, who had taken over the Grans-Fassian winery in 1982. A precise winemaker who limits his production to 80,000 bottles a year, he gave up his ambition to study medicine to run the winery, which has been in the family since 1624. The specialty is Riesling. "There is no region in the world that Riesling of such a high quality can be produced," Grans maintains. He is eager to make red wine as well, but for that he has a joint venture in South Africa.

The first Eiswein was made at Grans-Fassian in 1970 by his father. Gerhard Grans made his first vintage in 1983 and every year since when nature cooperated. "In 1991 the wild boar ate all the grapes," he remembers. In 1997, when the frost only came in the latter part of January, he made no Eiswein because the grapes, waterlogged and deteriorated during the long hang time, no longer met his standard of quality.

The Eiswein production at Grans-Fassian seldom is more than two hundred liters a year, although in the bounteous and early

1998 vintage he produced six hundred liters. Grans sells his Eisweine so sparingly — largely to collectors and top restaurants — that he still has some bottles of his first vintage, the 1983 Riesling Leiwener Klostergarten. Tasted in 1999, the wine had become deeply gold in color and the complex flavors recalled rich and spicy fruit cake. Grans no longer includes the site on its Eiswein label because he thinks that Eiswein is drunk as Eiswein and consumers are not looking for vineyard character.

Weingut Gunderloch Carl-Gunderloch-Platz 1, D-55299 Nackenheim

The Gunderloch estate, founded in 1890, is renowned for Rieslings from the 12-hectare Nackenheimer Rothenberg vineyard, of which Gunderloch's proprietors Fritz and Agnes Hasselbach own three-quarters and covet the rest. The steeply sloped red slate soil, not far from the Rhine, catches too much sun for Eiswein. Fritz Hasselbach first made Eiswein in 1989 from the cooler Oelberg vineyard in nearby Nierstein.

"My father-in-law made an Eiswein in 1952," he recalls. "That is the first Eiswein I remember he made. He did not try to make an Eiswein. He had some Riesling grapes he intended to pick late and it got very cold. He did not want to make an Eiswein. It was nature that made the first Eiswein. It is not a big tradition in this region; it is usually not cold enough." Nackenheim is at the eastern edge of Rheinhessen, influenced by the moderating temperatures of the Rhine.

Gunderloch has built its reputation with the more usual late harvest wines, Beerenauslese and Trockenbeerenauslese. It also was nature that forced Hasselbach's hand to produce the 1989 Eiswein. The harvest that fall was so abundant that every tank in his cellar was filled before the end of the normal vintage, with one more hectare to pick. Accordingly, those grapes were left for Eiswein. It did not get cold enough until early February and much of the fruit was lost through natural causes. He produced a mere three hundred liters of Eiswein that year, enough to whet the appetite of Gunderloch customers. Hasselbach set out to make it in all subsequent years when the weather cooperated. Often, it did not: for three consecutive years beginning in 1992, the grapes left hanging for Eiswein were rendered worthless by rain and rot.

In 1996 the Hasselbachs leased **Weingut Balbach** in Nierstein, a venerable estate dating from 1675 and a more significant owner of property in the Oelberg vineyard. Fritz's second successful Eiswein was made in 1996. Again in 1997 it failed to freeze sufficiently but, because of a dry winter, the grapes remained healthy as they shriveled into raisins and a late February harvest yielded a fine Beerenauslese. In 1998 Hasselbach was able to make his third successful Eiswein in a decade — almost five hundred liters — when the deep frost came early, in the third week of November.

Acquiring Balbach's 14 hectares doubled the vineyard area under Hasselbach's control. Now when he decides to make Eiswein, he is risking the loss of a much smaller portion of his harvest. The three-quarter-hectare plot set aside each year for Eiswein is a flat-lying vineyard just at the edge of the village of Nierstein, in a pocket where cold air tends to sit longer than anywhere else in the Balbach vineyards. "If there is a chance to make Eiswein, this vineyard is perfect."

Hasselbach's Eiswein now is always released under the Balbach label. The 1998 is a superb example. Made with entirely healthy grapes, it presents a powerful aroma of tropical fruits and a rich palate, with the concentrated fruitiness balanced by a piquant but not sharp acidity. Hasselbach attributes the fine acidity to the vineyard's red slate soil.

A skilled winemaker, Fritz Hasselbach has quickly reached firm conclusions about this latest addition to his wines. Eiswein should be big and intense, standing apart from other late harvest wines. "I want concentration in the wine," he says. "I don't like a light Eiswein." He achieves that by aiming for a natural sugar content significantly higher than the minimum allowed under the winemaking rules.

In common with many German winemakers, he does not care for

the taste of botrytis — a defining feature of many late harvest wines — in Eiswein, and botrytis-affected grapes are culled before the Eiswein harvest. "I just want the clean, healthy grapes." He also expresses reservations about some other producers in the Rheinhessen who, with the use of mechanical pickers, are producing thousands of liters of low-priced Eiswein each year with varieties other than Riesling. "The perfect grape for Eiswein is Riesling," he insists.

Weingut Louis Guntrum Rheinallee 62, D-55283 Nierstein am Rhein

Hans Joachim Louis Guntrum and his son, Louis Konstantin, represent the tenth and eleventh generations of a family that has managed this winery since 1648. "It has never occurred to me to work anywhere else," says Louis Konstantin, who was born in 1970, the year in which the winery, in a Christmas Day harvest, made a Riesling Eiswein of such superb quality that it was drinking well three decades later.

Hans Joachim, an informal man known universally as Hayo, says the first Guntrum Eiswein was made in 1962. There had been several good vintages of late harvest wines in the 1950s. As prosperity returned to postwar Germany, there was an attitude among consumers, Hayo says, of "what else can you do?" Eiswein was the ultimate challenge. The vintage he recalls best is the accidental one of 1965 when an unusually early frost of -8°C hit the vineyards on October 6.

"Overnight we had buckets full of Eiswein," he remembers. "We had fifteen thousand liters. Normally, we would have five hundred liters."

When it was ready to be sold, he took samples to the American army's commissary at Heidelberg. His asking price of 10 marks a half bottle, the equivalent then of three dollars, met resistance until the wine went on sale. In short order, Guntrum's Eiswein was sold out and the military buyers could not understand why he could not whip up another lot on demand.

With a few exceptions, such as the 1970 Niersteiner Auflangen Eiswein, the Guntrums now produce Eiswein exclusively from the Silvaner grape. Hayo explains: "Silvaner keeps healthy longer on the vines."

In general, the Nierstein vineyards, close to the Rhine, seldom achieve Eiswein temperatures. For this reason, the Guntrums have settled on a single vineyard called Oppenheimer Herrenberg on a hillside overlooking the village of Oppenheim and its beautiful baroque cathedral. The vineyard, several kilometers from the Rhine, has a better microclimate for Eiswein. A slight bowl at the bottom of the slope and a border of trees trap the cold air, giving this vineyard two degrees more frost than neighboring vineyards.

The first Silvaner Eiswein from the Herrenberg was made in 1985, followed next by a vintage in 1990. "Silvaner Eiswein takes a long time to develop in the bottle," Hayo asserts. "It takes longer [than Riesling] but it also keeps longer."

Guntrum produced Eiswein in most vintages in the 1990s. Perhaps the most challenging was 1999, the first Eiswein vintage fully under Louis Konstantin's direction. After a long warm autumn, windstorms around Christmas knocked many grapes to the ground. When the sharp frost finally came at the end of January — three nights of -11°C — Guntrum could salvage only three thousand kilograms of grapes, just enough for three hundred and fifty liters of Eiswein, half the usual quantity. "It was a matter of patience," Louis Konstantin says.

The winery's 350 years of tradition has not deterred the Guntrums from coming up with clever marketing ideas for their Eiswein. The 1996 vintage, picked on December 24, was bottled in elegant crystal decanters and sold as Cristallo Eiswein, a name inspired by a mountain in the Alps where Hayo likes to ski. A quantity of the 1998 Eiswein was packaged in bottles with penguins on the label, an idea so successful in New World markets that Penguin has become a Guntrum brand.

Weingut Höhn-Zimmermann, D-55450 Langenlonsheim

I n 1965 Roman Zimmermann was one of the earliest of Nahe winemakers to produce Riesling Eiswein. Now, he produces between three hundred and one thousand liters at least every second vintage. On occasion, he also has made Eiswein from the less aromatic Silvaner grape. While Zimmermann has won awards with Eiswein and blazed the trail for other producers in the Nahe wine village of Langenlonsheim, he still regards his Trockenbeerenauslese (or TBA) wines as the winery's flagship wines.

It is a viewpoint that is common among German producers and for good reason. Until Eiswein got its own Prädikat, this was the ultimate in sweetness and intensity among dessert wines. But Zimmermann acknowledges that Eiswein now deserves its own pedestal, its brightly vivacious character defining a style entirely different from TBA's honeyed complexity.

"It is almost a privilege to harvest Eiswein," he says. That privilege is shared by others in his family. His nephew, Gregor Zimmermann, makes Ehrenfelser Eiswein at **Weingut Königswingert** in the neighboring village of Guldenthal. Roman's younger brother, Joseph, produces icewine in Ontario.

Weingut Johannishof Grund 63, D-65366 Johannisberg

O wned by Hans Hermann Eser and his family, this winery is in the village of Johannisberg, just outside the gates of the historic Schloss Johannisberg. While there is no other connection between the estates, both have been making Eisweine for a long time — "more than 30 years," writes Sabine Eser. It does not get cold enough every year, but the Esers had a good run of favorable conditions in the 1990s, making Eisweine in six different years of the decade. Only Riesling is grown on this estate.

I n 1993 Peter Jordan, who comes from the computer industry, acquired an old Saar property, the Van Volxem estate, which had made Eiswein since the 1950s. The 14-hectare estate was purchased as "a fascinating hobby" and Jordan promptly set about changing its direction. "With the purchase, we decided not to make typical German wines," he says. "We produce dry, complex and austere wines for which we are considered — in Sweden, for example — as the German Angelo Gaja." Not totally lacking humility, Jordan quickly adds: "That is much too much honor."

There is no question, however, that the standards are high. When the small lot of Eiswein made in 1993 under Jordan's direction fell below his standards, it was not sold. "Our first 'real' icewine was in 1995," Jordan says. The must that year had a weight of 160° Oechsle, an unusually high sugar concentration for the Mosel/Saar/Ruhr and one-third sweeter than the minimum required for the region's Eiswein. The intervening years of 1996 and 1997 yielded such thin and light Eisweine that Jordan also kept them off the market. He topped his 1995 record in the excellent 1998 vintage, with a must weight of 164°. "An absolute top wine," he exults. "If we are lucky, we produce between 400 and 700 bottles, which we sell for about US$130 per bottle."

Weingut Karlsmühle Im Mühlengrund 1, D-54318 Mertesdorf

I n 1995 Peter Geiben closed one chapter on his family's history by converting the ancient flour mill into a charming hotel, all the better to show off the family's other historic pursuit, the growing of finely crafted Rieslings. Geiben's vineyards are on steep slopes in the Ruwer valley, not far from Trier and also include the choice sites of recently

WEINGUT
KARLSMÜHLE

1993
LORENZHÖFER
Riesling Eiswein
Qualitätswein mit Prädikat
Erzeugerabfüllung Weingut Karlsmühle
D-54318 Mertesdorf (L)A.P.Nr. 3 536 016 17 94
alc. 8.0% vol   375 ml e
MOSEL-SAAR-RUWER

acquired **Weingut Patheiger.** Eiswein was first made at Karlsmühle in 1970 by Geiben's father. Geiben now makes delicate but long-lived Eisweine under both winery labels. Depending on the weather, the quantity can be as little as one hundred liters or as great as one thousand liters a year.

Weingut Keller Bahnhofstrasse 1, D-67592 Flörsheim-Dalsheim

This acclaimed Rheinhessen winery has made Eiswein each year, weather permitting, since 1971. Klaus Keller will wait until February after the vintage for the necessary cold weather. He only produces between two hundred and five hundred liters a year, primarily of Riesling Eiswein and he strives to achieve a high must weight, at least 175° Oechsle — a sugar concentration more often found in Canada than in Germany. When possible, he also makes Eiswein with the Rieslaner grape (a 1921 cross of Sylvaner and Riesling). He concedes that the weak-stemmed variety is ill-suited in the vineyard for Eiswein because the grapes drop too easily. But when it is successful, he says, Rieslaner Eiswein has "an exotic charm and a special appeal."

Weingut Reichsgraf Von Kesselstatt Schlossgut Marienlay, D-54317 Morscheid/Ruwertal

This historic producer with vineyards near Trier was in the hands of the Von Kesselstatt family for six hundred years before changing owners in 1978. The Reh family, who now own it, have rejuvenated the cellars and made wines that burnished the estate's reputation. Annegret Reh-Gartner, the manager, believes that Eisweine may have been produced here in various vintages over the last century. In the last decade, Riesling Eiswein was made in 1993, 1995, 1996, and 1998, with the quantities ranging between one hundred and one thousand liters.

Weingut Kistenmacher-Hengerer Eugen Nägele Str. 23-25, D-74074 Heilbronn

This small Württemburg winery has been in the Kistenmacher family for five hundred years but the first Eiswein was only made in 1996. From a harvest on December 26 that year, one hundred liters of Riesling Eiswein was produced. Hans Hengerer, the current member of the family running the winery, was sufficiently satisfied with the result that he plans to make more in years favorable for Eiswein.

Weingut Reinhard und Beate Knebel August-Horch-Str. 24, D-56333 Winnigen/Mosel

The Knebel family tree has been traced back to 1604 in Winnigen, a community in the northern or lower Mosel at the outskirts of Koblenz. When the Knebel vineyards were split among branches of the family in 1990, Reinhard Knebel, a Weinsberg graduate, and his wife Beate nurtured their winery on less than three hectares of vines.

The vineyards are dauntingly steep, with few promising Eiswein sites. Knebel relies on just five hundred vines on the lower part of the Winninger Brückstück vineyard. His father made the first Eiswein in Winnigen in 1967, just to prove he could. Since 1989 Reinhard Knebel has made it almost every year, just as he does Trockenbeerenauslese (TBA). The latter wine requires immensely time-consuming hand selection of the best botrytis-covered berries for TBA when grapes are brought in from the vineyard at harvest. In contrast, Eiswein is a matter of luck: it either freezes early or it does not.

"It is much more difficult to produce a TBA than an Eiswein," Knebel believes. Accordingly, he sells his TBA at five times the price of Eiswein.

With either sweet wine, Knebel has a sure touch. His 1996 Winninger Brückstück Eiswein, for example, was made with grapes lightly affected by botrytis and harvested on Christmas Day at -11°C. He made about 90 liters of a wine that shows a finely balanced tension between bright acidity and honeyed apricot flavors.

Weingut Korrell Johanneshof Parkstrasse 4, 55545 Bad Kreuznach-Bosenheim

This family winery in the Nahe — three generations currently are employed — has produced between three hundred and five hundred liters of Eiswein almost every year since 1970.

Wilfried Korrell remembers 1983 as one of the earliest and best vintages and he still has some bottles for sale from that year. Perhaps his most intense Eiswein was made in 1991 when the must weight achieved 202° Oechsle, or close to double the minimum sweetness required for Eiswein. The winery relies primarily on Riesling but, on occasion, also makes Eiswein from Silvaner and Grauer Burgunder (Pinot Gris).

Weingut Peter Jakob Kühn Mühlstrasse 70, 65375 Oestrich

Young Peter Kühn has been hailed in the German wine press as "a new star in the Rheingau's wine heaven" ever since winning a 1991 competition for the best dry Rieslings. He also has been critically acclaimed for his Riesling Eiswein since making his first in 1994. He only sets out to make between two hundred fifty and five hundred half bottles in a vintage. Kühn takes pains to achieve an Eiswein that possesses both a high sugar concentration and that balancing degree of acidity that, as he puts it, creates fireworks on the palate.

Weingut Landmann Umkircher Strasse 29, D-79112 Freiburg-Waltershofen

This small but energetic Baden winery offers a broad range of wines from table wines to sparkling wines and supplements its trade with the sale of apple juice and other farm products. The first Eiswein was a 1986 Spätburgunder from a harvest on December 26 that year.

Weingut Freiherr Langwerth Von Simmern Langwerter Hof, D-65343 Eltville

This estate on the Rhine has been owned by the Langwerth von Simmern family for more than five hundred years and produces Riesling wines almost exclusively.

"The first Eiswein we produced was in 1965," winemaker Peter Barth says. "To be honest, it was by chance. In general, the 1965 vintage was so poor that the grape picking lasted until late November. It just happened that it got so cold that the grapes were freezing naturally and the decision was made to pick and press them this way."

The winery produced its first Eiswein from the distinguished Erbacher Marcobrunn vineyard. When a bottle of this long-lived wine with bracing acidity was sold at auction in 1994, it commanded a lofty price of DM600.

Barth explains that it is not possible for the winery to make Eiswein every year because many of its best vineyards are near the Rhine "which works like central heating in the middle of the valley." When it is made, the quantity seldom exceeds 150 liters.

The richest, most concentrated Eiswein he has made was the 1996 Eltviller Sonnenberg Riesling. It had the same acidity, about 19 grams a liter, as the 1965 Eiswein but almost double the must weight at 214° Oechsle, resulting in a highly acclaimed finished with a luscious 345.5 grams of residual sugar.

Weingut Carl Loewen Matthiasstrasse 30, D-54340 Leiwen

An estate with a history dating from 1803 and the secularization of church-owned vineyards, this winery made its first Eiswein in 1965 and then sporadically in the fol-

lowing decades. Since 1992 Karl-Josef Loewen has sought to make it each year from Riesling grown in Leiwener Klostergarten, a vineyard near the village. He was frustrated only in 1994 when wild boar got to the grapes before he did.

The volume ranges from three hundred to one thousand half bottles each year. Typically, the wines display peach and mango notes balanced with the racy acidity.

Weingut Dr. Loosen St. Johannishof, D-54470 Bernkastel

Trained as an archeologist, Ernst Loosen came directly from university in 1987 to take over a winery that his lawyer father had neglected. Brash young Loosen was sufficiently overbearing that his entire vineyard staff quit rather than take his instruction. That was a stroke of luck. The delay in getting new pickers meant the Loosen vineyards were harvested late, after the grapes had recovered from the heavy rains earlier in the vintage. Loosen's reputation was established with his better than average 1987 wines.

For Eiswein, Loosen believes in producing it from his best sites, not his marginal sites. "I want to concentrate *ripe* fruit and I want some botrytis in the Eiswein," he says. Having tasted Mosel Eisweine from vintages dating from the 1940s, he asserts that those with "monster acidity" are not good. Because of his demanding standards, Loosen only produces Eiswein two to three times a decade.

Moselland Winzergenossenschaft Bornwiese 6, D-54470 Bernkastel-Kues

This cooperative, with 3,500 grower members, represents 40 per cent of the production in the Mosel. Eiswein is produced in those vintages when nature provides the opportunity, typically in quantities ranging from 50 liters to 500 liters a year. However, 1998 is remembered as an outstanding vintage because frost came early — in the third week of November — when the grapes were very sound. The cooperative, getting grapes from three different growers, made a prodigious 5,000 liters of Eiswein that vintage.

The Eisweine show typical Mosel acidity. The 1998 Kröver Paradies Riesling Eiswein had a piercing 16.1 grams of acidity beautifully balanced by a rich 180 grams of residual sugar per liter, guaranteeing great longevity. The 1990 Kinheimer Rosenberger Riesling Eiswein from Moselland, tasted a decade later, still showed crisp, fresh acidity and little age.

Weingut Eugen Müller Weinstrasse 34a, D-67147 Forst

Like many small and friendly German winery owners, Kurt Müller and family offer affordable guest lodging for wine lovers who want to experience the daily life of an estate that has grown grapes for 250 years. "We will be glad to tell you personally about all our wines," he says.

WEINGUT
EUGEN MÜLLER

1989

PRODUCE OF GERMANY

Qualitätswein mit Prädikat

A.P. Nr. 5 112 070 003 93

Alc. 8.5% by vol.

FORSTER UNGEHEUER

SCHEUREBE EISWEIN

RHEINPFALZ

ERZEUGERABFÜLLUNG

WEINGUT EUGEN MÜLLER D-6701 FORST Deutsche Weinstraße Tel. 063 26/1301

375 ml

His first Eiswein was 310 liters of 1988 Riesling when an unexpected frost whipped across the Pfalz vineyards on November 5. The next year, Müller was able to make 650 liters of Riesling from a harvest on the morning of November 26, 1989; and when the cold snapped back on December 11, the winery picked Scheurebe and made another six hundred liters of Eiswein.

Müller waited until 1996 to make Eiswein a third time, only with Riesling but again in two pickings. The first chance came on the morning of December 23, 1996. The temperature was a frigid -15°C and the grapes were frozen so hard that they only yielded enough juice for 150 liters of wine. He picked again on January 5, 1997, this time at -13°C, and with slightly less petrified berries, made 320 liters. All of his Eisweine have won gold medals in German competitions.

Weingut Müller-Catoir Mandelring 25, D-67433 Neustadt/ Weinstrasse-Haardt

This estate has a colorful history dating from 1744, including a long stretch from 1897 to 1968 when three owners in succession were women, the great grandmother, grandmother and mother of the current owner, Jakob Heinrich Catoir. Regarded as one of Germany's best wineries, it has 20 hectares of vineyards in the Pfalz, more than half of which is Riesling.

Hans-Günter Schwarz, a winemaker widely respected by his peers, has been a leading proponent of the modern reductive wines that are clean, fresh and intense in their fruitiness.

Exploring the various styles of making cleanly fruity dessert wines, Schwarz made the first Eiswein here in 1962, as well as a superlative Beerenauslese. Müller-Catoir tries to make a small quantity of Eiswein each vintage and has only missed five or ten times since 1962.

"Eiswein — in our opinion — is a marvelous way of producing rich and aromatic dessert wines," Sabine Weyrich, the managing director, says. "In our area, it is a terrific way of producing a dessert wine with a natural pure and fresh fruit concentration — without any botrytis. One can taste the pure grape." Both Riesling and Scheurebe grapes are used.

Weingut Adam Nass-Franz Engelmann Hallgartener Platz 2, D-65375 Hallgarten

T his winery, an amalgamation of two small estates both three centuries old, was one of the earliest Eiswein producers in the Rheingau. The first vintage in 1965 was a Riesling Spätlese Eiswein made and bottled by the Engelmann branch of this winery. The grapes were harvested on November 16 that year and the must weight was only 93° Oechsle, making for a light wine. The 1979 Eiswein harvest, which took place on January 12, 1980, yielded a similarly light wine.

1983er
Hallgartener Schönhell
Riesling » EISWEIN «
Qualitätswein mit Prädikat
Erzeugerabfüllung · A. P. Nr. 30 010 008 84
Produce of Germany

German wine law no longer permits the production of Spätlese or even Auslese quality Eiswein. In both 1985 and 1987 Karl Josef Nass, the current owner, was unable to get the necessary sugar concentration he needed for Eiswein and had to settle for Auslese dessert wines.

He has succeeded in making Eiswein in the majority of vintages since 1988. "A high point for Eiswein production in our winery was 1998," he says. "Two Eiswein years happened in one year." The 1997 vintage was picked on January 28, 1998. Ten months later, on November 22, he picked the 1998 vintage. His production ranges from one hundred to six hundred liters.

Weingut Dr. Pauly-Bergweiler Gestade 15, D-54470 Bernkastel-Kues

This winery, fronting on picturesque Bernkastel's main street, occupies an attractive building called Noble House, built in 1743 by a prince from Trier. The property was expropriated by Napoleon in 1805 and, when auctioned in Paris, was purchased by the Mayor of Bernkastel. Ultimately, the house was acquired by Zacharias Bergweiler, the grandfather of Dr. Peter Pauly, the current owner.

A graduate of Geisenheim, Pauly did his doctoral thesis on economic development of viticulture in the Mosel. Noble House was not the most efficient place in which to make wine. The best decision of his life, Pauly maintains, was to build a modern winery in 1980 just outside Bernkastel, inspired by a visit to the Joseph Phelps winery in the Napa Valley in California. "California winemakers can be innovative because they have no restrictions," he says. "We have nothing *but* restrictions." His winery is one of the Mosel's best producers, including the Eisweine Dr. Pauly has made since 1961. The Eiswein style is classic Mosel: bracing acidity when young with fresh fruity flavors because, he insists, "you must make an Eiswein from healthy grapes, with no botrytis."

Weingut Prinz Im Flachsgarten 5, D-65375 Hallgarten

Fred Prinz made the first Eiswein at this tiny estate in 1991, the year in which he established it. Based on a vineyard of only 1.6 hectares, the winery's total production seldom exceeds 10,000 bottles of wine, of which Eiswein, always made with Riesling, comprises a mere one hundred to three hundred liters, depending on the vintage. "The earlier the harvest, the healthier the grapes are and the volume will be greater," he says.

Prinz is especially pleased with the 1996 vintage when he produced two lots of Eiswein — a lighter one made from juice of 156° Oechsle and his Gold Capsule Eiswein from juice with 213° Oechsle. Prinz believes that such highly concentrated juice is likely only every 20 to 30 years in his region of the Rheingau.

The late Nikolaus Weis was trained as a shoemaker but made a prudent career change in 1947 when he started this winery on the outskirts of Leiwen. It is now a quality leader in the Mosel and is managed by his Geisenheim-trained grandson who, in an old family tradition of giving the same name to every first-born male, also is Nik.

The winery also operates a large nursery and developed one of the world's best strains of Riesling, Clone 21-B, or the Weis clone. Naturally, the Eiswein is made with Riesling, grown usually in the Leiwener Klostergarten vineyard close to the village. Eiswein began with grandfather Weis.

In 1999, the winery still was selling an Eiswein from 1983, one of the first vintages in which Nik Weis, born in 1971, participated as a picker. The harvest took place before dawn on a Sunday morning after which young Nik went to church where he was an altar boy. He was so weary that, during the homily, he fell asleep in a chair beside the altar, in full view of the amused congregation.

Eiswein was not made every year, partly because the Weis family preferred to finish the vintage by mid-November to turn their attention to the demands of the grape nursery. Production became more systematic in the 1980s. The 1986 Eiswein, a seductive and delicate wine with a filigree of fruit flavors, was made from grapes picked on Christmas Eve. By coincidence, the winery picked its 1996 Eiswein grapes on the same date but at a slightly lower temperature, producing a more intense wine with lemon and apricot flavors.

Nik Weis believes that better Eiswein is made when grapes have a longer hang time, concentrating the flavors. However, a winemaker takes winter when it comes. The 1998 vintage took place at the end of November in conditions so wintry that Fritz, the winery dog, had to be sheltered in a car before he stopped shivering.

The winery also owns a parcel of the Ockfener Bockstein vineyard in the Saar valley and has made Eiswein intermittently from those grapes as well. The 1998 Eiswein from that vineyard, harvested at -15°C at 185° Oechsle, is rich and fruity, racy in its acidity and with complex notes of white pepper in the flavor. Only eight hundred half bottles were produced.

The Weis family's impact on Eiswein goes beyond the home winery at Leiwen. Nik Weis's sister Christine and her husband Klaus Lucas operate **Weingut Lucashof-Pfarrweingut** at the community of Forst in the Pfalz and its 1996 Forster Stift Riesling Eiswein has been scored highly by wine critics. As well, Nik Weis's father, Hermann — the family's name tradition skipped a generation — founded the **Vineland Estates** winery in Canada in 1979. That winery was an icewine producer by the time Weis sold it in 1992 and now is one of Ontario's leading producers.

Weingut Prinz zu Salm-Dalberg Schlossstrasse 3, D-55595 Wallhausen

N ow a certified organic producer in the Nahe, this winery is believed to be Germany's oldest estate under the ownership of the same family. Prince Michael zu Salm-Salm, the current owner, traces his family back to 932. The family has had vineyards near the villages of Wallhausen and Dalberg at least since 1200.

The ruined Dalburg (sic) Castle (still worth seeing), whose construction began in 1150, is shown in its full glory on the winery's labels. The family's current residence is the somewhat more modest Schloss Wallhausen.

Total annual production is about 50,000 liters a year, primarily Riesling and Spätburgunder. Despite its antiquity, this winery only began making Eiswein in 1981 and believes its four best vintages have been 1986, 1993, 1997 and 1998.

The Nahe region winery's Bockenau valley vineyards are notable for giving mineral tones to the wines. For this reason the winery believes that even its Eiswein is distinctive. A small family-owned winery, Schäfer-Frölich made its first Eiswein in 1983 with Ruländer (Pinot Gris) grapes. In 1995 they produced one from Weisser Burgunder (Pinot Blanc); in 1996 and again in 1998, Eiswein was made from Riesling.

Winemaker Tim Frölich has decided that he will only use Riesling in the future for Eiswein because, in his opinion, the fruit aromas are superior. He describes the character of his Riesling Eiswein as "very fine and filigree" in a picturesque phrase that captures the delicate brilliance of a cleanly made Eiswein.

Weingut Schales Alzeyer Strasse 160, D-67592 Flörsheim-Dalsheim

This Rheinhessen winery boasts the largest private Eiswein archive in Germany. The first Eiswein harvest was in 1961 and more than 40 different Eisweine have been made since then.

While Riesling and Silvaner are the primary varieties, the winery at various times has made Eiswein with Huxelrebe, Ruländer and Rieslaner. In 1998 it made Germany's first Eiswein with Kanzler, a locally produced crossing of Müller-Thurgau and Silvaner.

Ralph Bothe, the winery's manager, proudly claims that, in 1991, the winery made the world's first Eiswein-Sekt, a sparkling wine from Silvaner grapes with an Eiswein dosage. For the Millennium, Schales followed this with a sparkling wine made from

Riesling Eiswein. The grapes were harvested by a crew of 18 on the morning of Christmas Day, 1996, when the temperature was a crisp -12°C. It was fermented as Eiswein and then bottle-fermented in the classic method, left on the yeast for 26 months and finally disgorged in May 1999. Only 450 bottles were made. The gold-embossed image on the label of this wine is of a coin found in one of the Schales vineyards. It dates from 1783, the year the winery was established.

Schloss Johannisberg D-65366 Johannisberg

E ven if this were not one of Germany's most famous wine estates, it would still be worth visiting to view the baroque castle, say a prayer in the austere church and eat lunch in a restaurant with views of the vineyards that drape the hill to Geisenheim and the Rhine in the distance.

The estate's southern slope, an outstanding Riesling site, has too warm an exposure for Eiswein. However, the vineyards on the north side of the estate occupy a long, cool flat and here, Eiswein often is produced.

The reputation of Schloss Johannisberg rests with its great botrytized Rieslings, created here since 1775. It also was one of the earliest Eiswein producers, with the first recorded vintage being 1858 and with regular production in many years since 1966. In the latter year, the frost was unusually early; the grapes were picked on November 1, enabling the winery to release what was called an All Saints Eiswein. Unhappily, subsequent changes to the German wine laws ended the romantic practice of putting the religious feast day of the harvest on the label.

While the Schloss is a large winery, its Eiswein production is limited. Even in 1998 when the November 23 harvest also was relatively early, Wolfgang Schleicher, the estate's veteran manager, made a mere 320 liters of a brilliantly vibrant Eiswein. "It is not sound business to harvest and sell Eisweine," Schleicher maintains. "It is made for the reputation of the estate."

There is no better place to taste it than in the winery's candle-lit barrel cellars, cool and humid underground vaults in which wines live for decades, perhaps centuries. Schleicher made his first Eisweine at the nearby **Weingut G.H von Mumm,** which has been under the same ownership as the Schloss since 1980.

Weingut Heinz Schmitt Stephanusstrasse 4, D-54340 Leiwen

When young Heinz Schmitt, who was born in 1961, took over the family winery in 1983, he decided he needed more than just the technical training recently acquired in German wine schools.

"I thought I needed to have more experience but it made no sense just to go the Baden or Rheinhessen," he figured. So he went to California to work the 1985 crush at Napa's Pine Ridge Winery.

"People told me I was crazy," admits Schmitt, who returned to Pine Ridge for various periods over the next five years. It influenced his approach to making wine at his estate on the Mosel. Where his peers aim for the best vineyard-designated wines they can make, Schmitt often assembles cuvées because he believes that better wine emerges when the qualities of various vineyards support each other.

The California influence also has found its way into his Eiswein production; he ages some of it in oak. The winery's first Riesling Eiswein was made in 1970 by his father, Ewald, with the harvest being done on Christmas Eve. The Schmitts have sought to make Eiswein every year since, despite such occasional frustrations as 1996 when wild boar got to the grapes before the pickers did.

MOSEL SAAR RUWER

Heinz
SCHMITT
Riesling

1993
EISWEIN
Leiwener Klostergarten

Qualitätswein mit Prädikat
Gutsabfüllung • A. P. Nr. 3 529 179 10 94
Weingut Heinz Schmitt • Stephanusstraße 4
D-54340 Leiwen/Mosel
375 ML   ALC.9.0% BY VOL.

Heinz Schmitt has a practical solution for the boar problem: "Shoot them and eat them!"

The point of oak-aging the Eiswein is to give it some roundness, accentuating the wine's fat texture, unless the sugar and fruit concentration is so high that the wine already is lush and fat. In 1998 Schmitt experimented with Missouri oak for some of the Eiswein, adding an exotic tone to the wine. "You can always get better if you do some experiments," he maintains.

Schloss Schönborn Hauptstrasse 53, D-65347 Hattenheim

A sharp three-day cold snap on the third weekend of November in 1998 across most of Germany's wine regions enabled the most bounteous production of Eiswein ever. The unlucky exception was Schloss Schönborn at Hattenheim, frustrating the plan of Günther Thies, the youthful general manager, to make a special bottling of Eiswein for the anniversary of this estate which has been in the powerful Schönborn family (who once controlled abbeys and bishoprics across central Europe) since 1349. The winery was only able to make 30 liters because the broad Rhine, only a stone's throw from the Schönborn estate, kept the temperatures from plunging as deeply there as elsewhere.

"We are proud to have one of the best vineyard sites in the Rheingau," Thies says. "We don't often have frost in these vineyards." That was the case with the Rauenthaler Baiken vineyard in 1998, a prestigious hilltop vineyard. In the absence of sufficient frost, Thies made Auslese instead.

Despite its long history — the oldest wine currently in the 500-year-old cellar is from 1735 — Schönborn only began producing Eiswein after the Second World War, and only occasionally. One of its oldest is vintage-dated 1970–1971 because the grapes were grown in 1970 but were picked early the following year. (Such labels no longer are permitted in Germany.)

The preferred Eiswein vineyard is the Hattenheimer Schützenhaus, located in a slight frost-catching depression about a kilometer from the winery. Proximity to the winery means the frozen grapes can be processed promptly before they can begin to warm up.

In the rare cold vintage of 1984 when grapes were picked at -13°C, Eiswein was made at the Erbacher Marcobrunn, Schönborn's most esteemed vineyard. Tasted 15 years later, the richly golden wine's vibrant acidity suggests that its complex honeyed-orange-peel flavors will develop well into the twenty-first century. "This is a good example of how long you can keep Eiswein," says Thies.

While collectors seek out Eisweine from famous vineyards like Marcobrunn, the character of specific vineyards generally is submerged in the wine's exuberant aromas and flavors. "The wine is influenced more by the picking date and by the healthiness of the grapes and by the cold temperature, much more than whether it is Marcobrunn or the Schützenhaus," Thies maintains.

In an average year, of which 1998 was not an example, Schönborn will make a mere five hundred half-liter bottles of Eiswein, a drop in its total annual production of 35,000 cases of mostly Riesling.

"Producing Eiswein usually has nothing to do with getting a lot of money," Thies says. "It is first to develop an image and build up a reputation and only second to earn money." With his biggest export market in Japan, Thies tantalizes select buyers with Eiswein.

Even at a property as traditional and historic as Schönborn, the mystique of Eiswein has established itself. Where vineyard work in the rest of the year is done by hired employees (Polish guest workers are ubiquitous here as in other German vineyards), winter harvest grapes are picked willingly by the winery's clerical staff and their friends.

"Picking Eiswein is something special," Thies says. "It is fun. We start at four o'clock in the morning and we finish at seven. We have breakfast later on together and we have some of our Schnapps to get warm. We have a lot of customers who ask to come out with us. There is a special atmosphere and there is a story that they can tell later, that they have been part of the Eiswein picking at Schloss Schönborn or wherever. You can see in the newspapers that a lot of politicians go out, doing Eiswein picking for publicity."

Weingut Schloss Sommerhausen Ochsenfurter Strasse 17-19, D-97286 Sommerhausen am Main

This winery in Franconia, near the city of Würzburg, is at the fifteenth-century Schloss Sommerhausen. The attractive castle, now with a guest house open to the public, has been owned since 1968 by the Steinmann family, whose nursery is one of Germany's largest suppliers of grape vines. The vineyards supporting the winery cover 20 hectares and many varieties in addition to Silvaner, the leading vine in Franconia.

Martin Steinmann, the general manager, says that the winery has sought to specialize in dessert wines. "Our first regular Eiswein vintage was 1989 with Riesling," he says. Over the next decade, he has been able to produce Eiswein in eight different vintages, not only with Riesling but also Silvaner and Gewürztraminer — "and our favorite, Scheurebe."

In 1996, the coldest winter since 1961–62, the winery made a phenomenally powerful Eiswein by picking the Scheurebe at -18°C. The juice had a staggering sugar reading of 245° Oechsle (almost 60° Brix) and really bracing acidity — but necessary to balance the sweetness — of 23 grams per liter. Only 210 liters were made.

Schmitt Söhne Weinstrasse 8, D-54340 Longuich

Founded in 1919, this Mosel producer has become one of Germany's largest exporters. Among other clients, it is a supplier to Disneyworld in Florida. The first Eiswein by this producer was made in 1921 (one bottle remained in the winery cellar in

2000). Recent Eiswein vintages include 1995 and 1999, with the quantity limited to about one thousand half bottles from the Longuicher Herrenberg vineyard.

Weingut Schwab Bühlstrasse 17, D-97291 Thüngersheim

At this small winery in Franconia, Thomas Schwab continues the tradition of making Eiswein begun by his father, Gregor, who in 1972 made about 250 liters of Ruländer Eiswein, followed in 1978 by a Riesling and 1986 by a Scheurebe.

Thomas Schwab took over the winery in 1990. He produced Scheurebe Eiswein in 1991 and in 1995 (a mere 120 liters) and then made 180 liters of Silvaner in 1996.

Weingut Selbach-Oster Uferallee 23, D-54492 Zeltingen/Mosel

Johannes Selbach was a brash 24-year-old University of Cologne business student in 1983 when he urged his father, Hans, to make Eiswein. His father took the less risky route of making fine Auslese Rieslings instead, fending off his son with a Selbach aphorism: "You cannot make gold more golden." In that year, one could, since 1983 was one of the best Eiswein vintages of the decade.

"Beautiful, beautiful Eisweine," Johannes Selbach, who now runs the wine business, said 17 years later, still regretting that he could not sway his father. "The '83 Eiswein is a textbook example to show people today how good an Eiswein tastes. The '83 Eisweine are now showing beautifully."

The family, in wine production in the Mosel for at least 350 years, made its first Eiswein in 1985 and now are consistent

Eiswein producers, with 13 vintages between 1985 and 1999. The winery also made Eiswein in 1995 and in 1997, two very late harvests, but declined to release them because the wines were unbalanced. "Rather than put our name on a wine we didn't like, we didn't bottle it," Selbach says.

Good Eiswein sites have been identified in two vineyards, Bernkasteler Badstube and Zeltinger Himmelreich, sites that are more assured of getting the required frost than more renowned vineyards. In 1999, when the harvest took place on December 22, only the juice from the Badstube Riesling had sufficient sugar (135° Oechsle) for Eiswein; at Himmelreich, which got less frost, the juice, at 122° Oechsle, was considered by Selbach to be "too weak" for Eiswein.

"The majority of our vineyards are excellent vineyards where you can always make very good wines and where the microclimate is so that it does not really freeze deeply," Selbach notes. The winery learned the hard way not to leave Eiswein grapes in its very best plots. "We've paid our dues with failed Eisweine in top vineyards."

Selbach sets out to make Eiswein every year, not because it is especially profitable (small-volume Eiswein seldom meets an accountant's standard for profit) but because it is the pinnacle of the vintage: "Eiswein is like the sportsmanship effort to achieve the ultimate."

For Selbach, the Eiswein year begins in the spring when the designated vines are pruned specifically for Eiswein (more canes and more buds remain on the vines). Those vines are managed differently throughout the season.

"Over the years we've learned that you have to write off that vineyard. You have to say, *this* is crossed out. If the boars eat it, if the birds take it, or the wind or the rain takes it, we won't weep," he explains. "With that attitude you can really make Eiswein. It is feast or famine."

Selbach-Oster is a typically small Mosel winery, making about seven thousand cases of wine a year. Selbach also operates a much larger négociant company, J & H Selbach, which distributes popular-priced wines made by other growers, including estate-bottled Eiswein. Selbach has been reluctant to join other German négociants in bottling and distributing so-called bulk Eisweine.

"We will not buy Eiswein in bulk," Selbach says firmly. "Eiswein in bulk is a new phenomenon. It comes from people who have surplus grapes. They leave them hanging and wait for a frost and make them more or less by accident. You get Eiswein which fulfills the letter of the law but it does not taste how I would like it to taste. And before I sell something I don't like, I'd rather not! It's a very simple but very successful business principle in our family."

True to his word, he produced three lots of wine in 2000 from Eiswein grapes but decided that only one lot, a mere 60 cases, had the power to be Eiswein. The remainder was bottled as Auslese. "Great Auslese," Selbach is quick to add.

Staatliche Weinbaudomäne Oppenheim Wormser Strasse 162, D-55276 Oppenheim

This winery was established in 1895 as an experimental station and, true to those roots, the winery's Frank Doka brings the detail of a scientist to the discussion of Eiswein. It is a risky business, he observes, with more than one cold day of at least −10° Celsius needed to freeze the grapes properly.

Production is necessarily small, with a hectare of vineyard yielding only two hundred to three hundred liters of wine.

"The best grape variety for Eiswein is Riesling," Doka maintains. "The high degree of acid, the content of residual sugar and the amount of extract — minerals and other components — make the wines full-bodied and guarantee maturing over a long time." Ten years after it was made, he described the winery's 1989 Riesling Eiswein as a juvenile. "We estimate that it will take more than 30 years to get this wine to its optimum."

Staatsweingut Bergstrasse Grieselstrasse 34-36, D-64625 Bensheim

The appellation north of Heidelberg known as Hessische Bergstrasse is comically tiny, with only 450 hectares of vines, but it contains a surprising number of quality producers. Possibly the most notable is the Staatsweingut Bergstrasse, owned by the state of Hesse. It harvested its first Eiswein in 1972 and, since 1977, succeeded in producing such a wine annually, both with Riesling and with Spätburgunder (Pinot Noir), from its renowned Heppenheimer Centgericht vineyard.

The winery's earliest and latest Eiswein harvests both occurred in 1983 when grapes from the unusually late 1982 vintage were picked on February 16, while the 1983 vintage was picked on November 13.

German wine commentators have called this winery the *Eisweinkönig* or Icewine King because of its unbroken string of vintages. The wines have won accolades in the market as well. At a 1997 wine auction, an astounding DM1200 was bid for a bottle of the winery's Spätburgunder Weissherbst 1996 Eiswein which was picked on Christmas Day that year. A mere two hundred to three hundred liters of Eiswein is made each year.

Weingut Tesch Naheweinstrasse 99, D-55450 Langenlonsheim

WEINGUT   SEIT 1723

TESCH

1997
RIESLING
LANGENLONSHEIMER LÖHRER BERG
EISWEIN

Gutsabfüllung
Qualitätswein mit Prädikat   375 ml
D-55450 Langenlonsheim
9,5% vol   NAHE

A.P.Nr. 7 738 166 14-98

The Tesch family has owned this estate since 1723 and has records of Eiswein production reaching back to the nineteenth century. Unfortunately, no Eiswein made before World War II remains in the cellars. Dr. Martin Tesch explains: "During the war, we lost nearly all our wine, so we cannot offer very old Eiswein. ... We still have Eisweins from nearly every possible vintage after the Second World War."

Over the years, the family has acquired

vineyards in what Martin Tesch calls "privileged top locations." Two of these, Königsschild and Löhrer Berg, produce the winery's modest quantities of Eiswein, between two hundred and four hundred liters a year, a drop in the winery's total annual output of 150,000 bottles, most of it Riesling and dry.

"The ideal site to produce Eiswein in our estate is the Löhrer Berg," Tesch explains. "Here the Riesling vines grow on top of the mountain and we obtain the lowest temperatures in our estate. In other sites we can only pick Eiswein if we get a very early, very cold night like in 1998." In that year the vineyards were hit by a sharp -13°C cold snap on November 19. "We obtained a must weight of 180° Oechsle at the Löhrer Berg and 160° Oechsle at the Königsschild. This was one of the best years for Eiswein in the last decade."

In contrast, the previous winter was so mild that few German producers made Eiswein. Tesch got just barely enough of a freeze at the Löhrer Berg on December 19 and the 1997 Eiswein juice had a sweetness of only 129° Oechsle. Tesch describes that Eiswein as "bright and light" compared with the concentrated 1998.

Martin Tesch, who manages the estate with his father, Hartmut, is a microbiologist and it shows in the almost surgical care he takes with Eiswein. The vines set aside for Eiswein are protected by plastic sheets against wind and rain. The vines are inspected twice a week and any grapes that become botrytis-affected are removed. The grapes, which are picked just before dawn at the coldest point in the night, are crushed into a pre-cooled press. The wine is fermented in stainless steel tanks, with the temperature precisely controlled.

"We are ranked among the German top estates," Tesch says proudly, "and we have received over 800 prizes and medals for our products."

Dr. H. Thanisch D-54470 Bernkastel-Kues

Two wine estates in Bernkastel operate side by side under the Thanisch name, sharing ownership of the renowned six-hectare Doctor Vineyard, so named because in the fourteenth century, the ailing archbishop of Trier recovered after drinking a glass of Riesling from this vineyard.

The Thanisch family, with a wine history extending back to 1636, split the estate in 1988, creating **Dr. H. Thanisch-Erben** and **Dr. H. Thanisch-Erben Müller-Burggraef**, now operating independently from each other.

The latter estate is owned by Margrit Müller-Burggraef and directed by her niece Barbara Rundquist-Müller, who researched the Thanisch Eiswein history and found that the first one was made in 1964. "I thought it had a much older tradition," she said. "It was one of the first made in the Mosel." There was then a rising popularity for late harvest wines and the Thanisch estate produced the complete range.

Until 1983, when German wine law set a minimum sweetness for Eiswein must, it was possible to produce less intense winter-harvest wines than are permitted today. Natural freezing was a way of concentrating the sugars and flavors of grapes that were not as fully mature. "You could have a Spätlese Eiswein, an Auslese Eiswein," Rundquist-Müller says. "In most cases, they were more sour than pleasant. Today, it must have the minimum must weight of a Beerenauslese."

The now-divided Doctor vineyard is where Rundquist-Müller's staff and family try to make Eiswein in a thousand-square-meter patch of south-facing vineyard that rarely gets the required deep freeze.

"One just does it, it's a question of prestige," Rundquist-Müller says. "You try to limit your losses. If it is not cold enough by the beginning of or the middle of December, we just harvest them."

In 1998 the freeze came in mid-November and three hundred liters of Eiswein were made, the first Doctor Eiswein since 1989. It is a flagship wine, always with a hefty price. "Basically, you want it on the best wine lists of the world." However, Rundquist-Müller offers popular-priced wines through **Zimmermann-Graeff & Müller**, the much larger winery in Zell (not far from Bernkastel) of which she also is a director. ZGM, which distributes the Thanisch Müller-Burggraef wines, is both a producer and a négociant.

In 1998, ZGM began purchasing Eisweine from independent growers in the Pfalz wine region, where Eiswein can be made almost every year. This more commercial product is sold internationally under such names as Rudolf Müller, who was Rundquist-Müller's grandfather and one of Germany's most successful wine exporters of the twentieth century.

TauberFränkische Winzergenossenschaft Beckstein Weinstrasse 30, D-97922 Lauda-Königshofen

A cooperative in Baden, this winery has made Eiswein since 1958, often with an annual production ranging from two to three thousand bottles. What is most unusual is the number of varieties its member growers have agreed to set aside for this purpose. The winery has made Eisweine in various vintages from Riesling, Schwarzriesling (as the Germans call Pinot Meunier), Silvaner, Kerner, Scheurebe and Gewürztraminer. Located in the quaintly beautiful community of Beckstein, the winery greets the public with a grand, candle-lit *weinstube* that is open until midnight.

Valckenberg Weckerlingplatz 1, D-67513 Worms

This is the winery that turned Liebfraumilch into a household word, somewhat to the regret of the Valckenberg family and its heirs. In the Middle Ages pilgrims came to worship the Madonna at the Church of Our Lady, the Liebfrauenkirche at the Capuchin monastery just outside the city of Worms. The vineyards around this church produced wines so pleasing that they came to be called Liebfraumilch, the "Milk of Our Lady."

In 1808 when church vineyards were being secularized, a Dutch wine merchant, Peter Joseph Valckenberg, bought the Liebfraumilch vineyards. A century later the first German wine law decreed that wine had to be denominated strictly from the area in which it was produced. By this time Valckenberg had established such a large international market for Liebfraumilch that grapes were being purchased from many vineyards in addition to those around the church. Rather than limit sales, the Valckenberg family allowed the use of Liebfraumilch as a generic synonym for Rhine wines.

The unfortunate result was that the reputation of Liebfraumilch was damaged by a glut of simple and inexpensive German white wines. However, the winery still controls most of the vineyards around the church and produces fine wines that are sold under the Madonna brand. These include Eisweine from the church vineyards, made since the 1960s in years when there is sufficient frost.

Weingut Robert Weil, Mühlberg 5, D-65399 Kiedrich

It is a challenge to say whether the village of Kiedrich's most attractive feature is its majestic church or this white-walled winery in its quiet park-like setting next to the cemetery. Under the direction of Wilhelm Weil, the fourth generation of his family to run the winery, it has emerged as a leading Rheingau producer. Robert Weil owns 60 hectares, including Gräfenberg, an 11-hectare slope just at the edge of the village. Weil owns most of the vineyard and produces the full range of Riesling wines there, including some of German's best late harvest wines.

Eiswein was first made in 1973. When Wilhelm Weil took over responsibility for the winery in 1987, he decided that he would try each vintage to make every possible Prädikat, or grade, of Riesling, including an average of 650 liters annually of Eiswein from the lower, frostier sections of the Gräfenberg. Elegant wines with the vibrant acidity that suggests good aging potential, the Weil Eiswein is prized by collectors.

"No risk, no fun," says Bernhard Werner on his philosophy toward late harvest wines, which he makes very well indeed. Born in 1958, he is one of a group in Leiwen that formed the Association of Young Winemakers in 1985 to improve the quality and the reputation of their Mosel community's wines. He labels his best table wines as "Par Excellence," a conceit, perhaps, but also a statement of his dedication.

The winery was started by his father, Oswald, who made Eiswein only as a hobby and could not be persuaded to set aside enough grapes for a significant quantity. "He never had the nerve to take the risk," says young Werner, who took over the winery in 1987 and made his first Eiswein the following year. With two hectares of grapes now dedicated to Eiswein and other late harvest wines, he seeks to make Eiswein every year and usually succeeds.

Clearly, Werner is not given to worrying. As the regular harvest finishes in late October or early November, he selects the healthiest unpicked grapes for Eiswein, deploys the foil that protects them from rain and then, as he puts it casually, just forgets about the grapes while awaiting a frost.

"You must play poker," he says. In the wonderful vintage of 1998, nature dealt him a full house. The frost was early, lasted for at least three days and was at its sharpest on the third day, a Sunday, when grapes were picked at -12°C — "Perfect," he says, "absolutely perfect."

As a result, Werner made five hundred liters, double the usual quantity, of Leiwener Klostergarten Riesling Eiswein, but in three lots, one for each harvest day. All are classic examples of the art. The Friday Eiswein is the lightest, the Saturday version is fat and spicy and the Sunday Eiswein is luscious, with ripe apricot flavors and with a lively acidity to balance the sweetness. Werner took a lot of fun from that vintage.

Weingut Wilhelmshof Queichstrasse 1, D-76833 Siebeldingen

I t was an excellent marriage that brought Herbert Roth in 1975 to Wilhelmshof where he now is the winemaker and one of the proprietors. Roth acquired the art of making sparkling wine through studies in Champagne. This Pfalz winery produces only 80,000 bottles a year, but a third of the production is sparkling wine that has gained Wilhelmshof considerable acclaim.

Roth has applied himself to Eiswein with similar careful attention; whether he makes one each year depends on the selected grapes being sound enough to hang late into the year, if not longer. His 1997 Silvaner Eiswein, made from grapes harvested on January 28, 1998, won several major awards. Roth also was able to make Eiswein twice that year because the 1998 Eiswein grapes — Riesling this time — were picked on November 22, 1998.

Weingut Des Hauses Württemberg Schloss Monrepos, D-71634 Ludwigsburg

E ven royalty cannot resist the challenge of Eiswein. This winery, with a history dating from 1677 and vineyards that are much older, belongs to the royal house that governed the former Kingdom of Württemberg which existed from 1805 to 1918.

The winery is near the castle which is set in an expansive park-like setting. The extensive production covers the gamut of what can be made with grapes, from wines to brandies to vinegar. Despite the long history, the first Eiswein was made in 1996, a Riesling Eiswein harvested December 26 in the Stettener Brotwasser vineyard, one of the many distinguished properties owned by the Württembergs.

5

The Austrians

Austria's first Eisweine were made in the mid-1960s. Heidi Schröck, the talented young Rust winemaker behind the revival of Ausbruch, the legendary dessert wine from Rust, says that Klosterkeller Siegendorf produced a vintage in 1965 by taking advantage of an unexpectedly early frost.

Other producers in Austria soon were making Eiswein deliberately because, Schröck believes, German tourists asked for it. "For a time, Ausbruch was in danger of being replaced by Eiswein," she laments. It is perhaps an exaggeration to blame Eiswein for the near-extinction of Ausbruch, but it is not exaggeration to credit Ausbruch for laying the foundation on which rests the Austrian reputation for growing some of the world's finest sweet wines.

The medley of Austrian dessert wines has specific gradations of sweetness defined in the Austrian wine law. The summit of sweetness is Trockenbeerenauslese, made from overripe botrytis-affected grapes that have shriveled on the vine; the minimum must weight is 32° KMW. (This refers to Klosterneuburger Mostwaage, a measurement of grape sugar developed in 1869 at the Klosterneuburg wine school. One degree KMW is equal to one per cent sugar. A dry table wine is made from grapes with a minimum of 13° KMW.)

Grapes for Ausbruch have a minimum sweetness of 27° KMW and must be botrytis-affected. A minimum sweetness of 25° KMW is required for Beerenauslese, Strohwein and Eiswein, although it is not unusual for Eiswein, when made from overripe grapes frozen hard by a deep frost, to reach sugar levels even of a Trockenbeeren-auslese. The difference is that both Eiswein and Strohwein usually are made from grapes unaffected by botrytis.

Strohwein achieves its concentration because the grapes are placed on beds of straw (*stroh*) after being picked and allowed to dehydrate for some weeks before being crushed. If the grapes are dried instead on the reeds (*schilf*) that grow at the edge of Neusiedler See, the wine is called Schilfwein.

All of these wines are labor-intensive — only Eiswein grapes can be harvested by machine — and all are fraught with the risk of failure from natural causes. Botrytis cinerea, the so-called noble rot, works its magic by dehydrating grapes on the vine, not only concentrating the flavors but as well adding a characteristic taste and aroma (honey and tobacco). Noble rot flourishes in those microclimates where the mornings are misty but the afternoons are dry.

Few areas in the world have a better microclimate for noble rot than the vineyards around Neusiedler See, in particular the four hundred hectares at Rust, the tiny city of seventeen hundred persons on the southwest shore of the lake. Thirty-five kilometers long, Neusiedler See has an area of some three hundred square kilometers but seldom is more than one and a half meters deep. It loses half its volume by evaporation each year, creating morning mists that promote noble rot.

Winemakers have used this phenomenon for a long time to make distinctive sweet wines. The wines of Rust were already so well-known in the sixteenth century that in 1524 the wineries received a special trademark — the letter "R" which still is stamped on the corks of Rust wines — to certify the origin of the wines.

Early records refer to noble rot wines in 1617 and Ruster Ausbruch in 1634. The term "Ausbruch" means carefully selected berries that are affected by botrytis.

As Rust's charming architecture shows, the city so prospered from its unctuous wines that in 1681 it gained free city status by paying the emperor 60,000 gold guilders and 30,000 liters of Ruster Ausbruch.[1] In the Habsburg empire, the only other wine of equal repute was Tokaji Aszú, a comparable noble rot wine from north-eastern Hungary. These were among central Europe's earliest record-ed noble rot wines, certainly predating the storied "discovery" of noble rot Riesling at Schloss Johannisberg in 1775 and perhaps even preceding the systematic production of Sauternes.

Like Tokaji, traditional Ausbruch was made primarily from a grape called Furmint, notably useful for sweet wines because it reaches good sugar levels while retaining high acidity. Other Austrian white varieties, such as Welschriesling, now also are used for Ausbruch but Heidi Schröck and her colleagues in the Cercle replanted Furmint after the variety almost vanished from the vine-yards of Rust.

Ausbruch was near extinction at least twice before it was chal-lenged by Eiswein. In 1865 the shallow Neusiedler See dried up entirely and remained dry until 1871, putting a temporary end to noble rot. Sweet wines still were made from very ripe grapes but they missed the complexity added by the noble rot flavors. Then phylloxera ravaged the vineyards of Burgenland in 1897.

Farmers did not replant many of the vineyards for half a cen-tury as Austria itself stumbled through one impoverishing political crisis after another: dissolution of the empire after World War I, followed by the depression, World War II and Soviet occupation which ended only in 1955. The occupying troops plundered the wine cellars and almost no pre-war wines can be found anywhere in the country.

Sadly, there was a precedent for this brigandry: Napoleon's troops at the beginning of the previous century blew up the cellar at Klosterneuburg and drank so much wine elsewhere that they came to be called the thirstiest army in Europe.[2]

A turning point for the sweet wines of Austria was the vintage of 1969, when Burgenland experienced extensive noble rot across the vineyards. Stephen Brook, in his 1987 book called *Liquid Gold*, recounts how several winemakers got such high sugar readings on their grapes that they assumed their instruments had malfunc-tioned.[3] The winemakers of Burgenland produced 12,225 hectoliters of Beerenauslese and 3,500 hectoliters of Trockenbeerenauslese, astonishing quantities of excellent dessert wines that were sold comparatively cheaply. Almost instantly, the Austrians came to be known as suppliers of bulk quantities of good, reasonably priced sweet wines, usually to bottlers in Germany. Even larger quantities were made in the vintages of 1973, 1976 and 1981.

These dessert wines were as well made as comparable sweet wines of France and Germany but were much less well known around the world because, in the fragmented Austrian wine business, few producers exported their own wines. If they did, they typically wholesaled their wines to one of the handful of large firms such as Lenz Moser at Rohrendorf near Krems, which had its own vast estates and, as a reputable négociant, purchased from others.

The success of the Austrian sweet wines set the stage for the wine scandal of 1985 when wines adulterated with diethylene glycol were uncovered. The practice, which may have been going on for several years, came to light when an auditor investigated why a winery was buying unusually large quantities of this substance, normally used in benign chemical applications. A minute addition of this chemical — at first the Austrian authorities lacked instruments calibrated to measure for it — is very hard to detect by chemical analysis. With a few drops of this and a sweetening agent, it was a simple matter to raise the apparent quality of a Spätlese by one or two levels from its minimum 19° KMW.

The Austrian authorities became aware that this might be happening in April 1985 and, after confirming tests, warned the market. Word flashed around the world in July after the Germans, who were then buying two-thirds of Austria's wine, mostly in bulk, impounded and tested wines — and advised consumers not to drink them.

The world's media treated the matter first with alarm and then with cynical witticisms. For example, *The Economist,* the influential British weekly, wrote that some Austrian wine traders had been caught adding "a substance commonly used in antifreeze for car engines." The magazine, and many other wine writers, confused the adulterating but not especially dangerous chemical with toxic ethylene glycol, which is used in antifreeze. Sweet wine from Austria became unsaleable.

Big wine exporters such as Lenz Moser, none of whose wines were involved in the scandal, saw business collapse overnight. (Lenz Moser had been established by the respected Moser family since 1848; it was taken over by its bankers and then sold to other commercial interests.) In the United States, the Bureau of Alcohol, Tobacco and Firearms released a long list of Austrian and German wines (including eight Austrian Eisweine and one German Eiswein presumably reinforced with Austrian blending stock) in which diethylene glycol had been detected.

The Austrians promptly prosecuted and jailed the culprits and imposed a tough new wine law in August 1985. Among other measures, the authorities banned the export of sweet wines in bulk, requiring it to be bottled in Austria where its soundness could be assured. In the years immediately after the scandal, Austrian producers concentrated on fine dry table wines. But in the 1990s producers once again dared to increase sweet wine production, with a revival of Ausbruch and a significant increase in Eiswein output.

The community in Austria where wine production first was recorded, in 1217, is Mönchhof on the Pannonian Plain, 50 kilometers southeast of Vienna. Here, Weingut Hafner claims that in 1971, it made the first Austrian Eiswein produced deliberately, rather than as a result of accidentally early frost. The variety employed was Weissburgunder. Since then the winery has been a consistent producer of Eiswein, in quantities ranging from three hundred liters to five thousand, depending on the circumstances of the vintage. The only break in the winery's record of Eiswein production are the vintages from 1985 to 1989, the years following the wine scandal when few in Austria made sweet wines. The Hafner winery was among those that failed after 1985, to be re-established when Julius Hafner III, tutored by his father, began making wine.

The Hafners have a history of making multiple Eisweine when the conditions allow it. In 1983, for example, eight were made; five were made in 1991 and again in 1998; four were made in 1980 and in 1997. Only twice in the 1990s was the winery unable to make Eiswein at all. The consistency is due to the vineyards around Mönchhof being far enough from Neusiedler See that the grapes are less likely to be affected with noble rot than, for example, those at Rust.

The winery's Eiswein production records provide a glimpse into Austrian Eiswein. Typically, the Austrians employ a great number of grape varieties; the grapes are very ripe when picked and the resulting wines often achieve higher alcohol levels, and may have slightly lower acidity, than German counterparts.

The Hafner Eisweine

Year	Harvest date	Variety	KMW*	Residual sugar/g/l	Acid /g/l	Alcohol %
1971	Nov. 23	Weissburgunder	32	125	7.2	11.5
1973	Jan.5, 1974	Weissburgunder	28	108	6.5	10.7
1976	Jan.6, 1977	Gewürztraminer	29.5	112	6.1	10.2
1977	Jan.6, 1978	Gewürztraminer	32	118	7.4	10.5
1978	Dec. 12	Weissburgunder	31.5	126	8.1	11.7
1980	Dec. 28	Weissburgunder	31	107	7	12
1980	Dec. 28	Sämling	31.5	117	7.3	11.8
1980	Jan.12, 1981	Gewürztraminer	27.5	109	6.9	11.1
1980	Jan.12, 1981	Traminer/Bouvier	28.5	113	7.2	11.5
1983	Jan.5, 1984	Sämling	30	119	6.9	12.1
1983	Jan.5, 1984	Gewürztraminer	29.5	122	7	11.8
1983	Jan.5, 1984	Welschriesling	28	110	7.8	11.2
1983	Jan.5, 1984	Neuburger	29	115	7.1	12
1983	Jan.6 1984	Müller Thurgau	31.5	121	6.5	12.1
1983	Jan.6, 1984	Weissburgunder	30	118	7.9	11.8
1983	Jan.6, 1984	Grüner Veltliner	28	105	7.3	11.2
1983	Jan.6, 1984	Goldburger	32	124	6.2	10.3

1984	Jan.1, 1985	Welschriesling + Weissburgunder	31.5	115	7.2	11.9
1984	Jan.1, 1985	Gewurztraminer	29	107	7.5	12.2
1984	Jan.1, 1985	Welschriesling + Goldburger	32	119	7	12
1984	Jan.1, 1985	Grüner Veltliner	27.5	104	8	11.4
1990	Dec. 4	Chardonnay + Traminer	27	132.1	6.5	10
1990	Dec. 4	Zweigelt	26	106	5.7	11.5
1991	Dec. 9	Ruländer	29.5	159	10.1	9.6
1991	Dec. 9	Ruländer (II)	37	175	10.9	11.9
1991	Dec. 9	Zweigelt	26	92	5.7	11.6
1991	Dec. 9	Muskat Ottonel	29.5	108	6.1	13.7
1991	Dec. 9	Chardonnay	30	115	6.7	12
1992	Dec. 29	Sämling	26.5	108	6	11.3
1995	Jan.5, 1996	Sämling	31	125	7.4	10.5
1995	Jan.5, 1996	Chardonnay	28.5	102	8.7	11.8
1995	Jan.5, 1996	Welschriesling	26	109	8.2	10.8
1997	Oct. 30	Sämling	26.5	136	8.9	9.2
1997	Oct. 30	Muskat Ottonel	33	109	8.1	13.2
1997	Dec. 12	Chardonnay + Welschriesling	26	112	5.4	11
1997	Dec. 12	Muskat Ottonel II	35	127	8	11
1998	Dec. 19	Ruländer	26.5	105	9.1	10.5
1998	Dec. 19	Muskat Ottonel	29.5	127	7.8	12
1998	Dec. 20	Chardonnay	27	115	8	11.5
1998	Dec. 20	Grüner Veltliner	26.5	109	7.5	11
1998	Dec. 20	Zweigelt	26.5	107	6.4	10
1999	Dec. 14	Sämling	28	130	7.6	10.3
2000	Dec. 22/23	Chardonnay /Sämling	28	135	N.A.	10.5

* KMW stands for Klosterneuburger Mostwaage, a scale of must measurement created at the wine school at Klosterneuburg near Vienna. 1° KMW equals approximately 5° Oechsle, the equivalent scale used in Germany.

6

A Parade of Austrian Eiswein Producers

What sets Austrian Eisweine apart from those of the rest of world is the proliferation of grape varieties that are used. As many as 20 may be employed, including indigenous grapes, such as Grüner Veltliner and Zweigelt, almost exclusive to Austria. The obscure Blauer Wildbacher grape, also known as Schilcher, is a traditional grape confined to the tiny viticultural region of West Styria in southeastern Austria. Sure enough, a Schilcher Eiswein appears among the wines made at Weingut Jöbstl, a well-regarded Styrian producer in the village of Wernersdorf. The wine is said to have an aroma of rose petals. This is typical of the cornucopia of fresh, even unique, flavors and aromas presented by Austrian Eisweine. Almost always, the wines are well made, reflecting Austria's long tradition for making excellent sweet wines.

Since nearly all Austrian producers have only small vineyards, wineries each seldom make more than one thousand liters of Eiswein in a single vintage; often, only enough is made to satisfy a winery's local market.

Austrian Eiswein also is distinguished by its price, typically selling for only half to two-thirds that of German Eiswein. This anomaly is inexplicable, since some leading wineries often ask aggressive prices (that are fully merited) for other powerful sweet wines such as Ruster Ausbruch. It may just be that Ausbruch has centuries of history behind it, while Eiswein still is novel. Most of the producers only began making Eiswein in the 1990s as a new generation of young winemakers took over, seeking to establish themselves by mastering one of wine's ultimate challenges.

Weingut Matthias Achs & Sohn Am Goldberg 15, A-7122 Gols

The father and son team running this family-owned winery, which traces its history to 1624, are both graduates of Austrian wine schools. From 20 hectares of vineyard, they produce about 150,000 bottles of wine a year. As if the quality were not enough to sell these wines, the Achs family also puts some of its production in 50 different specialty bottles; for hunters, there even is a bottle shaped like a musket.

"In our region, which is favored by the Pannonian climate — hot summers with a lot of sunshine and quite cold winters — it is possible to produce wonderful ice-wines," the winery states in its literature. The quantities are always small which is why the winery describes Eiswein as "an absolute rarity in international winegrowing."

The winery began releasing Eisweine under its own label in 1991, beginning with one made from a Neuburger-Riesling blend. By using harvesting machines, the winery has overcome the labor shortages that limited Eiswein production volumes. In the 1999 vintage, eight hundred liters were made from a blend of Sämling 88 and Riesling.

Matthias Achs Senior discovered that machine harvesting also has its hazards. In the 1996 Eiswein vintage, it was so cold that he suffered frostbite to two fingers while cleaning a harvester with wet gloves.

Winzerhof Familie Alt A-3471 Grossriedenthal 32

See Grossriedenthal, page 109.

This winery, thirty kilometers south of Vienna and with six hectares of vineyards, is about twenty-five years old, young by Austrian standards. Leopold Aumann, who was born in 1978, made his first Eiswein in 1993, a Grüner Veltliner picked very early on the morning of November 17 at -8°C. The result was a rich and muscular Eiswein (alcohol of 13.1 per cent but still 136 grams of residual sugar per liter). Leopold believes that the wine will live at least to 2020.

He points out that in his region good Eiswein years are also good red wine years for the same reason: an absence of botrytis. The other two fine years in the last decade of the century were 1997 and 1999.

The Aumanns average three thousand to five thousand small bottles of Eiswein in such vintages. They recommend the wine be served at the end of banquets, taken perhaps with Gorgonzola or Roquefort cheese or with one of the classic desserts of Vienna.

Weingut Anton Bauer Neufang 42, A-3483 Feuersbrunn

When he was only 20, Krems-trained Toni Bauer in 1992 assumed responsibility for the production at this family winery that is more than a century and a half old.

Bauer, who also spent five years as assistant winemaker at Weingut Dr. Unger in Furth, likes his wines bold. The winery's 1999 Grüner Veltliner Reserve had 14 per cent alcohol but also was packed with fruit. The 1999 Chardonnay, with a similar alcohol, was partially barrel-fermented.

Bauer's first Eiswein, six hundred liters of 1999 Grüner

Veltliner, was fermented in and aged two months in oak. With only 80 grams of residual sugar, it is comparatively dry for an Eiswein but appealing, with caramel flavor notes.

Familie Bauer Naturnaher Weinbau Hauptstrasse 68, A-3471 Grossriedenthal

See Grossriedenthal, page 109.

Weinbau Familie Bartl Hauptstrasse 40, A-3471 Grossreidenthal

See Grossriedenthal, page 109.

Weingut Bründlmayer Zwettlerstrasse 23, A-3550 Langenlois

U nder the hand of Willi Bründlmayer, who has managed this estate and its 60 hectares of vineyard since 1980, the winery has gained a reputation for its dry white wines, its sekt and, unusual for this region of Austria, for growing enough red varieties that reds make up a third of Bründlmayer's output.

The red varieties are described as a "hobby horse" of the family; the varieties were planted by Wilhelm Bründlmayer, Willi's father, because his wife preferred red wines.

Most of the vineyards are terraced on the hills around Langenlois, on soils whose ancient complexity adds to the character of the wines. For example, the soils of the Zöbinger Heiligenstein vineyard are 250 million years old and are a mix of sandstone and volcanic deposits. The vines are grown organically and vineyards are allowed to lie fallow five years between replanting

Bründlmayer produces powerful and complex sweet wines; recent notable examples include a 1998 Grüner Veltliner Beerenauslese aged 12 months in new 300-liter oak casks to accent the ripe, spicy fruit. The one Eiswein in the Bründlmayer cellar is a 1976 made when an early frost caught the estate with unharvested grapes. Produced with a cuvée of Chardonnay and Pinot Blanc, the wine a quarter-century later had evolved into a rich and complex compote of fruit flavors.

Weinbau Karl Diwald A-3471 Grossriedenthal 33

See Grossriedenthal, page 109.

Weingut Edelhof Hauptplatz 6, A-7093 Jois

The Wetschka family, now with six and a half hectares of vineyards, has been making wine in this area of Burgenland for five or six generations. The lack of precision reflects the fact that Martin Wetschka, who describes himself as the junior winemaker, is only 25. But he is a seasoned 25, having completed wine school and worked abroad, including with the legendary Paul Draper at Ridge in California. "I like the international style of wines," Martin says.

Leo, his father, began making Eiswein in 1990. Edelhof — the name comes from a small old castle that the family is restoring — only makes between eight hundred and twelve hundred half bottles of Eiswein on average every second vintage. The varieties include Goldburger, Neuburger and Welschriesling.

After nearly 40 years' experience making sweet wines, Johannes Holler has developed frank opinions. "I am not convinced about Eiswein," he says. The skepticism arises because, since he made his first Eiswein in 1987, he has lost at least two potential vintages to the abundant population of birds around Rust.

But Holler, who with his wife owns vineyards that have been in the family since 1642, also is a practical businessman who has 400,000 bottles of wine to sell each year. He often sets aside for Eiswein one to four hectares of the thirty-two cultivated by Elfenhof because his customers ask for Eiswein. It can only be produced in those years when the vineyards of Rust are lightly touched, if at all, by noble rot. In other years Holler, like his neighbors, produces the great Ausbruch and other dessert wines for which the community is renowned.

In markets like Japan, where the noble rot wines are not always well known, Holler's Eiswein is the carrot that draws customers into tasting all of the wines in Elfenhof's range. His white Eisweine usually are made by fermenting together the juice of Welschriesling and Goldburger (the latter a relatively recent Austrian-bred variety that achieves very high sugar at maturity). For red Eiswein, Holler turns to Blaufränkisch.

Weinbau Ing. Wilhelm Eminger Nr. 90-91, A-2224 Niedersulz

The Eminger family has been growing wine for generations in Weinviertel and, with nine hectares of vineyards, makes slightly more white wine than red, including a superb barrel-fermented Weissburgunder in the so-called international style. Wilhelm Eminger's first Eiswein was made in 1999, some fifteen hundred half bottles of Welschriesling Eiswein. "It was an experiment," he explains. "I wanted to try something new." The experiment succeeded: the wine, with 13 per cent alcohol and enough acidity to balance 116 grams of residual sugar, shows tropical fruit flavors and an exotic aroma; the texture is rich with the backbone of a mineral graininess.

Weingut Alfred Fischer Hauptstrasse 1-3, A-7023 Stöttera

This Burgenland winery was established in 1931 and is run today by the son and grandson of the founder, both of whom also bear the name Alfred (although the grandson, born in 1979, goes by Thomas). They have built a substantial business with grapes from their own ten hectares of vineyards and with grapes purchased from three hundred growers, filling each year a cellar with a capacity of seven million liters.

The Fischers began making Eiswein in the early 1970s, taking advantage of a year without botrytis to introduce a new product for the winery's extensive range. Now the winery makes between 20,000 and 40,000 small bottles a year.

While the first Eiswein was made with Welschriesling, Alfred Fischer has settled on Sämling 88 (Scheurebe) as the preferred Eiswein grape because of its dramatic perfume. His 1997 Eiswein, sold affordably in 200 ml bottles, has that beautifully exotic aroma with flavors of pineapple and melons and with a fresh, clean finish. The 1997 vintage was so bounteous that Fischer did not make any in the following three vintages.

Freie Weingärtner Wachau A-3601 Dürnstein

A cooperative owned by nearly eight hundred growers, Freie Weingärtner's cellars have been built within sight of castle ruins at Dürnstein on the Danube. It is recorded that, during the Crusades of the twelfth century, Richard the Lion-Heart was held hostage here for a year until he was ransomed.

The cooperative belongs to an organization called Vinea Wachau, founded in 1983 by winemakers concerned with defining the Wachau wine region and establishing the quality terms for the region's dry white wines. The three main categories, going from the lightest to the most intense, are Steinfeder, Federspiel and Smaragd. The latter is the strangest of wine terms: it is actually the name of an emerald-green lizard native to the stony Wachau vineyards.

Freie Weingärtner's range of wines extends to well-made Trockenbeerenauslese but rarely to Eiswein. Often when the winery seeks to complete a tasting, it will do so with an Eiswein from a Wachau producer such as **Weingut Franz Hirtzberger** at Spitz. And Hirtzberger makes a few hundred liters of Eiswein only in the largest of vintages.

Schloss Gobelsburg Schlosstrasse 16 A-3550 Langenlois

An estate whose history dates at least from the eleventh century, Schloss Gobelsburg today is an attractive baroque palace surrounded by vineyards. The winery now is managed by Michael Moosbrugger, who grew up in the hotel and restaurant trade. He switched to wine in 1996 when the Cistercian monks of Zwettl Abbey stopped operating this 10,000-case winery.

With advice from Willi Bründlmayer — who could want a better consultant? — Moosbrugger has modernized the cellar and the winemaking. He declines to pour a 1993 Eiswein made before his time, explaining that "the wine had a problem from the beginning." He is justly proud of his peach-flavored 1999 Eiswein, of which five hundred liters were made from Grüner Veltliner harvested by machine on at -11°C on December 23.

"It was a wish to get more experience in that very special category of wine," he says. "We have a long tradition for Eiswein in this region. We are very seldom able to make sweet wines from botrytis-affected grapes but we can make Eisweine more regularly."

The community of Grossriedenthal (population five hundred) calls itself Austria's Eiswein Village, with perhaps fifteen wineries now making Eiswein routinely. Only 30 kilometers east of Krems, the village emerged from a heritage of raising pigs and dairy cattle. Despite the charm of its cobbled Hauptstrasse, Grossriedenthal does not yet exude the prosperity of established Austrian wine communities. Here, the rising winemakers are well-schooled and ambitious young people who have taken over the family businesses, determined to play a bigger role than their ancestors.

The sleepy town nestles in a valley below a ridge called the Wagram, a feature that runs for many kilometers with southern slopes ideal for vineyards. The vineyards seldom are touched with botrytis and that is one reason why, when the producers make top sweet wines, Eiswein is a logical choice.

Alfred Holzer, the owner of **Winzerhof Alfred und Maria Holzer** at Hauptstrasse 17, was one of the first Eiswein producers, making one in 1989 from Roter Veltliner, a comparatively rare grape almost exclusive to the Wagram, where Holzer has his 12 hectares of vineyards. "It has good acidity and good extract," he explains. "It has more acidity than Grüner Veltliner." This shows in the remarkable freshness of the Holzer Eisweine. Tasted 11 years later, the 1989, while gold in color and showing aromas of caramel and apricots, had a frosty crispness to the fruit flavors.

A similar style could be seen in the Eisweine that Holzer was able to make in 1991, 1992, 1993, 1995 and 1999. His output is as rare as the grape: between eight hundred and eighteen hundred half bottles in each vintage. In the initial years, Holzer's artistic daughter, Claudia, drew a gold hand-crafted label on each bottle.

Karl Schuster, once a choir boy at the majestic monastery of Göttweig, also made

Eiswein 1991
Großriedenthaler Sand
alc. 11 % vol   Prädikatswein   süß
Österreich   L/F 0558792   ℮ 0,375 L
Weingut Fam. H. u. I. Holzer,   A-3471 Großriedenthal 30

an Eiswein in 1989. "We were young," he laughs (he was then 29). He makes between one hundred and fifty and one thousand liters of Eiswein a year. His 1991 Grüner Veltliner Eiswein, harvested at -15°C, remains a hugely concentrated tour de force.

Now that he is older, Schuster complains that making Eiswein is too much work, even though his two-hundred-year-old **Weingut Familie Schuster**, at Hauptstrasse 61, only has a total production of about 50,000 liters a year. He puts such effort into his hand-crafted wines that his wife calls him an artist.

Several producers joined the group making Eiswein in 1991, including **Weinbau Josef Mantler** at Hauptstrasse 25, with a Grüner Veltliner still showing fresh fruit and a peppery finish a decade later. At **Weinbau Karl Diwald** at Hauptstrasse 33, a winery established in 1925 with 10 hectares of vineyard, the first Eiswein was made in 1991 with Grüner Veltliner. Karl Diwald, only 25 in 2000, was in the vineyards with his family on November 20, 1991, to pick the grapes in the pre-dawn darkness, with the temperature at -20°C. "Fortunately, there was absolutely no wind," he remembers. The deep cold at picking resulted in an intense Eiswein with 195 grams of residual sugar per liter and layered with honeyed tropical fruit flavors.

The Diwald 1993 Grüner Veltliner Eiswein stands in absolute contrast, with only 112 grams of residual sugar. The Diwald 1998, the winery's third Eiswein, was made from grapes picked December 11 at -14°C and, with the peppery richness of Grüner Veltliner, shows the most elegant balance of the trio with 149 grams of residual sugar. The winery seldom makes more than two hundred liters in each Eiswein vintage.

Yet another occasional Eiswein producer in this village is **Winzerhof Familie Alt** at Hauptstrasse 32, a winery dating from 1900, which made a 1992 Zweigelt Eiswein. Almost a decade later, the wine remained a fresh, rose petal–hued, spicy-sweet confection tasting of plums and cherries. Andreas Alt, 29, another of the wine-makers trained in Krems, recalls his father making an opportunistic Eiswein in 1981 during a late October cold snap. Because there was little market for it, the resulting wine was not sold as Eiswein but went into Alt's late harvest wines. Recent Eisweine have been made with Grüner Veltliner, the dominant grape in the Alt vineyards.

One of the stars in Grossriedenthal is Josef Bauer, the serious young man born in 1973 who's in charge of **Familie Bauer Naturnaher Weinbau**, located at Haupstrasse 68. Long grape growers, the Bauers only focused on making wine in the mid-1980s. Their traditional cellar is more than two centuries old but in 1995 they built a new cellar, gleaming with temperature-controlled stainless steel tanks set on a pristine tile floor.

This equipped the soft-spoken Josef, after four years studying winemaking in Krems, with the tools to continue making the wines which have placed the winery among Austria's top one hundred producers.

The Bauer family's first Eiswein was made in 1991, taking advantage of a -17°C freeze. In every subsequent year but one, they produced Eisweine from their vineyards, using such varieties as Riesling, Blauburgunder and Grüner Veltliner. As Bauer offers a glass of his 1997 Grüner Veltliner Eiswein, he observes proudly that in one American tasting, it matched a score of 93 points gained by an Eiswein from Alois Kracher, one of Austria's most acclaimed dessert wine producers.

Josef's uncle, Franz Schneider, whose **Weingut Franz Schneider** at Hauptstrasse 103 has three and a half hectares of vineyard, made an Eiswein in 1999 from Sauvignon Blanc, the first time this variety has been used for Eiswein in Grossriedenthal.

Weinbau Familie Bartl at Hauptstrasse 40 is more than 50 years old and produces from about six hectares. Franz Bartl, the winemaker, made his first and only Eiswein of the last century in 1993, some five hundred half bottles from Grüner Veltliner. In the new Millennium, this wine remained fresh and lively, with a classic pepperiness balancing the sweet peach flavors.

Others in or near Grossriedenthal who make Eisweine include **Weingut Familie H. und I. Holzer** at Hauptstrasse 30; **Winzerhof Obenaus** at Hauptstrasse 53, whose 1994 Zweigelt Eiswein recalls a bowl of sweet cherries; **Weinbau Othmar Passecker** at 3471 Neudegg 32 with a 1994 Grüner Veltliner; **Weinbau Riegler** at Hauptstrasse 77 with a 1998 Zweigelt; **Weinbau Wöber** at 3471 Neudegg 40, with a 1999 Eiswein made with Grüner Veltliner and Sämling 88; and **Weinbau Zeiner,** one of only two Grossriedenthal producers (Bauer was the other) who managed to make Eiswein in the difficult vintage of 2000.

Weingut Hafner Halbturner Strasse 17, A-7123 Mönchhof

The Hafner family has made wine in Mönchhof for five generations which, for this community, is a blink of the eye. Mönchhof claims to be the oldest winemaking town in Austria, with winegrowing recorded as early as 1217.

Julius Hafner III maintains that his father, also named Julius, was in 1971 the first Austrian winemaker to make Eiswein deliberately. Those few that predated Hafner resulted when unexpected frosts caught grapes still in the vineyard. Hafner's inspiration came from Germany where he has been impressed by several early examples he tasted. The first Hafner Eiswein was made from Weissburgunder grapes harvested at -8°C in a one-acre vineyard near this Burgenland community.

A quarter century later, young Hafner, who was born in 1975, still had four or five bottles of that wine along with a comprehensive selection of other Hafner Eisweine made over that period. The range is amazing because the Hafner winery was among those businesses swept away by the 1985 wine scandal.

The original Hafner winery now is in other hands while the self-confident young Hafner has rebuilt the business, including the winery's position as one of Austria's leading makers of kosher wines. In 2000 the winery's Chardonnay Eiswein was harvested on the night of the Jewish festival of Hanukkah, with the picking and pressing supervised by Rabbi A.Y. Schwartz of Vienna. Triumphantly, Hafner described this as a "world sensation — the first kosher and kosher for Passover Eiswein."

Hafner sets aside as much as 12 hectares of vineyard for sweet wines, with Scheurebe — or Sämling 88 as the variety is called in Austria — a preferred Eiswein grape. The late-maturing variety remains healthy on the vine and resists botrytis. "Botrytis flavor in Eiswein is not good," Julius Hafner believes. "Eiswein should be fruity and refreshing."

It is a challenge to avoid botrytis among the vineyards around the vast Neusiedler See, so shallow that it freezes in cold winters. Such cold weather does not occur reliably. Hafner says that growers should expect to make Eiswein only every second year in his region. "Top qualities will be produced three times in ten years," he warns.

Schlossweingut Graf Hardegg A-2062 Seefeld-Kadolz

In the flat rural landscape of northeastern Austria, the ochre-hued baroque Hardegg castle, built in 1704, commands the countryside, a reminder of the authority of the Hardegg family. "My ancestors became Count Hardeggs in 1492," says Count Maximilian Hardegg, recounting their services of bravery to the emperor.

The current count was born in 1966 and studied agriculture. Since 1991, he has managed his 2,500-hectare estate, one of the single largest farms in Austria. The vineyards comprise only 43 hectares; however, Hardegg, who has recently modernized the estate's winery, is leading the quality improvement in the Weinviertel region of Austria better known as the source of tart base wines for sparkling wine. The Graf Hardegg whites —

Weissburgunder, Riesling and Grüner Veltliner primarily — are crisply fresh wines; some are barrel-fermented to achieve more richness and complexity. The reds — Zweigelt, Merlot, Cabernet Sauvignon and Syrah — show the bright cherry flavors and leanness of cool climate wines.

Hardegg's winery began making Eiswein in 1994 and was able to make it every year of that decade, usually from the Steinbügel vineyard just behind the estate's winery. "Eiswein has no tradition in this region but we saw the rising international interest in sweet wines."

The harvest has been as late as January 28 in 1997. In 1999, it turned cold on the night of December 21. Under a full moon so bright that artificial lights were not needed, the count, his winemaker Peter Malberg and a group of friends harvested about two thousand kilograms of frozen Riesling between 11 P.M. and 1 A.M., enough to yield six hundred liters of wine.

In most of the vintages, the Hardegg Eisweine, all made with Riesling, display both a racy acidity and a remarkable intensity of fruit and sweetness. The 1998 benefited from an early harvest, December 10, when the grapes were healthy and solidly frozen at -10°C, yielding a perfect Eiswein, with fresh, spicy flavors of virginal purity. Unfortunately, serious hail in the autumn of 2000 so damaged the vineyards that the winery could make no icewine from that vintage.

Weingut Martin Haider Seegasse 16, A-7142 Illmitz

Established in 1870, this is one of the oldest producers in Illmitz. Martin Haider was only 21 in 1967 when he took over the family's three hectares of vineyards, then growing only three varieties of grapes for white wine. As his impeccable winemaking brought him awards and accolades, he has acquired a further seven hectares and expanded to fifteen varieties. "Against criticism you can defend," Haider likes to say. "Against praise you are powerless."

In 1981, the year in which he won his first wine championship at a competition in Ljubljana, he began making Eiswein: nine hundred liters of Welschriesling and three hundred of Zweigelt. The Zweigelt had become too ripe for a standard table wine and he had no choice but leave them for Eiswein. "It was a good accident," Haider recalled 19 years later during an extensive tasting of his wines that left no doubt about the ability of Eiswein to age. The Zweigelt, bronze in color, showed a powerful aroma of cassis, a silken texture and berry flavors that were very much still alive. The Welschriesling, gold in color, had a honeyed aroma and rich spicy flavors.

Because the Illmitz vineyards often are touched with botrytis, Haider finds that, on average, his style of Eiswein can be made once every four years. His style is fresh, with moderate alcohol, clean flavors of fruit and a hint of frost in the aroma. The wines never are aged in wood and, when possible, grapes with more than 20 per cent botrytis are avoided. In 1997, he produced a voluptuous Chardonnay Eiswein with a hint of noble rot because his pickers, who are paid by weight of grapes picked, gathered the noble rot grapes with the sound ones. The other grapes that Haider has employed for Eiswein are Welschriesling, Grüner Veltliner, Neuburger and Muskat Ottonel.

Schlosskellerei Halbturn Parkstrasse 4, A-7131 Halbturn

One of Austria's storied castles, baroque Schloss Halbturn is set in an expansive park in this village close to the border with Hungary. The castle belonged to the Hungarian royal court for about four hundred years until 1746 when it was purchased by the Austrian emperor. The current owner, Baron Paul Waldbott-Bassenheim, traces his lineage back to the court through a succession of ancestors, many of them field marshals in momentous campaigns.

Wine production dates at least from 1214. Today Halbturn, which manages a 2,000-hectare estate, produces about 200,000 bottles a year from 40 hectares of vineyards. The first Eiswein was made only in 1980.

"Nature gave it to us," admits Hans Beck, the cellarmaster at Halbturn for more than 30 years. "At the end of October, it suddenly turned cold. We had not planned to make Eiswein."

The wine was sold cheaply in bulk because the winery had no immediate market for it. In the 1990s, however, Halbturn began trying to produce Eiswein each year, often from Ruländer grapes, yielding a style in which flavors of peach mingle with citrus with elegant balance.

Hans Beck maintains that the 1999 Eiswein at Halbturn is the finest he ever has made, because the grapes were healthy and frozen hard at harvest. Picked on December 23 at -10°C, the wine has an aroma of pears and an intense sweetness balanced to perfection with piquant acidity. From ten thousand vines, Beck got enough fruit for two thousand half bottles of Eiswein. Individually numbered, it was his Millennium wine. "The year is 2000 and I have 2000 bottles," he said.

Weingut Heiss Untere Hauptstrasse 12, A-7142 Illmitz

At this small winery with its guest house on the main street of Illmitz, Franz Heiss and his family have been bottling well-regarded wines under the family label since 1970. The first Eiswein was made in 1972.

Even though he only has nine hectares of vines and a large portfolio, Heiss attempts two Eisweine every year. In 1999, for example, he made a Blaufränkisch Eiswein from grapes picked November 21 and a Welschriesling Eiswein from grapes picked just before Christmas. It is not always possible to harvest Eiswein at that time, or at all. One year the grapes remained on the vines until late January before Heiss accepted that a suitable frost would not come in time. Instead, he made a dessert wine whimsically called *Januarlese,* or January harvest.

The latest Eiswein-picking date Heiss has experienced was January 27, 1998, when he brought in Welschriesling and Sauvignon Blanc together, producing an intriguing wine tasting of fresh sweet melon covered with honey.

Weingut Familie H. und I. Holzer Hauptstrasse 30, A-3471 Grossriedenthal

See Grossriedenthal, page 109.

Winzerhof Alfred und Maria Holzer Hauptstrasse 17, A-3471 Grossriedenthal

See Grossriedenthal, page 109.

Weingut Höpler Hauptstrasse 52, A-7092 Winden am See

Few Austrian winemakers are as cosmopolitan as Jost Höpler. He was born in Vienna in 1938 with a wine pedigree in his family. His uncle was Dr. Robert Schlumberger, the bookish doctor of both law and philosophy who was the last Schlumberger to manage the famous sekt house that still bears the family name but now is corporately owned.

Höpler, after studying agriculture and working in French and Italian wineries, spent several years making Schlumberger sekt. That led to a job crafting sparkling wines at a South Australian winery named Kaiserstuhl for three years. After returning to Austria and briefly to his uncle's firm, Höpler in 1973 became the marketing spark plug at Klosterkeller Siegendorf, a successful wine exporter until the 1985 scandal (in which the winery was not involved) ruined the overseas sales of Austrian wines.

Leaving his partners at Siegendorf, Höpler in 1987 opened his own winery in a charming old farmhouse in the village of Winden. Here, he has established a style of pristinely clean wines which he sells to leading hotels and other prestige clients around the world. He leaves no export sale unexplored. One of the surprising customers for Höpler Eiswein is a retailer in Narvik, serving ships and oil platforms off northern Norway. "You would think they would like Glühwein," he laughs.

Höpler first tasted Eiswein when, as a young apprentice winemaker, he worked briefly in the Mosel in the 1960s. He made his

first Eiswein in Austria in 1974 for Siegendorf and in 1992 began making it consistently at his own winery. In style, his Eisweine are cleanly fruity but unctuously rich on the palate.

He has employed a host of varietals, including Sämling 88 in 1992; a blend of Muskat Ottonel and Grüner Veltliner in 1994; Cabernet Sauvignon in 1995 when that variety did not get too ripe; both Grüner Veltliner and Welschriesling in 1997; and in 1998, about 4,200 liters of Eiswein in a cuvée combining Grüner Veltliner, Welschriesling and Sämling 88.

"Eiswein is not the most difficult wine to make," he suggests. "It just happens." He takes special pride in the winery's Eiswein labels because they are designed by his wife Doris, an architect.

Weingut Hubertushof Heidegasse 4, A-7062 St. Margarethen

Charming St. Margarethen, just a few kilometers north of Rust, is known for the Passion Play which has been held every five years since 1926, staged on fine summer evenings in the rugged Roman quarry at the edge of the village. The actors all are diligent amateurs from the town. In the summer of 2000, the role of Peter was taken by Josef Kugler, 40, the third generation of his family to operate Hubertushof.

The winery is named for St. Hubert, patron saint of hunting, one pursuit of earlier generations of the Kugler family, as shown by the images of game on the family crest. Proud of his heritage, Kugler has had the crest molded into the bottles for some of his top wines. He also has been inspired by the quarry to register Vinum Saxum — saxum is Latin for stone — as a label for some of his best wines, including Eiswein.

The winery made its first Eiswein in 1975 when Kugler, still a teenaged student, urged his father to do so. If nature allows him, Kugler tries to produce between five thousand and ten thousand half bottles of Eiswein each year. The variety used most often is Welschriesling; occasionally Grüner Veltliner or Pinot Blanc and, for red Eiswein, Blaufränkisch. His Vinum Saxum Eiswein 1997, a blend of Welschriesling and Grüner Veltliner, won a gold medal at an international competition in Paris.

Johanneshof Reinisch Im Weingarten, A-2523 Tattendorf.

S ince establishing their winery in 1923 at Tattendorf, a village just 30 km south of Vienna, the Reinisch family has emerged among the leading winemakers in the region. A new winery with an airy tasting room and vaulted cathedral cellar for six hundred barrels opened in 1995, attractively placed in a garden setting just outside Tattendorf.

The setting draws visitors from the big city who, on arriving, find Austrian wines, notably the reds, that bear a touch of California. During much of the 1990s the consulting winemaker was Gerhard Reisacher, who also worked at Clos Du Val in the Napa Valley and then developed his own winery there.

Youthful Johannes Reinisch, who now makes the wines with his father Johann and is eldest of four Reinisch siblings at the winery, was the understudy, gaining experience during two vintages in California. "I met André Tchelistcheff once and got him to taste two of our wines," Johannes says, recalling the distinguished California winemaker who died in 1994. The stylistic influences of California ranged from what Reinisch learned about barrel-fermenting Chardonnay to techniques for crafting some of the biggest reds in Austria. The winery's Zweigelt is a dark, swaggering red layered with flavors of plums, blackberries and cherries after 25 days of skin contact. "If the skins are ripe, why not?" Johannes asks.

The Reinisch family's sure touch with Eiswein is largely home-grown. The first Eiswein vintage here was 1977, followed by 1979 and 1983. "Then we had the 1985 problem," says Johann Reinisch, referring to Austrian wine scandal that devastated sweet wine sales even for producers like Reinisch that were not involved in adulterating dessert wines. It took the winery some years to sell its large 1983 Eiswein production. Johann was philosophic: "It got better with age."

In the 1990s, Reinisch resumed making Eiswein in years with favorable conditions. The wines often are blends of Grüner Veltliner and Neuburger grapes. The former, employed because it has good acidity, is fermented in stainless steel tanks, while the Neuberger, used for its high sugars, is fermented in barrels.

The object is to make Eisweine that express harmony rather than varietal character. However, in 1997 when it froze at the end of October, Reinisch made single variety Eisweine from Neuburger and from a rare red-fleshed Austrian variety called Blauburger. "We had intended to make a table wine but the grapes froze," Johannes confesses. The outcome was a dark rose-colored Eiswein oozing fresh flavors of cherries and strawberries.

Weingut Jurtschitsch
Rudolfstrasse 37-39, A-3550
Langenlois

F or a long time this winery was called Sonnhof until, starting with wines from the 1999 vintage, the three Jurtschitsch brothers who run it began giving the family name prominence on the labels.

Difficult as it may be to pronounce, the name is unique in the world of wines, while there are several other wineries sharing Sonnhof. The name is thought to have originated in Slovenia. A Jurtschitsch took over Sonnhof in 1868. The property, which exists at least since 1541, once belonged to a monastery and the cool, humid 600-meter-long underground cellar remains in use.

The three brothers currently in charge have divided their duties with exemplary intelligence. Edwin, a graduate of Geisenheim in Germany, looks after the 55 hectares of vineyards which include some of the finest sites in the Kamptal, or Kamp Valley, around the medieval town of Langenlois. Paul, a graduate of Klosterneuburg, makes the 30,000 or more cases produced each year. Karl, with a doctorate in business management and a considerable flair for public relations, handles marketing.

Nearly a third of the production is from Grüner Veltliner. For Eiswein, first made here in the 1970s, Sonnhof has used both Grüner Veltliner and Riesling. The winery makes Eiswein every fourth year on average. "Some years we say, 'Let's have a try,'" Karl says. "Some years we haven't got the nerve for this. So we make Trockenbeerenauslese or Strohwein." There is more to the decision than just nerves. "It is not good for vines to have the grapes too long," Karl believes. "It costs the vine a lot of energy. So we give the vines a rest for the next two or three years."

The cavernous cellar still contains a few bottles of the 1977 Sonnhof Riesling Eiswein, a lean wine made from an October harvest that, two decades later, remained fresh with a balance that gave the impression of dryness. More characteristic is a 1997 Sonnhof Grüner Veltliner Eiswein, with 125 grams of residual sugar and rich toffee flavors.

Weinhaus Kaisergarten Kreuzjoch 1, A-7123 Mönchhoff

This winery, now one of Austria's largest bottlers of sweet wines, has emerged from the economic ashes of Weingut Hafner, which slipped into the hands of a bank after the 1985 wine scandal. (The Hafner family have since re-emerged with a new winery down the street.) Kaisergarten resumed production in 1991 as a state-sponsored cooperative and was acquired in 1997 by a small group of individual winegrowers and businessmen. The name of the winery recalls the era in the nineteenth century when this fertile area of Burgenland was the garden that produced choice vegetables for the Kaiser and the other members of the Imperial family.

While Kaisergarten today makes dry table wines, the emphasis is on sweet wines. The two hundred growers who banded together in the 1991 cooperative agreed that their best dessert wines would be sold under the Seewinkler Impressionen label, with an independent committee selecting the qualifying wines. The marketing of the label was assumed in 1997 by Kaisergarten. The preferred style of the Eiswein, which is based on Grüner Veltliner and Welschriesling, is vivid fruitiness with moderate alcohol. "No more than 11 per cent," says Peter Münzenrieder, the youthful managing director. "The customers prefer it that way."

Weingut Kollwentz-Römerhof
Hauptstrasse 120, A-7051 Grosshöflein

A nton Kollwentz, the proprietor of this modern winery, had made his reputation with table wines from varieties like Chardonnay and Zweigelt, but especially with red wines. A producer of dry reds since the 1960s, Kollwentz considered himself ahead of the times; many of his peers were then still making de-acidified reds with residual sugar while he planted the first Cabernet Sauvignon grown in Austria. His son Andi, who now has joined in the family winery, acquired valuable experience at wineries elsewhere in the world. The winery's Steinzeiler 1997 — a blend of Blaufränkisch, Cabernet Sauvignon and Zweigelt — won the Austrian Red Wine trophy at the 1999 London Wine Challenge.

The first Eiswein at Kollwentz estate was made in 1980 from the Neuburger grape, an Austrian specialty. "This vintage was less ripe and therefore the balance between alcohol, sweetness and lively acidity was perfect," Andi Kollwentz says. "With dessert wines, if the vintage produces insufficient botrytis, the winemaker resorts to Eiswein if a timely frost permits it."

Throughout the 1990s, the winery employed Welschriesling for sweet wines, both Eiswein and, as in 1996, a Trockenbeerenauslese from an unusual blend of Chardonnay and Welschriesling. Kollwentz describes the Welschriesling as a late-ripening grape that achieves medium sugar levels along with spicy acidity. The Eiswein harvest in this region frequently is in November or December. In 1999, Kollwentz picked its grapes on November 27 with the temperature at -7°C. This winery is one of several producers in Grosshöflein to make Eiswein when the conditions allow. Others include **Weingut Josef Leberl** and **Weingut Wagentristl.**

Weingut Alois Kracher Apetlonerstrasse 37, A-7142 Illmitz

Alois Kracher has become one of Austria's best producers of sweet wines since taking over his father's vineyards in 1981. A chemical engineer, he waited until he was 40 in 1991 to work full-time in wine. It was a good choice: his wines have won him four "winemaker of the year" awards at the London Wine Challenge, among many other accolades. Eiswein is made only in years, such as 1998, when there is little botrytis. In most years, his seven and a half hectares of low-lying vineyards around Illmitz are nobly endowed with botrytis. A relative of Willi Opitz, another of Illmitz's star winemakers, Kracher shares some of the same marketing flair, giving his wines proprietary names such as *Nouvelle Vague* (a sweet wine) and *Days of Wine and Roses* (an ethereal cuvée of Chardonnay and Welschriesling).

Weingut Kummer-Schuster Erzherzog Friedrichstrasse 9, A-7131 Halbturn

Traude Schuster (her maiden name is Kummer) does not have much patience with Eiswein, which this winery began making in 1992. "It is hard for one to wait for the frost," she says. "That is not good for my soul." Take the winery's 1997 vintage: on the first three occasions when it was cold enough to harvest, Alois Schuster, her husband, was abroad on business. It was not until January 27, 1998, that a picking opportunity coincided with him being home. "I get gray hair waiting," Traude laughs.

Both are winemakers trained at Klosterneuburg which is perhaps why Alois, who has been president of the Austrian Wine Marketing Board, is able to travel, confident that Kummer-Schuster's cellar is in capable hands.

The 1999 vintage was not nearly so stressful. The weather turned cold on December 23 and beginning at 4 A.M., under a clear sky, a full moon and -9°C, the Schuster family hand-picked 2,900 kilograms of frozen Sauvignon Blanc during the next five hours.

The outcome was 1,200 liters of an Eiswein with flavors of ripe pineapples. For Rainer Schuster, their son and the next generation at the winery, it was his first Eiswein. With 11 hectares of vineyard, Kummer-Schuster always will have a few grapes set aside for sweet wines. However, the winery is best known for its well-made dry table wines and sparkling Riesling, wines less likely to test Traude Schuster's patience.

Weingut Lackner-Tinnacker Steinbach 12, A-8462 Gamlitz

Fritz and Wilma Lackner-Tinnacker, with grapes grown in 13 hectares of steeply sloped vineyards in southern Austria, have a solid reputation for their aromatic white wines. That includes an acclaimed Traminer Eiswein from the 1999 vintage, which one Austrian critic described as being both "massive and supple and very polished."

Weingut Lang Quergasse 5, A-7142 Illmitz

The fiercely independent Helmut Lang — he refuses viticulture subsidies from the European Union — began making wine in 1976 when he was 16, having learned from his father. In 1991 he took responsibility for all the winemaking and three years later he took over the family's winery. Now, the father prunes Lang's 13 hectares while the son specializes in making some of Burgenland's most delectable sweet wines.

"Everybody in the world can do *some* good wine but not everybody can do sweet wine," Helmut Lang explains. "In my vineyards, I always have botrytis." With his emphasis on botrytized wines, Eiswein is made sporadically in those years when there is little botrytis. He believes that the first Eiswein produced in the winery was a 1983 Welschriesling. In 1990 the winery produced 1,200 half bottles of a cuvée of Sämling 88 and Welschriesling, a honeyed Eiswein with a note of botrytis.

By that vintage Lang had acquired a Nikon and become an accomplished photographer. One of his Eiswein harvest images, an atmospheric photograph of a grape cluster entombed in hoar frost, was pirated for publication. Always quick to remedy an affront, Lang ended the trespass with legal action.

He produced three thousand half bottles of Eiswein in 1997, blending purchased juice with his own. He declines to pour a taste because, in his opinion, the wine is not as fine as the 1990.

Weingut Melitta u. Matthias Leitner Quellengasse 33, A-7122 Gols

Matthias Leitner is one of eight winemakers in Gols who belong to Pannobile, an association dedicated to quality wines. The winemakers critique each other's wines, releasing only the best under the Pannobile label.

This focus on quality shows in the Eisweine that Matthias Leitner has been making since 1978, three years after he and his wife took control of the family winery. His production, in years when nature and birds allow Eiswein to be made, ranges from one thousand to eight thousand half bottles, almost always from Welschriesling.

Leitner's 1989 Eiswein won a gold medal at the 1991 Vinexpo in Bordeaux. In style the Leitner Eisweine are powerful, with voluptuous structure and rich caramel flavors. His 1991 Welschriesling Eiswein, even with a muscular 13 per cent alcohol, is a languidly fat wine, as chewy as toffee. His 1998 Welschriesling Eiswein is rich in tropical fruit flavors. When the acidity of his super-ripe grapes is low, he ferments and ages the wine in barrels, relying on the oak to add complexity and structure.

See Grossriedenthal, page 109.

Weingut Mantlerhof Hauptstrasse 50, A-3494 Gedersdorf

Josef Mantler and his wife Margrit bring a family winegrowing tradition dating from 1365 to managing this estate near Krems. However, the first Eiswein was made only in 1992, followed by the second in 1999, about one thousand liters of a honeyed Grüner Veltliner showing layers of tropical fruits and a classic note of pepper. Somewhat controversially, Josef Mantler makes a distinction between Eiswein and botrytis-affected late harvest wines. "Eiswein," he says, "is not a noble wine but it is an interesting wine."

Weingut Mayer am Pfarrplatz Pfarrplatz 2, A-1190 Vienna

Rare among world capitals, the city of Vienna includes more than three hundred wine producers cultivating more than seven hundred hectares of vines. These are primarily in the western suburbs of Grinzing, Nussdorf and Heiligenstadt where the family of Franz Mayer has lived since 1683. Beethoven, a notoriously irrascible tenant, lived here in 1817 and rented rooms in numerous other homes in the neighborhood during his greatest creative years.

Today music lovers doing homage to Beethoven often dine at Mayer's hearty heuriger restaurant, enabling Mayer am Pfarrplatz to sell half of the wine it makes right at the restaurant. The winery, with 26 hectares of vineyard, is one of Vienna's largest and, as the new Millennium began, still was being managed energetically by Franz Mayer, 72. "This is my work," he says. "I have known my vineyards since I was five or six years old."

Mayer produced his first Eiswein in 1995 from Traminer. He has admired this grape since 1952 when, as a young graduate from Klosterneuburg, Mayer was at his first wine fair in Germany. He still vividly recalls tasting a 1936 late harvest Traminer from the Gustav Adolf Schmitt winery. "The whole room smelled of Traminer," Mayer says, remembering the spicy and floral aromas.

In 1953, over his father's objections, Mayer converted a Vienna vineyard to Traminer. But when the young winemaker made the first vintage of Traminer in 1956, his father soon invited all of his friends to "taste my boy's wine." Over the years Mayer has produced the full range of dessert wines from his precious Traminer, including between eight hundred and one thousand liters of Eiswein in 1995, 1998 and 1999. "It was really great," he says of the 1999 Eiswein.

Schlossweingüter Metternich-Sándor A-3491 Strass

Even historic properties like this one cannot resist the challenge to produce one of the most difficult of wines. "We produce icewines in certain years — but not often," says Angela Tragauer, one of the winery's managers. "It is not business — just a thing about gaining 'more image.'" The estate has employed both Grüner Veltliner and Sauvignon Blanc for Eiswein. It is a big risk, Tragauer notes, because the grapes often cannot be picked until January.

Weingut Karl Mitterer Kirchgasse 3, 2523 Tattendorf

Thirty kilometers south of Vienna, Tattendorf formerly was a retreat for Vienna's most celebrated citizens (including the composers Brahms, Liszt and Richard Wagner), attracted by good wines and the pleasant heuriger cafés. The community was heavily bombed during the Second World War but has since restored its charm.

The Parkheuriger Dumba-Park, whose facilities include a reclaimed mill and an expansive garden, serves the wines of many members of the Heuriger Association, including Weingut Mitterer. Proprietor and winemaker Karl Mitterer III, schooled as a wine-maker at Krems, cultivates just over six hectares of vineyards. His reputation with dessert wines rests on the range, from Auslese to Eiswein, he produces from the Traminer grape, depending on the vintage. In 1998 he was able to make both.

Weingut Hermann Moser Bahnstrasse 36, A-3495 Rohrendorf

The Mosers are one of Austria's largest wine families. Martin Moser, 26, who manages this 15-hectare winery, is a distant cousin of Sepp and Nikolaus Moser, perhaps Rohrendorf's best-known winemakers. Ambitious to develop his own stature, Martin made his first Eiswein in 2000, about five hundred liters from Sauvignon Blanc harvested on December 23. The result was a rich-ly textured wine with flavors of peach and lime. "It was an experi-ment," he says modestly of this considerable success. "It is my hobby to make sweet wines every year."

Weingut Sepp Moser Untere Wiener Strasse 1, A-3495 Rohrendorf

The partnership of brothers Sepp and Laurenz Moser was severed after the 1985 Austrian wine scandal when their Lenz Moser company, along with other major Austrian wine exporters, almost collapsed after markets dried up. While Laurenz established a new export business, Sepp, then 57 and older of the two, restored the family winery. In the

sprawling country mansion their father had built in the 1960s, Sepp Moser and his son, Nikolaus, established the Sepp Moser winery. Now with 50 hectares of vineyards (more than half of them in Burgenland), Moser again is a significant producer and in quantities that have required the addition of new cellars to the old house.

Moser's Eiswein is made primarily from grapes in a Chardonnay vineyard only six-tenths of a hectare in size, just across the street from the mansion, beside a busy road that usually deters birds and other predators.

"I remember a situation in 1982," Sepp Moser recalls. "We had eleven and a half hectares of Grüner Veltliner hanging for Eiswein until January 6 of 1983. It was quite a quantity of grapes but 1982 was a very big harvest, so we left them because our cellars [at Lenz Moser] were completely filled. On a Friday it was snowing and getting cold. I looked forward to harvesting on Monday." The snowfall was so heavy on Sunday afternoon that it completely covered the ground where the birds had foraged, driving them onto the vines. "Almost the complete Eiswein harvest was finished by the birds. On Monday morning, there was nothing left, just a few kilos. It could have been a very high-quality Eiswein."

From the Lenz Moser era, he can still produce a 1978 Riesling Eiswein grown in a Burgenland vineyard near Apetlon. More than two decades later, the gold-hued wine remains fresh and vibrant with a powerful and complex aroma.

The Sepp Moser era is marked by Chardonnay Eisweine made four times during the 1990s. These include a light 1992; a fat and spicy 1993 Eiswein; a botrytis-touched 1997 with smoked-meat flavors that caused one restaurateur to declare it perfect with a cigar; and an unctuous mango-flavored 1999.

On the night of November 20, 1999, when it started to turn cold enough to pick the Eiswein grapes, Moser was entertaining about 20 hunting friends. By early morning it was -9°C in the vineyard. The hunters were roused, the grapes were picked in two hours and the party resumed with Glühwein.

A forceful entrepreneur, Johann Munzenrieder began producing Eiswein at this family-owned winery in 1991 because Eisweine could be sold for more than dry table wines. In 1960, his father, who planted the first few hectares of what now is the family's 18 hectares, was a pioneer in converting Burgenland's hay fields to higher-value production.

Busy with other activities — selling building supplies and farm supplies as well as operating a small fleet of commercial trucks — the Münzenrieder family sold its wines in bulk until 1990 when it became more profitable to sell them under the winery's own label. In addition to selling under the family label, Münzenrieder also is one of the owners of the Weinhaus Kaisergarten in Mönchhof, which distributes the Münzenrieder wines.

Never one for half measures, Johann Münzenrieder quickly has become one of the largest Eiswein producers in Apetlon, making between 8,000 and 10,000 liters a year in those years when nature cooperates. To achieve this volume, the winery operates two harvesting machines to take in its own frozen grapes and those of neighboring Eiswein producers. The primary grape varieties used for Eiswein at Münzenrieder are Grüner Veltliner and Sämling 88.

Weingut G.&R. Nastl Gartenzeile 17, A-3560 Langenlois

Surrounded by vineyards spreading northwards from the Danube, Langenlois is being known for producers of table wines. Nastl, with 6.5 hectares of vineyard, has specialized in Riesling, St. Laurent, Zweigelt and Grüner Veltliner. Usually the latter variety produces crisply dry white wines with a characteristic aroma of white pepper. But in 1992 Nastl also made a fine Eiswein with Grüner Veltliner. The wines can be sampled in the casually rustic Nastl heuriger which is open for three-week periods five times a year.

Weingut Nehrer St. Georgener Haupstrasse 16, A-7000 Eisenstadt

This family winery has operated for more than four hundred years but under a series of names because succession passed primarily through the mothers. It has been Nehrer now for two generations, managed since 1989 by Hans Nehrer (an agricultural engineer whose thesis was on the Welschriesling grape) along with the vivacious red-haired Eva, his wife and mother of their three children.

Together, this attractive couple manage 15 hectares and produce a commendable range of table wines, along with the occasional Eiswein. The last one of the decade was a 1997 Eiswein from Sämling 88, of which one thousand half bottles were made.

With her small children, Eva is excused from picking Eiswein grapes. "I am the one who stays at home and makes the Glühwein," she laughs.

Weingut Nekowitsch Schrändlgasse 2, A-7142 Illmitz

Since 1990 Gerhard Nekowitsch has juggled a government job in Vienna with the management of four hectares of vineyards near Illmitz. He specializes in sweet wines, including a wine called The Red One — a Schilfwein (the grapes are dried on reeds before being pressed) from Zweigelt and Blaufränkisch. In the 1999 vintage, Nekowitsch extended his exploration of sweet wines with a Welschriesling Eiswein.

The Nittnaus surname is rare in Austria — except in the Burgenland village of Gols where several families of that name own competing wineries. Christine and husband Hans have been making wine together since 1986, successfully enough that the winery's street-front grocery now has been leased to other operators.

Christine's first Eiswein was made in 1978 at her family's winery, **Weinbau Norbert Schmelzer**, with her brother, still an occasional Eiswein producer. At the time she was 18 and brother Norbert was 21.

"We were young and we had just come home from school," she recalls. "We wanted to do something new and different for this area. Our parents thought we were arrogant." A four-day cold snap that fall enabled them to make enough Neuburger Eiswein that, twenty-two years later, she still had a bottle to share at a tasting with her husband and a visitor.

At Weingut Nittnaus, where Hans and Christine make about 75,000 bottles of wine in total each year, Eiswein has received increasing attention since 1990. In 1995 the vineyards were extensively touched with noble rot. Even so, Hans Nittnaus was able to make two hundred liters of barrel-fermented Eiswein from Blaufränkisch, yielding an almond-and-orange-peel–flavored Eiswein whose color is gold rather than red.

In 1998, when there was little botrytis to leach the color from the skins of red grapes, the same variety yielded a salmon-pink Eiswein with fresh raspberry flavors. In that vintage, Nittnaus also produced two white Eisweine, blends based on Welschriesling, Neuburger and Grüner Veltliner. In 1999 they made seven thousand liters of Grüner Veltliner and two thousand liters of Muskat Ottonel Eiswein.

Their winemaking style is clean and fresh, with seductive aromas and flavors of pineapple and other tropical fruits. "When we make Eiswein, we work the vineyards specially," Hans Nittnaus says. "We try to grow more grapes so that they will not be ripe at the normal time of harvest." Slightly immature grapes are less susceptible to noble rot.

After the normal vintage, the grapes left for Eiswein get particular attention, with pickers removing the significantly under-ripe grapes and those infected with noble rot, leaving only healthy grapes.

The sure hands of Christine and Hans Nittnaus extend across the winery's range of table wines, including the flagship Vigor Albus (a barrel-fermented white) and Vigor Rubeus (a barrel-aged red), so named because these are table wines with power.

Weingut Hans u. Anita Nittnaus Untere Hauptstrasse 49, A-7122 Gols

Only an occasional producer of Eiswein, Nittnaus is esteemed for its red table wines, with 90 per cent of the winery's 21 hectares of vineyard in red varieties.

Hans Nittnaus (not related to the other Hans Nittnaus in Gols) also has a creative way with wine names. Since the wine region around Gols is known as Pannonia and since Nittnaus has sought to ennoble the quality of the wines, he devised the term "Pannobile" for one of his best blended reds (Blaufränkisch, Zweigelt and St. Laurent). The term, having grown into a quasi-appellation, now is used by seven other producers for their best and most powerful wines.

Nittnaus's other top red, a Merlot-Cabernet-Syrah blend made only in the best vintages, is called "Comondor." That name is inspired by a large Hungarian sheep dog breed named Komondor.

Weingut Matthias u. Nelly Nittnaus Obere Hauptstrasse 32, A-7122 Gols

Matthias and Nelly Nittnaus first made Eiswein in 1990, eight years after taking over his family's vineyards and developing their own winery. "We were young and we wanted to try a new thing," Nelly explains. "It was very exciting for us." Their début, five hundred liters of Welschriesling Eiswein, sold quickly. "Everybody who came to taste bought a bottle," she says. A decade later, it remains a polished wine, with the aroma of spiced apples and flavors that remind Nelly Nittnaus of apple strudel.

The winemakers have had more than their share of frustration since then with Eiswein. None was made in 1991 because the grapes were drenched with rain in the autumn. In 1992 cold weather settled across the vineyards on the afternoon of December 24, with -7°C in the afternoon and pickers were alerted to be in the vineyard before dawn on Christmas Day. As they gathered, Matthias decided the grapes were not frozen hard enough. All he could do was exchange Christmas wishes with his friends. The conditions remained marginal on December 26 but, finally, on December 27, enough Welschriesling and Sämling 88 was picked for two hundred liters of wine.

Five years passed before they set out again to replenish their Eiswein inventory. This time, they harvested on the first cold night in mid-December rather than waiting for perfect conditions; the grapes — Sämling and Neuburger this time — were not frozen as hard as in the previous years. "The wine is a little bit thinner," Nelly says, "but most of the customers like it more because they can drink more." Five hundred liters were made.

In 1998 they netted the vineyard against birds and harvested on November 21, not long after some late season rain. Unhappy with the dilute quality of the wine, they chose not to bottle it. In 1999, the first freeze again was marginal. They waited for colder weather, only to experience three freeze-thaw cycles by Christmas. By that time, the grapes were so dehydrated that they abandoned the harvest. Matthias increasingly has focused on making red table wines but the couple has not given up on Eiswein.

Winzerhof Obenaus Hauptstrasse 53, A-3471 Grossriedenthal.

See Grossriedenthal, page 109.

Ing. Willi Opitz St. Bartholomäusgasse 18, A-7142 Illmitz

The charismatic Willi Opitz is a mechanical engineer who once earned a living selling confectionery for an international candy maker. He exploded onto the world's wine scene in the 1990s, both as the creator of exquisitely crafted dessert wines and a man with a flair for promotion. On one occasion he recorded a compact disc of fermentation sounds in his small winery. He later boasted that the disc, entitled "Sound of Wine," sold briskly enough to pay for a new tractor.

A fan of Formula One racing, Opitz often quotes Ron Dennis, the owner of Team McLaren, who says: "Second place is the first of the losers." Opitz wines have been made for McLaren or named for McLaren and some of the team's sponsor's have been persuaded to fix their logos onto Opitz wine. He makes wine for other distinguished partners, including Vienna's famed Hotel Sacher and Harrods of London. Sixty per cent of Opitz wines are sweet, the biggest seller being a red dessert wine called Opitz One.

A cousin of both Helmut Lang and Alois Kracher, two other stars of Illmitz wine, Opitz was born in 1956 and began making wine in 1975, as a sideline, from a tiny one-hectare vineyard. It was not until 1995 that Opitz and his wife, Maria, committed themselves fully to wine production (with a comfortable guest house providing a little more cash flow). They now own five hectares of vineyard and they add to their holdings from time to time.

His first Eiswein, a red, was made in 1978 from 550 kilos of Blaufränkisch grapes that had remained on the vine for Trockenbeerenauslese until the vineyard was touched conveniently by an early frost. "Accidents help," laughs Opitz, who made 120 liters of wine. "At the beginning we just gave it to some of our friends. We had to find out what people were thinking." He took his next Eiswein, a 1983 Muskat, to the 1991 Vinexpo at Bordeaux and was encouraged by the good critical reception. By Vinexpo, he also had made Eisweine in 1986, 1988 and 1990; subsequently, he made five more vintages in the 1990s, all barrel-fermented, along with a broad range of other creative sweet wines such as Opitz One, an ultra late harvest barrel-fermented Zweigelt.

"In our winery, we always have a way out," he says, explaining that he usually decides whether to allocate grapes for Eiswein or another of his sweet wines in September. A poor outlook for noble rot is a good one for Eiswein; the reverse is equally true. "The risk is very high," he says. In the 1999 vintage birds got under the netting on his vines to devour a hectare's worth of grapes. This is a particular hazard of Illmitz, a once poor farming town now prospering from the bird-watching tourists who come out from Vienna to enjoy the national bird sanctuary. "If you take good things from nature, you should be prepared to give something back to nature," Opitz says. Besides, the winery guest house does a good business accommodating bird watchers.

Rosenhof Florianigasse 1, A-7142 Illmitz

This compact winery is integrated with a restaurant and a charming 15-room hotel, all grouped around a rose garden — Rosenhof — in the center of Illmitz. Three businesses under one roof give the prudent Haider family the economic security the family sought when grandfather Josef Tschida settled here just after the Second World War.

"Before the war, Illmitzers were poor people," says Reinhard Haider, the grandson. After the war, the Soviet army of occupation had barracks nearby and winegrowers like Tschida readily sold all their wines in barrels, not bothering to bottle them. One harvest was so abundant that Tschida

built a house with the proceeds. "In those days," Reinhard says, "when you had wine, it was better than money." Vinzenz Haider, his father, was one of the first Burgenland winemakers with a professional diploma in winemaking. He was also one of the earliest — Reinhard is uncertain whether it was in 1971 or 1973 — to produce an Eiswein, a wine which has remained in the Rosenhof assortment.

The winery's 1977 Welschriesling Eiswein, when tasted almost a quarter century later, had aged to a silken elegance but still showed a freshness that belied its deep gold hue. A bronze-hued 1989 Zweigelt Eiswein, with a hint of chocolate in the aroma, still had the taste of tart plums. With its 1990 Traminer Eiswein — a wine with rose petals in the aroma and clean, spicy flavors — Rosenhof won a Grand Prix d'Honneur at the Vinexpo competition in 1993. Reinhard remembers the 1990 Eiswein vintage as the one he missed because he was honeymooning in Mexico with Renata, his new wife. He has been around for the winery's remarkable Eisweine since, including the 250 liters of a richly fruity 1995 Welschriesling, picked on December 30 at -17°C.

In 1998 the Rosenhof Eiswein was made with Grüner Veltliner and the bottle displays a label with the constellation Orion because it was visible in the sky during the harvest. In 1999, 1,200 liters of Grüner Veltliner Eiswein was produced here. In 2000, Reinhard wanted to make a Welschriesling Eiswein but failed to get a good freeze.

St. Georghof-Weingut Georg Wind Hauptstrasse 191, A-7062 St. Margarethen

A producer with an extensive range, this winery has made Eiswein from Welschriesling and Blaufränkisch. The former is a white variety seldom found outside the wine regions of central Europe; it is widely planted in Austria, both for fruity dry wines and for charming botrytis-affected dessert wines. The winery describes its 1994 Welschriesling Eiswein as "spicy" with an amber hue. The Blaufränkisch (grown as Lemberger in North America) is another middle European variety yielding substantial, racy red table wines or, in the case of St. Georghof, an Eiswein. It described its 1995 as "light pink in color similar to cherry [with a] perfect balance of alcohol and acidity." In 1998 the winery produced 1,000 half bottles of a slightly peppery Blaufränkisch Eiswein.

Weinbau Peter Schandl Haydngasse 3, A-7071 Rust

The Schandl family has grown wine at Rust since 1741 and in that time has acquired 15 hectares of choice vineyard and a reputation for good wines. Ludwig Schandl, Peter's father, brought Cabernet Franc and Cabernet Sauvignon vines to the Rust area in the 1970s.

Peter, a graduate of the German wine school at Weinsberg, has given special attention to making dry white wines. Peter's son, Paul, whose apprenticeship included making wine in New Zealand at Seifried Estate, is one of the young winemakers in the Cercle Ruster Ausbruch. Founded in 1991 and now with 15 members, the Cercle is dedicated to promoting Ausbruch, the highly regarded botrytis-affected dessert wine of the region.

In years when there is little botrytis, the Schandl family also produces Eiswein. "We make it every five years, more or less," Paul Schandl says, recalling the vintages of 1992 and 1997. In the latter year, the Schandls made nearly two thousand liters of Gewürztraminer Eiswein from grapes harvested one night in mid-December at -10°C.

In the 1999 vintage, the Schandls gambled that they could make a Millennium Eiswein with grapes picked on January 1, 2000. However, it snowed heavily three days earlier, driving foraging birds from the ground to look for sustenance among the vines. The grapes were all gone by New Year's Eve.

Weingut Franz Schneider Hauptstrasse 103, A-3471 Grossriedenthal

See Grossriedenthal, page 109.

Weingut Schuckert Wilhelmsdorferstrasse 40, A-2170 Poysdorf

Winemakers since 1763, the Schuckert family made its first Eiswein on Christmas Day in 1992 from Grüner Veltliner, the predominant variety in the winery's 16 hectares of vineyards and the best for Eiswein, in the opinion of Rainer Schuckert. The winery made small quantities of Eiswein in each subsequent vintage but made the plunge into significant production in 1999. From a December 22 harvest, Rainer and his father made about five thousand small bottles of Eiswein, achieving a fresh and delicate wine with appealing peach and pineapple flavors.

Weingut Familie Schuster Hauptstrasse 61, A-3471 Grossriedenthal

See Grossriedenthal, page 109.

Weingut Johannes und Maria Söll Steinbach 63, A-8462 Gamlitz

This is one of a handful of producers in Styria, Austria's south-ern-most wine-producing area, that make Eiswein from time to time. Johannes Söll's boast is that he was the first in Styria to make Strohwein, an Austrian dessert wine, and Eiswein seemed an obvious encore.

Söll, which was established in 1939, made its first Eiswein, a Traminer, in 1995 and repeated the feat with the same variety in 1997 when the harvest could not be done until January 28 the fol-lowing year. In 1999, the winery made two Eisweine: a Riesling harvested December 22 and a Sämling 88, with a New Year's Eve harvest. Söll released it as a Millennium Eiswein. Unhappily for collectors, Söll made only 750 bottles of Eiswein in total in 1999.

Weingut Stadt Krems Stadtgraben 11, A-3500 Krems

N ow owned by the picturesque town of Krems on the Danube, this claims to be Austria's oldest wine estate, dating at least from the thirteenth century. The 32 hectares of vineyards were united under the town's ownership in 1915. Heinrich Redl, the general manager, significantly improved the quality of the wines during the 1990s.

These included the winery's first Eiswein in 1999, seven hundred liters of Riesling Eiswein from grapes picked just after dawn on the morning of December 22 in the walled Weinzierlberg vineyard which is within the Krems boundary. Because Redl anticipated difficulty getting pickers, he decided to harvest the grapes by machine. He maintains this is preferable in any event because machine harvesting effectively destems the grapes on the vine, gathering only clean fruit for the crusher. However, other grapes are harvested only by hand.

Weingut Familie Studeny Number 174, A-2073 Obermarkersdorf

E stablished in 1968 in Austria's Weinviertel, this winery, with 15 hectares of vineyard, is small but ambitious. "I want to make really good quality wines," says Herbert Studeny, who was born 10 years after his father, also named Herbert, started the winery. Young Herbert has graduated from Klosterneuberg and gained work experience in both Australia and California.

The winery made a small quantity of Eiswein in 1990 and made a serious commitment in 1999 with nine hundred liters of Welschriesling Eiswein harvested on Christmas morning, producing a fat wine with flavors of sweet pineapple superbly balanced with good acidity, bold alcohol and rich mineral undertones. The family grows that thick-skinned variety in three different vineyards, considers it the perfect Eiswein grape and intends to make some every year.

Terra Galós Weingüter Achs-Tremmel Obere Hauptstrasse 103, A-7122 Gols

The double-barreled name of this large winery (300,000 to 400,000 bottles produced annually) reflects the owning families, Achs and Tremmel. But in a community full of individuals bearing his surname, Hans Achs decided to feature on his labels a variant on the former Hungarian name for Gols, which was *Galós*. An ancestor named Michael Achs appears in both the local tax lists and the church records of 1670 but the family only became wine producers about 70 years ago.

Hans Achs believes that a grandfather who lived in Rust (across Neusiedler See from Gols) may have been the first in the family to make Eiswein but it was blended into more marketable Ausbruch. Today, Terra Galós makes Eiswein in years when the frost comes before the end of December, with a target of about 10,000 half bottles annually.

The grape varieties used for Eiswein include Neuburger, Traminer and Furmint; in 1999 a red Eiswein was made from a blend of Zweigelt and Blaufränkisch. The 1999 Eiswein vintage is memorable at Terra Galós because, as the weather turned cold, the family was hosting a large party in the winery for the seventy-fifth birthday of Hans's father, Georg, on November 21. Some guests went directly from the party to the vineyard to pick frozen grapes.

Weingut Dr. Unger Kirchengasse 14, A-3511 Furth

In Austria's Kremstal wine region, the tradition of the cellar cat is carefully observed by Petra Unger, the charming young woman who took charge of this winery when her father died in 1999. The tradition requires a winemaker to crown the best vat of wine in the cellar with a cat; in practice, it is the image of a cat carved in wood or made from ceramic material.

After the 1999 vintage Unger's cat reposed on a large barrel of Eiswein resting in cool, moist cellars built at least three hundred years ago by winemaking monks at Stift Göttweig. Dr. Wolfgang Unger, Petra's father, who ran one of Austria's largest chemical companies but also was an enthusiast for wine, leased the Göttweig cellars and winery in 1987 and combined them with his family-owned Weingut Furtherhof.

The imposing monastery of Göttweig, built on a height of land that commands a view of the Danube and the city of Krems, has made wine for nine hundred years. With a dwindling labor pool, the monastery leased the business to Dr. Unger. The professional staff hired by him and retained by his daughter raised the wines to the top rank of Austrian wine. "He was a winemaker in his heart," she says of her father.

Dr. Unger's Eiswein 1991, a cuvée of Neuburger and Roter Veltliner, was the first of several gold medal Eisweine that the winery has made. The grapes were picked on December 12 at -17°C, a deep freeze that concentrated everything — aroma, flavor, acidity and natural sugar. The 1991 is decadently luxurious, with spicy caramel aromas and intensely sweet but well-balanced fruit flavors. The winery's first Eiswein, it burnished the Unger reputation. Since then, the winery has made Eiswein in every year when the weather was suitable, always from a blend of the same two grapes, both of which are old regional varieties.

ICEWINE: *The Complete Story*

Österreich
WEINRIEDER

1998

RIESLING

EISWEIN
Poysdorfer
Schneiderberg

Weingut Weinrieder Untere Ortsstrasse 44, A-2170 Kleinhadersdorf-Poysdorf

The community of Poysdorf, 60 kilometers north of Vienna and almost at the Czech border, proclaims itself as Austria's "Sektmetropole" or the metropolis of the tart wines needed for making sekt. With a population of 5,600, Poysdorf's thriving wineries, some with a history of several centuries of production, are based on 1,700 hectares of vineyards.

There is much more going on here than sekt production. A case in point is the impassioned Friedrich Rieder, who claims that even his pulse rises as he approaches a new Eiswein for a first taste. Born in 1958 in Poysdorf, he was the first winemaker in this region of Austria (the *Weinviertel* or wine quarter) to make Eiswein, in 1979. His interest had been stirred by wines he had tasted in Germany where he studied before taking charge of his winery.

Rieder has such a complete cellar that, two decades later, he and his wife Melanie can still host a tasting of 18 of these confections, beginning with a lush 1983 made from Neuburger, an old Austrian variety. Self-taught as a winemaker and self-assured, Rieder has ten hectares of vineyards and, in favorable years, will chance two to three hectares for Eiswein. "I love risk," he says. "I *need* risk." As cold as winter can be in the Weinviertel, it also can be late. In the 1990 vintage, as an example, he harvested the last Eiswein grapes on January 16, 1991. So dedicated is Rieder to Eiswein that, in the month before the harvest, he begins rising well before dawn to check the temperature in the vineyards.

Not surprisingly, there is a memory with every vintage. One of his most successful is the 1986 Welschriesling Eiswein which, as it matured, developed a mocha aroma and rich flavors of coffee and chocolate balanced with a fine acidity. The grapes were harvested early on Christmas morning. "On the 24th of December, I went into the vineyard at midnight," Rieder recalls. "There was snow on the ground, stars in the heaven and three deer in the vineyard. I could hear *Silent Night* being played in the church."

In the 1998 vintage, he was able to produce three Eisweine, from Welschriesling, Riesling and Zweigelt, because a deep cold under a clear sky with a full moon persisted for several days. "Every year is new," he says. The 1996 vintage was difficult, with grapes that did not ripen fully, leaving sharp-edged acidity in the wine. Weinrieder's 1996 Riesling Eiswein has a tart 18 grams of acidity per liter. To the extent that nature permits, Rieder endeavors to make Eisweine which are plump with residual sweetness brightly balanced with clean acidity, a good example being his superb 1999 Riesling Eiswein.

In years when acidity is low, Rieder will let the Eiswein ferment to a higher alcohol which he believes helps balance the wines. His 1997 Zweigelt and his 1997 Welschriesling Eiswiene both were finished with a strapping 14 per cent alcohol. The Zweigelt in particular has a pronounced red wine character, the kind of Eiswein that Reider recommends be enjoyed with dumplings and strawberries, an Austrian summertime dessert.

"Top quality and their unmistakable style make these Eisweine classics in the Austrian wine scene," he says proudly of his wines. He has the awards to prove it, including a near-perfect score of 98 for his Poysdorfer Schneiderberg Riesling Eiswein 1998 from the Beverage Testing Institute of Chicago.

Several of Rieder's colleagues in Poysdorf also make Eiswein, including **Weinbau Ing. Manfred Ebenauer** and **Weingut Emmerich und Herta Haimer**, which has been in the family since 1722.

Weinbau Familie Weiss Hauptplatz 28, A-7122 Gols

Georg Paul Weiss is a professor in the wine school at Eisenstadt as well as one of the owners of this winery; if his students turn out as capable as their teacher, the future of Austrian wines is assured. The winery showcases not only his skills but those of his daughters Elisabeth and Beate and her husband Erik, all of them professionally trained winemakers.

Eiswein, says Beate, is the high point, with the preferred varieties being Muskat Ottonel and Welschriesling. "If it is possible, we make it every year."

Georg Paul's recollection is that the first Eiswein in his estate was made in 1965 and it was an accident. The family, which now has seven hectares of vines, then had fifteen hectares, all of which was being picked by hand. The vintage was late, not yet completed when the first hard frost hit on November 21. When frozen Sauvignon Blanc grapes arrived from the vineyard, the decision was made to press them.

"We were astonished," Georg Paul remembers. "This was high quality juice." The result was an acceptable light Eiswein, sold in bulk to other bottlers. However, there was not much market for the style and it was not until 1978 that Weiss again made Eiswein, this time deliberately.

Since 1990, the Weiss family has released Eiswein under its own label. The 1990 vintage was memorable for the family. The grapes were picked on a bitterly cold night in December, with two tractors — one of which broke down — lighting up the vineyard.

The outcome was worth it. Weiss won a gold medal at Ljubliana with an Eiswein made from a little-known Austrian white variety called Goldburger, a grape used primarily for sweet wines. It yielded an Eiswein with soft acidity but voluptuous toffee-like sweetness. Because the vines were old, that vineyard has since been replanted with Muskat.

Weingut Weiss Untere Hauptstrasse 17, A-7122 Gols

Youth Andreas Weiss and his wife Christine took over this century-old family winery in 1990. They cultivate eight hectares of vineyards between the village of Gols and Neusiedler See, producing wines that range from table wines to sparkling wines. For Eiswein, Weiss has employed Neuburger which is grown exclusively in Austria. A white grape, it is a cross of Weissburgunder and Silvaner that ripens earlier and achieves higher sugars than Grüner Veltliner, one of Austria's most widely grown whites.

PART III

Icewine in North America

7

The Canadians

The man credited with making Canada's first commercial icewine was a German, a former textile salesman from Hamburg named Walter Hainle who had emigrated in 1970 when his doctor ordered a career change to cure a bad case of ulcers. The prescription was sound. Before he died in 1995 in his eightieth year Hainle spent 25 vigorously productive years as the proud patriarch of a winery that he and his family established in British Columbia's Okanagan Valley.

Like most Europeans who arrived in Canada a generation ago, Hainle made his own wines because the Canadian table wines then available seldom pleased European palates. "He came at the whole subject of wine from an amateur enthusiast's point of view," Tilman Hainle says of his father. "Growing some grapes on his own property and making some wine from it was a dream from a long time ago."

In 1973, before Walter Hainle took delivery of all the Okanagan Riesling grapes he had ordered from a grower in the Okanagan, an early frost caught them on the vine. He seized the opportunity to make between 30 and 40 liters of icewine. It became an annual tradition. In 1988 when the Hainle Vineyards winery opened, with his professionally trained son Tilman as the winemaker, the vintages for sale included 265 bottles of 1978 icewine. "My dad's belief was that it always has to be a rare item," Tilman says. The majority of Canadian wineries, including Hainle, now make icewine each year, occasionally on the grand scale made possible by the famously cold winters.

Hobby lots of icewine may have been made in Canada even before Walter Hainle. One of the earliest icewine hobbyists may have been a French-trained dairy scientist named Adhémar De Chaunac who was the chief enologist for T.G. Bright & Co. from 1933 until he retired in 1966. Now absorbed into Vincor International Ltd., Brights sought to improve Canadian wine quality with research projects in both Ontario and British Columbia. At De Chaunac's urging, Brights in 1947 planted a large number of European grape varieties, including such important vinifera as Chardonnay, and a range of French hybrid varieties, including Vidal, which today is the mainstay of Canadian icewine production.

As a European, De Chaunac knew that he could never make decent table wines with the North American labrusca grapes on which the pre-war Canadian industry had been based. The imported hybrid wines for the De Chaunac–inspired planting in fact did improve Canadian wines in the 1960s; they had the same impact in New York State after growers imported cuttings from Canada. Grateful Ontario growers honored De Chaunac by attaching his name to a red hybrid, Seibel 9549, when wineries began selling it as a named varietal. Unfortunately, the De Chaunac grape was one of the least satisfactory of the hybrids and it now has been replaced with vinifera grapes.

It has been a much different story with Vidal — named for a French plant breeder called Jean Vidal. Among the varieties imported by Brights, it was successful because it is a hardy, thick-skinned, disease-resistant variety that makes white wines with voluptuously fruity aromas. Brights planted a significant quantity in its Niagara-area vineyards. According to George Hostetter,[1] a protégé of De Chaunac who became the company's research director, De Chaunac always asked that a small quantity of the Vidal grapes be left on the vines for his personal use, some of which he made into late harvest wine and some of which he picked when the grapes were frozen, making icewine for himself and his friends. According to Hostetter, he sought to interest his employer in this wine, without success.

The next icewine trials for Brights were conducted by John Paroschy. As a young wine scientist, he went to Germany in 1975 to work on his doctorate with Helmut Becker at Geisenheim. Paroschy helped pick Eiswein grapes and that, along with Becker's encouragement, led him to conclude that Canadians, with their colder winters, could produce icewine more easily than the Germans. When he returned to Canada, he experimented at home with cryo-extraction and then, after joining the research unit at Brights in 1979, made an experimental vintage with Vidal from the Brights research vineyard. "It was quite good," Paroschy recalls the wine. None of it was sold because "the owners took it all home."[2]

After Paroschy moved on to become a research scientist at Château des Charmes winery in 1982, Ray Cornell, an assistant winemaker at Brights, continued the research, making Vidal icewine in both 1983 and 1984. If the wines, under the label of Brights Research Cellars, were sold at all, it was only in the winery's retail store at Niagara Falls.

"We did them the right way," Cornell says. "There were no rules or regulations but we tried to pattern them on German practices."[3] Edward Arnold, who was president of Brights at the time, confirms that the winery's icewine trials were inspired by the existence of German Eiswein. The winery's first commercial release from the 1986 vintage even was labeled "Eiswein," with the change to "Icewine" being made in 1987.

The trials were substantial: Arnold believes that between one hundred and two hundred cases were made in each vintage. "We would not have done it just for ten cases," he says.[4] Vidal has fallen out of favor as a grape for dry table wine because the wine, while attractive, seldom fetches an adequate price. But when Vidal is transformed to icewine, the selling price approaches that of classic Riesling icewine. In New York state, the comparable workhorse hybrid for icewine (and other voluptuous dessert wines) is Vignoles, also known as Ravat 51 after its breeder.

Walter Hainle made his first icewines from a grape called Okanagan Riesling, a vine of uncertain origin that formerly was the ubiquitous white variety in the Okanagan. Some believed it to be a vine imported in the 1920s from Hungary. More likely, it was a chance hybrid with native labrusca grapes in its parentage. A hardy and productive vine, it yielded rustic and mediocre table wines; the icewines from the variety were only marginally better, possessing pungent aromas that recalled inexpensive after-shave lotion. There was nothing subtle about an Okanagan Riesling icewine; it was the wine's exotic character that created a sensation among the friends who sampled Walter Hainle's creations.

When he purchased raw land on a slope above Peachland as the foundation for the family's future winery, Hainle planted the true Riesling. By the 1990s, Okanagan Riesling had been eliminated almost totally from British Columbia vineyards in favor of vinifera vines, all of which make better table wines and, in some cases, excellent icewines as well. In 1982, after his son Tilman returned from enology studies in Germany, the Hainle winery began making icewine only with the true Riesling.

For the next decade, only two wineries in British Columbia made icewine regularly: Hainle in the Okanagan and the reclusive St. Lazlo winery at Keremeos in the nearby Similkameen Valley, which also began making icewine in 1982.[5] It was only in the 1990s that other Okanagan wineries, encouraged by icewine's rising star in Ontario, went down the path blazed by the Hainle family.

At first, it was the keen amateurs that began icewine trials in Ontario vineyards in 1982. A young winemaker named Peter Gamble, then working with a cottage winery now known as Hillebrand Estates, made icewine when grapes were offered to him for personal winemaking from a vineyard with unharvested second-growth Riesling. It was typical of amateurs that they scavenged what the commercial wineries had left behind. "This was, however, just a personal batch, not anything specifically for Hillebrand," Gamble stresses. He got enough juice to fill a 25-liter glass carboy which he placed in a home sink to ferment. Unfortunately, the carboy tipped, broke its neck and Gamble lost the juice down the drain.

In 1983 Ontario icewine-making lurched into the hands of the professionals. At a vineyard beside the Niagara River, Inniskillin's

Austrian-born winemaker Karl Kaiser and a neighboring German-born grower named Ewald Reif set aside several rows of Vidal for icewine, none of it protected with nets. "I didn't know where to buy nets here," Kaiser admitted later. "And I didn't know how ravenous the birds were either." The birds ate all of the Vidal.

Meanwhile, Walter Strehn, another Austrian and the winemaker at the new Pelee Island winery near Windsor, had the foresight to import netting from Europe that year for the vines he set aside for icewine on Pelee Island, a 4,000-hectare island positioned in Lake Erie on two major migratory flyways for birds. He draped the white nets across at least eight rows of vines, protecting a quantity of grapes that, if made into icewine, would have created a sensation.

But the netting worked *too* well, trapping birds as well as protecting the grapes. Strehn's nets were dismantled by conservation officers from the province's Ministry of Natural Resources, who charged Strehn with trapping birds out of season. While the charges were dropped later, birds ate about $25,000 worth of Strehn's unprotected grapes, primarily Riesling.

Even so, Strehn salvaged enough Vidal to make a commercial quantity of icewine in 1983, shipping about one hundred cases to the Liquor Control Board of Ontario where the wine retailed for $12.50 a half bottle. After little was sold, the LCBO returned it to the winery for a refund. Subsequently, Pelee Island found more remunerative markets in the United States and when the icewine began selling there for more than $100 a bottle, the LCBO begged to have it back.[6]

Hillebrand made its first icewine in 1983. The winery had been started in 1979 as Newark Wines by an engineer named Joseph Pohorly who sold control of the winery in 1982 to a large German firm. Jurgen Helbig, the young German winemaker dispatched to work with Pohorly at the winery, saw the grapes left hanging by Reif and Kaiser in the 1983 vintage and also decided to make icewine.

"They chickened out," Kaiser maintains. "They harvested the grapes in October and put them in cold storage and brought the grapes out in bushel baskets in December." The grapes spent a month or so in a cool room, secure from ravenous birds, and were placed outside overnight on a December evening when the mercury dropped below -10°C. They were pressed outside the next day. "There were no rules," Pohorly defended himself later, pointing out that the grapes had not been frozen artificially.[7] Sixty cases (12 half bottles per case) of icewine were produced that year by Hillebrand.

The same technique was used in 1984 when the winery's German consultants argued that this enabled them to harvest the Vidal at better acidity. In 1985, at a banquet at the Inniskillin winery, Pohorly and Kaiser presented their icewines in the company of Hans Joachim Louis Guntrum, who had come with a German Eiswein for the event. When Guntrum heard how the Hillebrand 1983 had been made, he growled — as Kaiser recalled the event years later — that if Pohorly had done that in Germany, he would have gone to jail.

It was another decade before the Canadians adopted icewine standards but when they did, they deliberately made them more rigorous than the German wine law. Since the 1985 harvest, Hillebrand icewine grapes have been frozen on the vine before being picked. (Guntrum recalled the evening somewhat differently 15 years later. "It was a very convincing tasting," he says. "The wines were dangerously good compared to our own."[8])

In 1982 Klaus Reif made his first Eiswein as an apprentice at a state winemaking school in Neustadt, Germany. "I thought it was very special," he remembers. The juice that dripped from the press has a sugar concentration of 36° Brix, double the sugar concentration that German growers usually require for conventional Riesling table wines. Armed with newly acquired winemaking skills, he came to Canada in 1987 to help his uncle, Ewald — Karl Kaiser's friend — who had opened a winery that Klaus since has taken over.

After the 1983 fiasco, Kaiser and Reif had both deployed nets in 1984 and icewines began to emerge each vintage. The volumes at first were modest as the winemakers learned the art. Young Klaus Reif (born in 1963) arrived at his uncle's winery in time to help bottle the 160 liters made in 1986 and then to take charge of pressing the 1987 vintage. He was surprised at the enormously concentrated liquid produced by Vidal grapes harvested under a deep frost.

"I was just — even my wife took pictures of me because I was just *stunned!* Now, we were not talking just of 36° Brix, we're talking about 48° Brix. Sometimes at the beginning, when I was just starting to press, it was 50° Brix. That was not juice anymore, it was honey."

Reif grasped the fundamental difference between Canadian and German icewine. "We treated the icewine back in Germany as more like a wine," he says. "I don't want to put it down. It was a very good product. It was more like a wine, it was treated like a wine, regular fermentation like a wine. Over here, you worry about whether you can ferment it because it is so sweet. It was a new world. You have to take the production of Canadian icewine really separately. It is harder to do because of that higher sweetness but, quite often, it is a higher quality product." Since that day in 1987, Reif always has made his icewines in the big, luscious style made possible by very ripe Vidal grapes and a crisp Canadian winter. His Vidal icewine, he says, "hits you like a two-by-four" and he is proud of it.

Along with his peers who began testing the waters in the late 1980s with a few hundred liters of icewine, Klaus Reif was in for a surprise when he began selling it: "You could not sell it." It was an unknown wine style in Canada and consumers, who suspected the quality of all Canadian wines, were not prepared to pay $20 or $30, then the selling price, for a flashy novelty from an industry still struggling for credibility. In 1989, desperate for recognition, Reif shipped a bottle, unsolicited, of his 1987 Vidal Eiswein (as it was then labeled) to Robert M. Parker, Jr., the American writer who authored *The Wine Advocate,* perhaps the most influential bimonthly wine guide in the United States. After Parker, reviewing the wine, included it among the "best" he had tasted in 1989, the sales of Reif's icewines exploded.

With Reif, Inniskillin and Hillebrand wineries leading the way, others now edged into icewine production. German-born Herbert Konzelmann, who had built a winery on the south shore of Lake Ontario with a view of Toronto on the horizon, made his first Vidal icewine in 1986. Willowbank, which was absorbed later by Marynissen Estates, joined the icewine producers in 1987, followed by Château des Charmes and Vineland Estates in 1988.

"The guys that jumped into it first were the German group," says Paul Bosc, Jr., a member of the family that operates Château des Charmes. "Our extraction is French and we just found it very strange —'Why are these guys picking grapes in the wintertime?' We thought we worked hard enough as it is."

His father, Algerian-born Paul Bosc, Sr., had come to Canada in the mid-1960s after the war in Algeria forced out French wine-makers like himself. The family's subsequent success, now evident in their grandly conceived winery near Niagara Falls replicating a Loire chateau, came from being alert to opportunity. In 1988, convinced that icewine was gaining acceptance, they made two hundred half bottles of Riesling icewine and priced it aggressively at $40 a half bottle. "In the first couple of years, we stayed within ourselves," Paul Bosc, Jr., recalls their learning experience. "If we did screw it up, we would not have told anybody we even made it." The wines succeeded, the Boscs being capable winemakers, and production expanded until, in the bountiful 1998 vintage, Château des Charmes made 140,000 half bottles of icewine.

Every winery's icewine production was tentative at first. "I think we made 25 cases in 1989," says Paul Speck, one of the three brothers who operate the Henry of Pelham winery near Jordan, Ontario. The nearby Cave Spring winery made a mere four cases that year.

Most winemakers had no experience with icewine or very little at best. Allan Schmidt, who with brother Brian, runs Vineland Estates Winery near Vineland, Ontario, had made a trial 50 liters of Riesling icewine in 1984 at Sumac Ridge in British Columbia, where he began his career. The icewine tutor that year was Walter Hainle but there was a limit to what a former textile salesman turned hobby winemaker could teach. "There have been no books," Brian Schmidt says, "Even in the old world, there have been no reference manuals. It has all been trial and error."

The first error that the Schmidt brothers made was trying to press grapes picked at extremely cold temperatures, only to discover that at -18°C, the juice yield is extremely low, the juice is too sweet to ferment properly and, especially with Vidal, the finished wine had less grace than Klaus Reif's two-by-four. "We quickly realized that there is a terminus [in picking temperature] at which you can make quality icewine," Allan Schmidt says. In subsequent vintages, the Schmidt brothers have aimed for a picking temperature no lower than -12°C.

Initially, Vineland Estates rewarded volunteer pickers with numbered, personally signed bottles. Each volunteer was given a label numbered in the order of arriving at the vineyard, beginning with 001, to be fixed subsequently to each picker's personal bottle. This remained practical only when the harvest was small enough to be completed by volunteers in one night. "Now, it takes up to 10 or 12 nights," says Allan, who hires pickers.

Novices all, the winemakers and the winery owners had much to learn and learned some of it the hard way. For a few years the Schmidt brothers obligingly sold unfermented icewine juice to other wineries. One buyer, whose identity the Schmidts will not disclose, sent its own truck for a small tank of this juice. In a scene reminiscent of a bad slapstick movie, the truck was backed down the steeply inclined ramp at the Vineland winery and a tank containing eight hundred liters of juice, worth $20,000, was loaded on the truck. As the vehicle pulled away up the ramp, the tank tipped, spilling its entire contents before the horrified eyes of the purchasers. "They put it through on their insurance," Brian Schmidt said.

"All you could talk about afterwards were the war stories," laughs Paul Speck as he recalls when he made icewine the first time in 1989. He was then a 22-year-old owner of a winery in its second vintage, making do with beaten-up equipment. "We literally picked in the dark with flashlights. We had a tractor but it had only one light that worked." In the bitter cold, he could not get the tractor running until jump-starting it with cables connected to a fully charged battery in an automobile. Their old pickup truck needed a similar boost to its weakened battery before the engine could be turned over and started.

The 1989 icewine harvest of Henry of Pelham, which took place just after New Year's Day in 1990, was done by the winery's staff and several of their friends. "I think I bought a Rieder Distillery Small Cask Brandy" — referring to a well-regarded spirit from a nearby distiller — "and we put it in the coffee, just to warm us up." The Speck brothers subsequently refined their icewine techniques, acquiring reliable equipment and a portable generator to power floodlights in the vineyard.

At Cave Spring, Angelo Pavan, a former philosophy teacher turned winemaker, made his first vintage of icewine, all of four cases, in 1989 and he never forgot the circumstances. The winery chose to pick on a night when the temperature was below -14°C. "It was cold. It was brutally cold," Pavan remembers. The frozen grapes yielded juice reluctantly, even under high pressure in the press. "It was just dripping out. I think we pressed out at 50° Brix."

Pavan got another surprise when, after pressing was complete, he opened the press to remove the spent pomace. "It was just a block of frozen grapes. I'm used to a regular harvest, you spin the press and all the skins come out. Well, this was just a cake of ice. We had to go in with sledgehammers and crowbars to break that cake. And it was awful. I was in head first, like a squirrel in a tree trunk. And it's cold. You want to cry, just about, because it is so unexpected. We have the hang of it now. What took 10 hours then takes a couple of hours now." The sugar concentration of the juice in 1989 was too high because the grapes were excessively frozen when pressed. "That one never fermented too well. It fermented until the end of June and it was still awfully sweet."

Before today's volume production of icewine, Canadian wineries relied on their own staff along with friends and even volunteers to do the picking. As in Europe, the icewine vintage often occurs around the Christmas or New Year holidays. At family-run Konzelmann Estate, export manager Jim Reschke, a son-in-law, remembers the entire family harvesting grapes one year after rising from Christmas dinner. "Two years in a row, we picked on Boxing Day, starting at six in the morning," Angelo Pavan says. "I'm phoning on Christmas Day to try and get pickers. It was burning us out." Ultimately, Cave Spring did what everyone else did: it hired picking crews which, unlike volunteers, could be counted on to show up and, what's more important, to finish the job. "The enthusiasts," Pavan adds, a note of exasperation in his voice, "last a couple of hours. The rest are here all night and it demoralizes them when the enthusiasts leave."

"In the early days, we grabbed anybody who worked in our retail store," Speck recalls. "And a lot of our customers liked to come out." The amateur pickers seldom are prepared for the cold, dark vineyards. "They actually get in the way sometimes," Speck admits. One year, a friend of the Speck brothers joined the harvest, fashionably garbed in a leather Stetson, leather western-style boots and no gloves. "Within half an hour, I had to bring him in," Speck says.

At nearly every Canadian vineyard, hired pickers now do the work that friends once did, but even that is no assurance that the harvest will go smoothly. During the 1997 vintage, the winter was so warm that there only were three or four picking opportunities in the Niagara region. Speck could not believe his good luck when, as one of the picking windows opened, an agent for a group of Vietnamese pickers called, looking for work. (Former refugees from Vietnam, these diligent farm workers are widely employed in Ontario's vineyards and orchards.) The winery owner told them to come along that night.

Speck also agreed to allow a television crew to film that evening's picking. When the cameraman flicked on his lights, the startled pickers scurried for their vehicles and disappeared down the road. "A lot of new immigrants want to be low-profile," Speck concluded. Within hours, the temperature rose and the picking window remained closed for several weeks while the Henry of Pelham grapes shriveled on the vine, losing most of the volume needed for icewine.

Among the large Canadian producers, a prolonged icewine campaign is routine. Sue-Ann Staff, who makes about 30,000 liters of icewine a year at Pillitteri Estate Winery near Niagara-on-the-Lake, describes the experience as physically demanding. "There isn't one part of making icewine that is easy, *not one part*," she says emphatically.

A tall, athletic blonde, Staff was a competitive figure skater as a teenager until, at 16, she focused her ambition on wine. "I'm the fifth generation of my family to be in the grape and wine industry in Canada," she relates. "We have vineyards over one hundred years old on our property at home." She equipped herself with a biotechnology degree from the University of Guelph and an enology degree from Australia's Roseworthy College before taking over at Pillitteri in 1997. She arrived just as the winery tasted success in aggressive efforts to sell icewine in Asia. "Our agent in Taiwan turned Pillitteri into an icon there and kept the Pillitteri name very prestigious," she says. "Taiwan was just the beginning." Pilliterri icewines now are found throughout Asia, even in Vietnam.

The Asian market is large and financially important. That is why the winery, also well regarded for its red table wines, throws its considerable resources at icewine. "It is a brutal and intense month," Staff says. "Nothing else exists. It's the number one priority and nothing else can come before it because who knows if it's going to get cold again." Her first icewine vintage at Pillitteri, in 1997, was an unusually mild winter. "There were five nights in the entire winter when we could pick — and the last night was on March 23. The grower was screaming because he wanted to prune his grapes."

In the 2000 icewine vintage, she received into the winery 175 tonnes of frozen grapes, all harvested by hand. While some vineyards have adapted mechanical harvesters for picking icewine grapes, Pillitteri believes that the machinery performs poorly at freezing temperatures for which it was never designed. "At -12°C, people will still go but a machine won't," Staff has learned.

The winery operates seven presses since the grapes must be processed promptly while still frozen. In 2000, the cellar crews worked around the clock for almost a month, beginning December 6. Pillitteri (and several other large Canadian producers) also extend the icewine harvest, extracting additional juice for late harvest wines by crushing the grapes a second time, and occasionally even a third time, after they have thawed partially. It is no wonder that Staff sometimes describes the icewine experience as brutal. "In every other wine region of the world, you have your harvest and then that's it. We're down for a month and then we start harvest again. The second harvest typically is six to eight weeks. It is two vintages back to back and it is a grueling time."

8

Inniskillin — The World's Largest Icewine Producer

No one has done more to turn icewine into Canada's signature wine than Karl Kaiser. The talented winemaker
was one of the two founding partners in 1974 of
Inniskillin Wines, an elegant estate downstream from Niagara Falls
and today the producer of about 100,000 cases of some of Canada's
best wines.

Kaiser's 1989 Icewine established the first international credibility for Canadian icewine in 1991 when it won the illustrious
Grand Prix d'Honneur at Bordeaux's Vinexpo wine fair. Almost
immediately, most of Inniskillin's peers in Canada also began producing icewine, with the larger wineries, Inniskillin included,
aggressively developing markets in Asia where Canadian wine previously had been unknown.

As the success of Canadian icewine rippled through the international wine world in the final decade of the twentieth century, many
European wineries — some who had been occasional makers of
Eiswein and some who had never made it — also joined a throng of
icewine producers around the world. It is not all Karl Kaiser's doing,
but he certainly played a role in starting the icewine avalanche.

Born in Austria in 1941, Kaiser intended to be a teacher. He
experienced vineyard work while in the novitiate of a Cistercian
monastery there and later, while helping in a vineyard owned by the
grandfather of his future wife. He immigrated to Canada in 1969,

planning to teach science after earning a chemistry degree and doing post-graduate work in microbiology. It was a choice of studies that equipped him well when his career switched to winemaking.

Kaiser arrived in Canada with a European wine palate and, dismayed at the sweet, foxy Canadian table wines, he planted a small home vineyard. While buying vines in 1971 at a nursery run by the Ziraldo family, Kaiser loudly disparaged Ontario wine as unpalatable. The combative Donald Ziraldo, a University of Guelph agriculture graduate seven years younger than Kaiser, loyally defended domestic wines. Kaiser made his point by returning with a well-made bottle of his home-vintaged Chelois rosé. Ziraldo conceded that better wines could be made in Ontario and proposed that he and Kaiser should make them.

The cottage winery they opened in 1975 was the first winery licensed in Ontario in nearly 50 years. Its success inspired a wave of estate producers in all Canadian wine regions and the quality of Canadian wine began improving.

In the 1970s, the avuncular Kaiser was one of the best-trained professionals among the German-speaking winemakers in Ontario. The other transplanted winegrowers from Austria and Germany gathered often at his well-equipped Inniskillin laboratory to share ideas and ambitions. In the summer of 1983, over several bottles of wine uncorked by the ever-hospitable Kaiser, the conversation turned to icewine. Kaiser and Ewald Reif, a German-born grower who owned a vineyard adjacent to Inniskillin, agreed to set aside vines for icewine. So did the Austrian winemakers then working at the nearby Hillebrand Estate winery and at the Pelee Island winery in southwestern Ontario.

Only Pelee Island and Hillebrand were able to save some grapes from the birds to make small icewine vintages in 1983. All deployed nets the following year. Kaiser, who made about nine hundred bottles (375 ml half bottles) in 1984, ultimately outdistanced his friends. By the vintage of 1998, he made or supervised the production of about 360,000 half bottles of icewine, undoubtedly a global record for any single winemaker.

Kaiser's seminal contribution has not been the volume he has made but the quality. His 1984 icewine — the label reads "EISWEIN Vidal (ICE WINE)" and it retailed for $18.50 when released on December 1, 1985 — was the only Canadian wine to win a gold medal at the 1986 InterVin International competition in Toronto. The Grand Prix in Bordeaux five years later, the first truly significant international medal won by any Canadian winery, firmly established Inniskillin's reputation.

Kaiser used the French hybrid, Vidal, for icewine, largely because it was grown in Inniskillin's Brae Burn vineyard adjacent to the winery. "It wasn't totally a coincidence," he adds, "because I considered the Vidal would have the right properties. It is fruity. It has a tough skins and hangs on well to the vines. It has relatively decent acidity." He considered several other varieties, including Seyval Blanc, which also were grown nearby, but none offered Vidal's perfect package. Over time, Kaiser has refined his view of what the ideal icewine grape must possess.

"It has to be aromatic because a sweet wine with no aromatic overtones is plain sugar water," he says. "It has to be late ripening. It has to have relatively high acidity and it has to have physiological properties to be durable against disease."

Besides Riesling and Vidal among the white varieties, Kaiser also has embraced Chenin Blanc, a fruity, aromatic variety "with the skin and stem of a tank." When Inniskillin established a second Canadian winery in the Okanagan Valley in 1994, Kaiser obtained Chenin Blanc for the 1994 and 1995 vintages for icewine. The variety was planted in Niagara and in 1998 Kaiser made a Chenin Blanc icewine there as well. Inniskillin Okanagan, where the winemaker now is Hungarian-born Sandor Mayer, also made Ehrenfelser icewine in 1996 and, in every vintage from 1996 through 2000, has made both Vidal and Riesling icewines.

At first, Kaiser took advantage of the frigid Canadian winters to make spectacularly big wines. His 1986 Vidal icewine was made from grapes that were deeply frozen to -17°C when pressed and the juice was 55° Brix, a honey-like sweetness. Kaiser concluded that the practical limit is -14°C; below that, the berries are so solidly frozen that the juice yield is minimal and the excessively sweet must is almost impossible to ferment. In the bitterly cold vintage of December 1996, the grapes again were picked at -17°C and Kaiser broke two presses at Inniskillin in a near-futile effort to extract juice. "We had to wait until it was -14 before we saw juice coming from the press," he says. He now prefers a picking temperature of about -11°C because it yields juice with 42° to 45° Brix, quite enough to make an icewine more sumptuously rich than many Eisweine.

The longevity of his Vidal icewines has delighted him. The 1986 "is one of the ones that is holding up amazingly," Kaiser said in 1999. "There is almost no sign of oxidation. I don't know how long Vidal lives. Our 1984 is still clean as a whistle."[1] He observes that Vidal, with a natural acidity lower than Riesling, takes on the golden hue of a mature wine earlier than Riesling.

Some Ontario winemakers, notably the Schmidt brothers at Vineland Estates occasionally, blend as much as 15 per cent Riesling into the Vidal must to brighten the acidity of the finished wine without changing its lush varietal character.

"That would make sense," Kaiser agrees. "The Riesling has a more steely acid and would give a slightly firmer structure. You can blend Riesling into Vidal but not Vidal into Riesling."

The broad flavors and aroma of Vidal overwhelm Riesling's delicacy. Many Vidal icewines owe their voluptuous flavors to the effect of a typical Ontario winter, with its succession of mild freezes and thaws before the hard freeze. The Vidal grapes on the vines turn bronze and become sweeter and richer in flavor. This causes caramel and maple flavors in Ontario icewines, dramatically differentiating their style from those of Europe.

While the homespun Kaiser honed the technique of making icewine, it was his partner, Donald Ziraldo, who sold them. A daredevil extreme skier in his free time, the suave Ziraldo is the silken salesman who gets both Inniskillin and Canadian wine in front of the world's most powerful palates. In 1998, to give a characteristic example, because he was pursuing Asia's icewine market, he arranged to be invited to a private reception that Canada's prime minister had in Toronto for the visiting Chinese head of state.

To give another example, Ziraldo enlisted Georg Riedel, the

brilliant Austria creator of fine crystal wine glasses, to design the "perfect" glass for icewine. Riedel has made a career of producing elegant stemware tailored to improve the sensuous enjoyment of wines. Ziraldo arranged that the preliminary trials of existing Riedel shapes be done at a tasting with some of the world's most influential wine writers, yielding a fine harvest of publicity. The long-stemmed Riedel icewine glass, with a bowl like a just-opening tulip blossom, was launched in 2000.

Ziraldo, who has received the Order of Canada, one of his nation's highest awards for achievement, made his first trip to Vinexpo in 1989. This Bordeaux exposition, properly known as Le Salon Mondial du Vin et Des Spiriteux, has become the most important of the international wine fairs. In Ziraldo's luggage were samples of Inniskillin's 1987 Vidal icewine, another powerhouse almost as concentrated as the previous vintage.

"We didn't have our own booth and there was no other Canadian winery there," Kaiser recalls. But Ziraldo, with his easy talent for mixing with the rich and famous, found influential people to taste the icewine, including an individual who identified himself as a personal friend of Jean Vidal, the breeder of the grape. "He said, when he sat down and tasted the icewine, that he would rate the wine among the five best sweet wines in the world," Kaiser recounts. This extravagant compliment spurred Ziraldo to enter an icewine at the 1991 Vinexpo.

At Kaiser's suggestion, Ziraldo took the 1989 Vidal. It was not nearly as voluptuously sweet as the previous vintages, with only about 160 grams of unfermented sugar, but with a hint of botrytis, it possessed more finesse and complexity. "It is very unusual for Vidal to get botrytis because it has a tough skin," Kaiser says. "But we had this warm Indian summer, with fog in the morning." This was ideal for the development of noble rot and the Vidal grapes had a 10 to 15 per cent infection. Kaiser had been pleased with that wine from the beginning and believed it was Inniskillin's best shot at winning a medal.

As it happened, Kaiser, ever the scientist, went instead to a technical conference in Seattle rather than Vinexpo, sending his daughter Andrea to Bordeaux with the Inniskillin delegation. She called from France with the stunning news that Inniskillin had won not only one of just seventeen gold medals but what she termed "the big medal." Her mother, Sylvia, thought it was more like "the Academy Award." The publicity sent Inniskillin's icewine sales rocketing.

"We were incrementally increasing our production of icewine every year," Kaiser says. He continued to be conservative in quantity, however, until the 1995 vintage, after Inniskillin had been acquired by Vincor International Ltd., Canada's largest wine group. "It became a corporate objective to make a lot of icewine," he says. That year, Kaiser made about five thousand cases or sixty thousand half bottles of icewine. Production rose to sixteen thousand cases in 1996, then declined to four thousand in 1997 when the harvest was delayed by warm weather until January 1998 and most of the grapes were lost.

But in 1998, with favorable harvest conditions in both Ontario and British Columbia, he was responsible for making an astounding 30,000 cases for Inniskillin or for Vincor under the Jackson-Triggs label. "We have more icewine under this roof than all of Germany makes together," Kaiser asserted after that vintage. Subsequently, Vincor has delegated its huge icewine production to the team of winemakers employed at half a dozen Canadian wineries the company owns, each with its own icewine program.

Such production volumes are possible at Inniskillin and at the several other large Canadian producers because the Vidal grape is so widely grown in Ontario. The major growers have installed presses on their vineyards so that the substantial volumes can be processed quickly, while remaining frozen.

A government-backed inspection system has been developed to police each year's icewine harvest and prevent cheating. (In British Columbia, the rules were tightened in 2000 to forbid trucking inadequately frozen grapes into the mountains in search of colder weather after one producer did exactly that — unsuccessfully — in the mild vintage of 1999.)

After limiting himself to just Vidal for some years, Kaiser has expanded to other varieties for icewine, including Chenin Blanc and the classic, Riesling. Since 1996, he also has sought to make red icewines from Cabernet Franc. After three vintages, he has concluded that the variety lacks the necessary physiological qualities — the ability to hang soundly on the vines into the winter. "We need a really dark-colored icewine for the Asian market," Kaiser says. Subsequently, he has begun experimenting with Dornfelder, a German vinifera cross with the rare attribute of having blood-red juice.

Making red icewines is difficult because almost all red wines derive their color from the skins of the grapes but icewine juice is pressed off before there is significant skin contact. A variety like Pinot Noir, with the desired acidity for icewine, produces light pink icewine in those years when its thin skin does not succumb to rot. "But if you had a suitable grape variety which is a teinturier — with color in the juice, not only in the skins — you would get red icewine juice," Kaiser says. Dornfelder grapes hang well on the vines and the juice is richly colored. "It's like ink, ink, ink."

Being large has not blunted the ability of either Inniskillin or Jackson-Triggs, the sister winery, to make award-winning icewines. With Kaiser protégés making the icewine, the Jackson-Triggs winery in British Columbia, one of the largest in western Canada, has won numerous gold medals for Riesling icewines from the vintages of 1996 and 1997. In an echo of 1991, the winery in 1998 won not only a gold medal but an award of excellence at Vinexpo for its elegant 1997 Proprietors' Reserve Riesling Icewine.

Inniskillin has been aggressive at introducing its wines to markets outside Canada, notably Asia. This market came to Inniskillin, as well as other wineries in the peninsula near Niagara Falls. This spectacular natural wonder is a priority attraction for Asian tourists (among others) who, when they fan out beyond the falls, discover wine touring.

At Inniskillin's quaint wine shop, the staff quickly noted that the icewine drew more notice that any other product; indeed, of every ten bottles of icewine sold at the shop, eight were being purchased by Japanese visitors. Very quickly, Inniskillin began attaching neck labels to the bottles, explaining icewine in Japanese. That was followed by supplying brochures in Japanese and employing Japanese-speaking staff to deal with the almost insatiable demand for bottles of icewine, a product ideally in tune both with the Japanese palate and with the Japanese tradition of giving each other prestige gifts.

Ever the silken salesman, Donald Ziraldo made the first of his numerous sales trips to Asia in 1997, introducing Inniskillin's 1996 Icewine in Hong Kong, Singapore and Beijing as well as Japan. In parallel with that, Inniskillin has begun its own team marketing its icewine in the United States. As European trade restrictions are lifted, Inniskillin icewines will be available there as well, including one of the few sparkling icewines in the world, created in 1999 for the Millennium.

Inniskillin Icewine History

Vidal grapes and Ontario harvests unless otherwise stated

Vintage	Harvest date	Harvest temp	Harvest brix	Harvest acidity grams per liter	Alcohol %	Res. Sugar
1983	Eaten by birds					
1984	January 8,1985	-15°C	51.6°	N.A.	N.A.	N.A.
1985	Dec. 15, 1985	-13°C	44.6°	N.A.	N.A.	N.A.
1986	January 23,1987	-17°C	55.0°	13.4 g/l	11	157
1987	January 5,1988	-15°C	52.0°	12.9 g/l	12	156
1988	Feb. 4, 1989	-10°C	38.0°	11.0 g/l	12.7	133
1989	Dec. 6, 1989	-12°C	38.0°	13.0 g/l	12.8	148
1990	January4,8, 1991	-13°C	44.0°	11.6 g/l	12	140
1991	Dec. 5,18, 1991	-16°C	37.3°	9.8 g/l	11	135
1992	Dec. 26, 1992	-13°C	38.0°	11.5 g/l	11.4	145
1993	Dec. 26-31,1993	-17°C	40.0°	11.5 g/l	11.4	155
1994	Dec.13,14, 1994	N.A.	46.0°	11.5 g/l	10.5	177
1995	Dec. 11-13, 1995	N.A.	42.0°	12.1 g/l	11	197
1995 Cab. Franc	Dec. 12, 1995	N.A.	42.0°	11.1 g/l	11	195
1996	Dec.20,31,1996, Jan. 1, 11, 12,16-19, 1997	N.A.	38.35°	12.5 g/l	10.5	192

1997	Dec.31 1997					
	Feb.15, 1998	-11°C	38.2°	12.3 g/l	10.5	225
1997 Cab.						
Franc	Dec.31,1997	N.A.	40.0°	N.A.	10.5	213
1998	Dec. 22, 1998					
	January1-12, 1999	-13°C	42.1°	13.1	10.5	247
1999	January13, 2000	-11°C	42.4°	12.9	10.5	246
2000	Dec.12, 13,20, 21,22,					
	28,29,	-11°C	40°	N.A.	N.A.	N.A.

Source: Inniskillin Wines Inc.

9
Icewine Harvest

The perception of Canada is of a wintry land locked in snow and ice. Sandra Oldfield, the winemaker at the Okanagan Valley's Tinhorn Creek winery, shared that notion when she was growing up in California. Subsequently, she experienced all of the Canadian seasons and discovered the advantage of bracing winters for icewine.

Unlike Germany, icewine temperatures are expected every year in Canadian vineyards. Exactly when is unpredictable. In some years Arctic cold grips the vineyards in early November. In 1997, a mild winter in much of the Northern Hemisphere influenced by the El Niño warm Pacific current, there was insufficient frost in the Okanagan before Christmas. The icewine window only opened for several days just after January 1, 1998, and then again briefly in mid-January. Because the harvest at Tinhorn Creek took place on January 3, 1998, Sandra Oldfield impishly declared on that year's icewine label that the vintage was "1997 + 3 days."

Harvest dates in Ontario's Niagara Peninsula have ranged from early December to late March. In the 1997 vintage, Inniskillin picked some of its grapes during a brief cold spell on December 31 but did not get another cold snap until February 15, 1998, when the remainder of the harvest was picked. It was the latest harvest in the 15 years in which Inniskillin had been making icewine and, even with protective netting, so much fruit was lost to birds or fell to the snow-covered ground that Inniskillin produced just 48,000 half bottles of the wine. By the standard of most European producers, that is a stupendous quantity — but it was only a quarter of what Inniskillin had produced the year before. In 1998, in a rare convergence of winter weather, both the Niagara producers and those in the Okanagan harvested almost the entire icewine crop a few days before Christmas.

Like those European wineries for which icewine is a niche confection, Tinhorn Creek only makes a few hundred liters each year. Its 1998 production was even more modest than planned because, a few weeks before harvest, cattle that had been foraging the dry mountainside grass of a neighboring ranch broke through the vineyard fence and devoured two tonnes of sweet Kerner clusters, about half the quantity set aside for icewine, before general manager Kenn Oldfield and Lucian, his exceedingly amiable dog, drove them off. "That was a first for us," said Kenn. In previous years, he had driven off bears, birds, deer and coyotes, all of which will devour the succulent icewine grapes. The persistence of hungry wild life is astonishing: the story is told of a grower who found three deer among the icewine grapes. He shot one and the others just continued to eat.

The 1998 vintage was only Sandra Oldfield's fifth icewine vintage. At the time of the 1994 vintage, she was still Sandra Cashin, a California native completing winemaking studies at the University of California's renowned Davis campus where Kenn Oldfield, a one-time engineering consultant turned vineyard manager, was a fellow student, learning viticulture prior to the launch of Tinhorn Creek. He persuaded the ever-cheerful Sandra to become Tinhorn Creek's winemaker (and subsequently to marry him as well).

Sandra was still in California on December 3, 1994, when Kenn telephoned from British Columbia that the temperature in the vineyard was -9°C and he was about to pick the Kerner grapes, the preferred variety for Tinhorn's icewine. She had little advice, other than suggesting which yeast to use. Neither had ever made icewine, as became evident a day or so later. Using the winery's new bladder press, Kenn Oldfield extracted enough juice for seven hundred liters of wine. In his inexperience, he had crushed the grapes before putting what had become an icy slurry into the press. Then he neglected to clean the press's horizontal drum promptly, allowing the slurry to freeze inside the press, which was anchored on a concrete pad beside the winery. The next day, when the press was spun in a misguided effort to dislodge the cake, the unbalanced drum tore the anchor bolts from the concrete.

Subsequent icewine vintages at Tinhorn Creek have gone more smoothly. Sandra Oldfield's 1996 Kerner Icewine, with an exquisitely clean balance of sugar and acidity, won numerous awards, including a gold medal at the Los Angeles County Fair where it was judged the best of all the dessert wines.

The icewine vintage of 1998, blessed with the right weather and a big crop, was among the most bountiful ever. In British Columbia, the wineries begin monitoring weather about the middle of November. In 1998 the Arctic front began descending from the Yukon on Tuesday, December 15, its progress catalogued on his winery's Internet site by Tilman Hainle, the technologically adept winery owner whose father, Walter, pioneered icewine in British Columbia. That Tuesday, even though the temperature outside Hainle's winery was still above freezing, icewine temperatures were forecast as early as Friday. On Wednesday, Hainle reported that a low of -12°C, perfect for icewine, was being predicted for the following Sunday. "Are we to believe this or will it be yet another tantalizing prognostication that falls apart as we draw closer to the date?" Tilman worried in his Internet posting for that day.

Sandra Oldfield was confident. She alerted her pickers, a small crew of about a dozen men and women, among them immigrants from India who now are Okanagan orchardists and French-speaking Quebeckers who moved to the Okanagan 20 years ago from the Gaspé as itinerant fruit pickers and remained as year-round agricultural workers. "I don't know anything about wine," one picker admitted in the vineyard. "I do it for the money."

The pickers arrived at Tinhorn Creek before dawn on Saturday morning, December 19, taking shelter from the biting wind in a tractor shed. They warmed themselves with hot chocolate while Oldfield periodically emerged from the shed to read her cheap household thermometer amid the vines. The mercury stalled stubbornly at -8°C and the fat, golden Kerner grapes remained springy to Oldfield's touch, not firm enough to allow her to produce another award-winning icewine. Oldfield wanted another two degrees of freezing. At 8 A.M., with a watery sun now rising in the pale wintry sky, she sought advice from the neighboring Gehringer Brothers vineyard where Walter and his younger brother Gordon had been making icewine 1991.

That morning, the Gehringers, watching eight meticulous acres of netted vines still heavy with unpicked grapes, also decided that the grapes would benefit from the extra degrees of frost forecast for that evening. Walter Gehringer, who lives at the edge of the vineyard, had been up several times during the night to check his vineyard thermometer. A scientifically accurate professional model, it corroborated Sandra Oldfield's kitchen thermometer. The Gehringers believed it would be cold enough to pick about three hours after nightfall. The Oldfields, who were hosting a wedding reception in Tinhorn Creek's elegant tasting room, asked their pickers to return at dawn the following morning. Most did come back, including several who had picked through the night's bracing cold at Gehringers.

While Tinhorn Creek approaches icewine on the modest and casual scale of the small European producers, icewine is a well-organized campaign at the Gehringer Brothers, a family-run winery that the brothers opened in 1986 after coming back from winemaking schools in Germany, Walter from Geisenheim and Gordon from Weinsberg. Their pristinely made white wines immediately placed the winery among the front ranks in the Okanagan and, with each vintage selling out before the following year's Christmas, it was 1991 before they got around to icewines.

They were plunged into icewine in much the same accidental way that the first icewines were made — by an unusually early freeze. With a cool growing season that summer, it had not been a good year for table wines. Late-ripening varieties, like Riesling, still

Grapes at Hainle Vineyards Estate in British Columbia, Canada, two months before the icewine harvest. Nets are used to protect the fruit from birds and strong winds during its prolonged hang time. *(Photo: J. Schreiner)*

Frozen grapes are harvested on a frigid night at the Gehringer Brothers vineyard in British Columbia. Finding ready, willing and able icewine pickers is one of the challenges of icewine production. *(Photo: J. Schreiner)*

Dr. Hans Ambrosi, the "father" of Eiswein. As director of the Hessische Staatsweingüter in Germany, he developed techniques for making Eiswein commercially viable. *(Photo: J. Schreiner)*

Eiswein for sale in Germany. *(Photo: J. Schreiner)*

The author *(right)* with Matthias Achs of Weingut Matthias Achs & Sohn in Gols, Austria. *(Photo: J. Schreiner)*

Hans J. Stiefensand, chairman of P. J. Valckenberg at Worms, Germany, standing in front of the Liebfrauenstift Kirchenstück, or the vineyard of the Church of Our Lady, from which Liebfraumilch originated. *(Photo: J. Schreiner)*

Frozen grapes ready for Ledeno Vino, the Slovenian version of icewine, at the Jeruzalem winery in Ormož, Slovenia. *(Photo courtesy Jeruzalem Ormož)*

Netted grapes at a Joseph Estates vineyard near Niagara-on-the-Lake, Ontario, Canada. Joseph Estates was at the forefront of icewine production in Canada. *(Photo courtesy Joseph Estates/Joseph Pohorly)*

Volunteer pickers at Weingut Sepp Moser in Rohrendorf, Austria, pose with the fruits of their labors. *(Photo Courtesy Sepp Moser)*

The Schmidt brothers of Vineland Estates celebrate reaching the North Pole with a drop of Vineland icewine. The trip would provide invaluable publicity. *(Photo courtesy Vineland Estates)*

The wine cellar of the legendary Schloss Johannisberg near Geisenheim, Germany.
(*Photo: Kurt L. Mayer*)

Schloss Johannisberg vineyard in winter. Botrytis cinera, or noble rot, is believed to have been discovered here in the 1770s. The Schloss was also one of the earliest producers of Eiswein. *(Photo: Kurt L. Mayer)*

were minimally mature at the end of October, and the Gehringers chose to leave a significant quantity unpicked, hoping to make icewine after a late Indian summer had added a few more degrees of ripeness. On the first day of November, the temperature unexpectedly plunged to freezing. The vines had not yet dropped their leaves and the perfectionist Gehringers first went along the rows, knocking off the canopy so that the cold could penetrate entire bunches and freeze the Riesling grapes uniformly before they picked them for icewine.

The ideal icewine temperatures continued the next morning and Walter Gehringer now seized the opportunity of the moment. A nearby vineyard, he learned, still had Ehrenfelser grapes on its vines for a producer that planned a late harvest wine but was not prepared to make icewine. Gehringer was, and he did. When it remained cold for a third successive morning, he and a small crew returned to the same vineyard for some Chancellor grapes, a red variety which the Gehringers had contracted for a dry table wine but had not harvested because the maturity was marginal. But because freezing concentrates the sugars and other flavors, the frozen Chancellor was fine for making a red icewine, one of only three red icewines made that year in British Columbia.

"You get bitten" is how Walter Gehringer explained the winery's subsequent decision to commit to icewine production on a scale unimaginable to many European producers.

On this December Saturday late in 1998, the Gehringer brothers, along with their father Helmut and their uncle Karl, had been bustling about the winery with last-minute preparations for the harvest that night. The telephone rang continually with calls from prospective pickers anxious to earn a few extra dollars before Christmas.

"Yes, we still could use some people tonight," Walter Gehringer assured one caller, warning: "You're going to have to dress well. The wind you are enjoying now is not going to stop." As the day progressed, the temperature edged down, clearly headed toward -12°C by midnight, and perhaps lower, made even more unpleasant by the wind knifing across the exposed ridge of the Gehringer vineyard.

When the gloved and heavily garbed pickers arrived in the

dark, about 7 P.M., they began working at the most exposed part of the vineyard and picked rapidly down the hillside to get out of the wind. With no moonlight and no reflective snow on the ground yet, the vines were illuminated by tractor-mounted light bars straddling eight rows at once. Hard bunches of grapes, snipped from the dry vines with little clippers, thudded into wheelbarrows, which were emptied into bins bound for the winery.

Everyone moved quickly. No one took time to view the diamond-bright constellations in the winter sky. The pickers were here, as the shivering French Canadian said, for the money. In the initial days of icewine production in Canada, when quantities were modest and grapes could be picked in hours, wineries augmented their own staffs with novelty-seeking friends of the winery and individuals from the restaurant trade. One year Inniskillin even was able to charge $1,000 a couple to a select handful of socialites who warmed up after picking with a party at the winery.

Walter Gehringer abjures such dilettantism. "The real world and the romance are two separate things." The scale of icewine production has quickly gone beyond where large producers can rely on well-meaning amateurs. This evening, with 25 tonnes to harvest, the hired pickers at Gehringers worked well into the early morning before going home. The two Gehringer brothers worked through the entire night and late into Sunday night without sleep.

The certainty that the cold will persist for several days facilitates the processing of the frozen grapes. By regulation as well as by necessity, they must be pressed while frozen and, if the sun has power, must not be allowed to warm up in the mid-day sun, for the juice then will become too dilute for icewine. Walter and Gordon Gehringer communicated this sense of urgency to their employees, seldom moving at less than a brisk trot about the vineyard or among the three presses, issuing orders, shifting equipment, preventing inexperienced workers from making costly errors like the one that damaged the Tinhorn Creek press in 1994.

With a weary note of resignation, Walter Gehringer paused to reflect that the production of icewine has turned winegrowers into gamblers who risk tonnes of grapes and costly winery equipment each vintage against the chance that nature will let them win the wager. It is the complaint of a tired and cold winemaker. It will be forgotten once the wines begin attracting the inevitable accolades.

With the temperature remaining cold, pickers returned on Sunday to finish the harvest in daylight; others fanned out to other vineyards as the temperature settled solidly in the icewine range well into the next week, exactly as the weatherman had predicted. It has been an ideal icewine harvest.

"It feels anticlimactic to have it so easy," Tilman Hainle grumbled over the Internet. "No uncertainty, no last-minute cancellations."

10

Polar Icewine

The 1992 expedition by dog team during which winemakers Allan and Brian Schmidt took icewine to the Magnetic North Pole began a few years earlier after Allan's divorce from his first wife. A friend advised that, before forming another relationship, he should first accomplish something that he considered a lifelong dream. For Allan, that dream was traveling to the Pole by dog team. After his younger brother, Brian, agreed to share the adventure, Toronto wine writer Tony Aspler suggested taking icewine on the trek. They took two dozen half bottles, divided equally between the expedition's two sleds, insurance against the possible loss of one sled.

Their Inuit guides were perplexed at the heavy cargo. Allan recounted their reaction to Aspler, who wrote about it later in *Wine Tidings* magazine: "When I told them it was wine we had brought with us, made from frozen grapes, they just couldn't understand it. They thought it was peculiar that these two men from the city would spend all this time, effort and money to bring bottles of wine to the Magnetic North Pole. When we got there and pulled out the bottles and placed them on the glaciers to take photographs, they said this must be very important wine if we went to all the trouble of carrying it here."[1]

For Vineland Estates, the Ontario winery where the brothers ply their craft, icewine indeed has become important. In the bounteous 1998 vintage, the retail value of the 14,000 liters of icewine they produced was estimated to be more than $1 million. Now among Canada's leading icewine producers, the Schmidt brothers mastered the art in a comparatively short time.

They were born in British Columbia, Allan in 1963 and Brian in 1968, and are so close that they finish each other's sentences. Grandfather Frank Schmidt was a pioneer grapegrower in the Okanagan and father Lloyd Schmidt was a founding partner at the Sumac Ridge Estate Winery where Allan, after an apprenticeship with Heitz Vineyards in California, began his winemaking career. "I made some icewine at Sumac Ridge in 1984," Allan recalls. "It was only 50 liters and it was never commercially available. We just drank it ourselves actually." Brian gained practical training in a German winery and joined Vineland Estates in 1991.

Vineland, where Allan began making wine in 1987, is based on vineyards planted in 1979 by the Weis family, long-established wine-makers and nursery owners in the Mosel. With their encouragement, Allan in 1988 produced his first icewine at Vineland from Vidal grapes. The following year, he made both a Vidal and a Riesling icewine. "We quickly realized that Vidal icewine when it is young is just a cornucopia of opulent fruit, peaches and apricot," Allan says. "In very, very ripe years Vidal can be accused of being too cloying. Riesling with its backbone of acidity doesn't have that problem."

He resolved the perceived shortcoming of Vidal with a cleverly obvious bit of winemaking. Since 1990 Allan and his brother, who helped him with the Vineland Estates icewine harvest at Christmas that year (they produced a mere seven hundred liters), have been blending as much as 15 per cent Riesling into the Vidal icewine.

"The characteristic of Vidal is so powerful that when you blend some Riesling with it, the minerally, flinty characteristics of Riesling are subdued and you have the nose of Vidal," Allan explains. "When you drink the wine, you have all of that Vidal character [in the mouth] but when you swallow the wine, you get a crescendo of acidity at the end which cleanses your palate and gives the wine more depth."

They improved the longevity of their icewine as well. Allan

suggests that Vidal icewine's life averages seven years while Riesling icewines are capable of aging at least twenty-five years. Therefore, he argues, the Vineland Estates Vidal with its backbone of Riesling is a wine for cellaring twelve to fifteen years.

The wines that were transported to the North Pole were from Vineland's 1990 and 1991 vintages. "I'd always loved the Arctic," explains Allan Schmidt who, like his brother, is a strapping, athletic man. He had devoured books on the great Polar explorers, men like Robert Peary and Frederick Cook, both of whom claimed to have reached the North Pole first, and the tragic Sir John Franklin, whose entire 1845 expedition perished. When Allan decided to realize his own Arctic adventure before remarrying, he and Brian took more than a year to plan their trek to the Magnetic North Pole, located over the ice beyond Grise Fjord, the most northerly inhabited community in Canada. They hired two Inuit guides, along with a pair of sleds, each packed with about two hundred pounds of equipment and each pulled by ten dogs.

"Three or four months before we went on the expedition," Allan recalled, "I was speaking with Tony Aspler and he said, 'Why don't you take icewine to the North Pole?'" The writer pointed out that they were setting out on a quintessentially Canadian pilgrimage and the newest star among Canadian wines deserved to go along. Besides, Aspler added, he would write about it in *Wine Tidings,* which then was Canada's only national magazine for wine consumers. "Done," agreed Allan, always alert to the value of publicity.

Since they were going to burden their dogs with unusual cargo, the brothers had to justify it. "We sort of tongue in cheek formulated this hypothesis that the reason why we would want to take icewine to the North Pole is because of the rich mineral content of icewine," Allan chuckles. "The magnetic polarization of the Pole would polarize all the minerals in the wine and we'd get the best-aged icewine in history — or whatever. We thought there could be a physiological change." Anything for science.

The winemakers flew to Grise Fjord, putting the Pole within practical reach in a trek that could be completed in 10 days under 24-hour sunlight. Under the bemused gaze of their guides, the duo celebrated their arrival at the Pole on May 19, 1992, toasting each other with icewine on a day when the temperature was -20°C and the viscous wine had become slushy. In their subsequent interview with Aspler, they said they decided against burying a second bottle at the Pole because it would be littering. When they returned home, they invited wine writers to a tasting, giving each one a sample from a bottle that had been to the North Pole and another from a similar vintage that had remained in Vineland's cellar.

"Everyone at the wine tasting concluded there was a difference between the two wines," Allan says. "They were split on which one they preferred." That is fortunate. Had the writers preferred the Polar traveler, Allan grins, he and his brother would have to take their icewine to the Arctic every year. "We can't take a 10,000-liter tank of icewine to the North Pole every year."

The publicity value of the *Wine Tidings* article proved unexpectedly crucial. Either the article or a news report based on the article — Allan Schmidt is not certain which — was read by a Japanese wine buyer. "He contacted us, to buy our icewine and use this story in selling the icewine to Japan," the winemaker recounts. "It resulted in our first export wine sale to Japan." Now, half of Vineland's icewine is sold to Asia and it has paved the way for its other wines. "It has given us access to markets which we would not otherwise have been able to provide ourselves," Brian Schmidt believes.

The brothers have prolonged the magic of that icewine by adding some remaining bottles to subsequent vintages of icewine. The brothers also have kept the magic alive since with their ready willingness to speak about the experience and show slides of Vineland's stubby brown bottle of icewine nesting in pristine polar ice. "We spent a truly inordinate amount of money [on the expedition]," Brian admits. They considered claiming their costs as a tax-deductible business expense until their accountant advised against it.

Along with the other new winemakers in Canada, the Schmidt brothers had to learn the icewine craft vintage by vintage. "There are no books, there are no journals that we can reference," says Brian, who joined his brother at Vineland Estates in September

1991 and gradually assumed the winemaking while Allan concentrated on viticulture and business. "It's been such a specialty product, even in the Old World, that there is no reference manual. It has all been trial and error. Every year is very, very different because the profile of the wines each year is different."

In 1995, the first year in which Brian was totally responsible for the vintage at Vineland Estates, the production of icewine was a substantial 8,000 liters, a quantity where a mistake would have been ruinous. "I remember my hands shaking," Brian recalls. "It is absolutely daunting." That was the year when many Ontario producers began increasing icewine production rapidly. Allan Schmidt estimates that his peers produced 10 times as much icewine in 1996 as the year before, were set back by poor harvest conditions in 1997, but took advantage of perfect icewine conditions in 1998 to produce five times as much as in 1996.

When the brothers first began making icewine, they belonged to the "bigger is better" school. While it is rare for German vineyards to get extreme freezing (anything below -12°C), Canadian vineyards can experience -18°C, a temperature that creates marble-hard grapes which, when pressed, yield must with extremely concentrated sugar and acidity.

"When we first started harvesting icewine, it would be -18°C and we thought, wow, we're going to get wonderful quality!" Allan recalls. But because the grapes at that temperature are so hard, the juice yield is poor, even when the press is cranked to an equipment-breaking pressure. "At maximum pressure, with a whole tonne of grapes in the press, you are able to count the drops, one at a time," Allan recounts. The juice yield is about a quarter of what it would be at -8°C and it is so sweet that it becomes almost impossible to ferment because the yeast cells collapse under the osmotic pressure of the juice's super-saturated sugar.

The brothers learned to aim for icewine harvests at -12°C and even then, Brian says, it may be necessary to inoculate the juice several times with fresh yeast to keep the fermentation progressing at a healthy pace. There is another reason, Brian adds, for not picking at an extreme of temperature: the finished wine is likely to be too sweet, lacking that taut balance between sugar and acidity that marks a great icewine.

Ultimately, the style of icewine depends on the conditions at vintage. "It would be negligent of us not to respect each vintage on its own, rather than have a blanket order of the sweetness or alcohol level at which each wine will be produced," Brian maintains. In 1998 the grapes were harvested generally at about -11°C, producing juice that averaged a commendable 42° Brix before fermentation. There were nights when it was too cold and harvesting was suspended until it warmed up. In general, they aim at alcohol of 10 per cent to 10.8 per cent in the finished icewine but are always flexible, depending on what qualities the vineyards deliver at harvest. "You have to determine the balance for every single vintage," he says. "You have to respect the vintage itself."

Six months after the Polar expedition, the Weis family sold Vineland Estates to John Howard, a Canadian entrepreneur. The winery, which formerly operated from a humble group of old farm houses, has been renovated and expanded into a grand edifice dominated by a tower in which the owner's office has a view of the mist of Niagara Falls on the distant southern horizon.

There was one year when the brothers could have used the tower to keep watch over the surrounding netted rows of icewine grapes in their vineyards. In a risky move, they opened the nets long enough to let the leaves fall from the vines rather than collect and decay in the bottom of the closed nets. To protect the grapes, they deployed bird bangers, loud devices that frighten birds with irregular artillery barrages of noise.

"Unfortunately, one Sunday morning, all the bird bangers stopped," Brian recounts. An employee had neglected to keep the devices charged with the necessary propane. Within hours, a huge flock consumed grapes that would have yielded icewine with a retail value of $100,000.

Initially, the brothers sold icewine juice to other producers because the cash was needed to buy additional vineyards. Their own icewine production, now substantial, then was crafted like an artisanal sideline, with friends and family volunteering for the harvest. "We wouldn't pay anybody for picking icewine," Allan remembers. The volunteer pickers — often restaurateurs and wine store employees — could expect midnight telephone calls informing them that the harvest was expected to begin before dawn the next morning.

"When they arrived, they would receive a label, with the numbers starting at 001," Allan says. "The first person who showed up would get bottle 001 of the vintage of that icewine they were producing." The volunteers would return for the bottling of the vintage, placing their individual labels on the corresponding bottles coming off the bottling line.

All the icewine labels then were hand-numbered in elegant penmanship by Noreen Schmidt, the mother of the two brothers, a practice finally discontinued after she numbered and wrote the date on 6,800 bottles from the 1993 vintage. Over the five years that Vineland Estates managed its icewine harvest in this manner, a growing number of the volunteers sought to collect the same numbered bottle each year, to the point of queuing at the end of Vineland Estates's long driveway in the appropriate order before proceeding to the winery.

"A couple of years ago we could do all our icewine harvesting in one or two nights and you could have some fun with that," Allan says, recalling festive barbecues with volunteers before the winery needed the reliability of professional picking crews. "Now our harvest of icewine can, quite conceivably, take us 10 to 14 nights."

In Ontario's Niagara vineyards, the icewine harvest conditions seldom occur before late December and not infrequently in January or February. "There have been times when Allan and I picked a couple of press loads on our own, either on Christmas Day or New Year's Day, where we didn't have the gall to phone anybody on Christmas Day to harvest icewine for us," Brian says.

In the warm winter of 1997–98, some winemakers could not pick until St. Valentine's Day in 1998 (Pillitteri finished picking on a rare cold day in late March). Brian Schmidt and two assistants worked for 68 hours without sleep in the first week of January 1998, frantic to harvest and press grapes before the weather warmed again. "We had brief moments when we hung out in the lab and had a bit of shut-eye, but that was the window of opportunity that we had and we had to do it."

Another challenging vintage was 2000, when Vineland produced 9,000 liters. Each time the temperature nudged toward the icewine threshold, a picking crew was assembled, only to be sent home when the weather moderated. Brian estimates that this happened two dozen times and the pickers were close to mutiny before the actual harvest took place. "In the end, we harvested nine times in December and in January 2001." He grouses that the harvest marathons are "very difficult on our marriages." But, so far, not so difficult as to send the brothers on another Polar icewine expedition.

11

A Parade of
Canadian Producers

anada is among the smallest wine producers in the New World, yet many Canadian wineries, in less than two decades, have emerged as the world's largest icewine producers. There are two reasons: Canadian vineyards benefit from famously cold winters that occur with a regularity unknown in Europe. Even in the occasional mild winters, producers can be certain that the necessary freeze for icewine will happen — even though it may not occur until February.

Secondly, the Vidal grape, from which about three-quarters of all Canadian icewine is made, has proven to be especially suitable for icewine. The grape is a white hybrid developed in France and was among the many hybrids imported to Canada and the eastern United States in the 1940s to improve vineyards then filled with native American varieties. The hybrids largely fell out of favor in the 1990s, to be uprooted and replaced with classic vinifera grapes whose wines have more acceptance with consumers.

The extensive Vidal vineyards, primarily in Ontario, were spared because of Vidal's icewine properties. Because the grape is thick-skinned, it resists disease and is somewhat unappealing to birds. The berries also cling well to the stalks. Thus, Vidal hangs on the vines, remaining healthy, longer than any other variety used for icewine. It yields plump, seductive icewines with powerful aromas of tropical fruits and flavors ranging from ripe pineapple to caramel. Canadian icewines, after winning numerous international awards in the past decade, have won global recognition for Canadian wines in general.

Andrés Wines Ltd.

See Peller Estates and Hillebrand Estates

Bellamere Country Wines 1260 Gainsborough Road, London ON N6H 5K8

Opened in 1998 by fruit farmer Don Mader, Bellamere primarily is a fruit winery although grape wines are made with purchased grapes. Bellamere's 24-hectare farm sold produce through a busy farmers' market on the outskirts of London, a university town in southern Ontario. When Mader decided to add some value, he recruited James Patience, a soft-spoken Edinburgh-trained brewer who began his winemaking career in Canada in 1964 as a laboratory technician at the London Winery. Patience took over as London's winemaker in 1978, remaining until the winery was sold 20 years later.

Several Canadian wineries, including Bellamere, simulate the icewine style by using fruits, primarily apples or pears, and commercial freezers. The technique, as Patience explains, is simple. The fruits are pressed to extract juice which goes into 60-liter plastic drums that then are placed into freezers for several weeks. The containers then are returned to the winery's cool cellar and allowed to warm slightly until sweet and concentrated juice congregates in the center of each drum. This is drained from holes that are drilled through the sides of the drums and the ice. Patience prefers juice with a sweetness of about 41° Brix and this is fermented to produce what the wineries called fruit ice. Appellation rules forbid calling these wines icewine. Fruit ice is deliciously refreshing and sells on average for half the price of icewine.

In its first decade, this winery has had three owners and three names. It began as **Willow Heights**. When Ron Speranzini relocated that winery to a nearby vineyard, he sold the Birchwood property in 1999 to Josef Zimmermann, who renamed it **Vine Court**. It became Birchwood in 2000 after being taken over by Diamond Estates, a winery management and marketing company that also owns **Lakewood**.

Some things remained constant at Birchwood, a rustic little winery beside the busy Queen Elizabeth Way highway. The inventory acquired by Diamond Estates included Vidal icewines from 1996, 1998 and 1999, all of them made in a style that displays plump caramel, peach and pineapple flavors.

Zimmermann, who remained the winemaker, extended the range in 2000 by also producing icewines from Riesling and Cabernet Franc. Zimmermann is a Geisenheim graduate who came to Canada in 1976 as a winemaker for Jordan & Ste. Michelle in British Columbia and Ontario until the winery was gobbled up in a merger. Zimmermann then became a consultant and a grapegrower in Ontario. His older brother, Roman, operates **Weingut Höhn-Zimmermann** in Germany and made Eiswein there as early as 1965.

Calona Vineyards 1125 Richter Street, Kelowna, BC V1Y 2K6

The oldest operating winery in British Columbia, Calona was established in 1932 as a fruit winery that soon switched to grape wines. In the 1960s it grew to be one of Canada's largest wineries by modeling itself on the product and marketing ideas of California's Gallo winery. In the 1990s Calona, still a successful marketer of generics, added premium wines and Ehrenfelser icewine to its portfolio.

Winemaker Howard Soon's debut icewine vintage was 1994 when he made 660 half bottles of icewine and promptly won two gold medals in international competition. "Beginner's luck," he says modestly. Except for Verdelet and Pinot Blanc in 1998, he has stayed with Ehrenfelser, preferring it because the grape's mouthfilling flavors of peaches and tropical fruits come through so well in icewine. In the fine 2000 vintage, just over 13,000 half bottles were produced. In that vintage, Soon also made his first red icewine, 2,400 half bottles of Pinot Noir.

Cave Spring Cellars 3836 Main Street, Jordan, ON L0R 1S0

With a premium reputation based particularly on Chardonnay and Riesling, Cave Springs produced its first vintage in 1986 from vineyards planted as early as 1970 on what is called the Beamsville Bench. The winery is operated by a partnership that includes president Leonard Pennachetti, a one-time professor of social sciences whose grandfather emigrated to Canada from northern Italy.

Another partner is Angelo Pavan, a fastidious winemaker in spite of having graduated in philosophy at university. What began

as a winery that produced 3,000 cases in its first vintage now is an integrated hospitality business that makes 50,000 cases a year, operates a fine wine country restaurant next door to the winery and a luxurious heritage hotel across the street in the quaint village of Jordan.

Angelo Pavan's initial vintage of icewine was in 1989, an experimental four cases of Riesling. The winery made icewine every year since then but one, gradually increasing its output. By the 1995 vintage, when the harvest lasted from late December to early January, Cave Spring made 330 cases (of 12 half bottles each) of Riesling icewine and 440 cases of Vidal icewine. "We are usually out of icewine for half the year," Pavan says, explaining his decision to make 2,500 cases in 1998, two thirds of it Riesling.

Production scaled back to 300 cases in 1999 and 450 cases in 2000, made with Riesling in both vintages. Pavan believes that Riesling is more elegant and ages better. His 1990 Riesling icewine a decade later remained vibrantly alive, its crisp acidity supporting tangy fruit with tangerine notes. The iconoclastic Pavan confesses that his teeth are too sensitive to tolerate much icewine without pain but while watching Sunday afternoon football, he likes to fortify dark beer with a few ounces of icewine.

CedarCreek Estate Winery 5445 Lakeshore Road, Kelowna, BC V1W 4S5

It is the familiar story of an unexpected frost. In 1991 this boutique winery still had some Riesling in its vineyard on October 27 when the temperature plunged suddenly to -10°C. "Necessity is the mother of invention," concedes Gordon Fitzpatrick, the winery's president.

CedarCreek's young winemaker at the time was Ann Sperling, now at the Malivoire winery in Ontario. After quickly getting guidance from her peers in the Okanagan, she made about 840 half bottles of an icewine with a piquant freshness reflecting the unusually early picking. The wine won a gold medal the following October at the Okanagan Wine Festival and, with other prestigious awards later, established icewine in CedarCreek's portfolio.

The winery followed with 1,800 bottles in the 1992 vintage (picked December 9); 7,000 bottles in 1993 (picked between November 22 and November 28); and only 500 bottles in 1994 (picked December 6), the small volume (all half bottles) reflecting the winery's desire not to overwhelm its market after the previous bountiful year.

CedarCreek has employed only Riesling, except for 1995, when it also produced a Chardonnay icewine. The latter was popular with customers but too sweet for Fitzpatrick. "It was pretty succulent," he recalls. "It was almost over the top." CedarCreek's tingling Riesling icewines have an almost sharp acidity when young but possess the balance and freshness to last for years. The production volumes now average about one thousand half bottles a year. "It is very much a specialty item for us," Fitzpatrick says. "We sort of maintain the fun of it." The pickers are friends of the winery, each rewarded with a bottle of icewine and a hearty breakfast.

Chapelle Sainte Agnès 2565 chemin Scenic, Sutton QC J0E 2K0

In 1997, Montreal antique dealer Henrietta Antony decided to plant a picture-postcard vineyard to complement the replica twelfth-century chapel she had had built four years earlier on this hillside near the Québec-Vermont border. The extraordinary slate-roofed chapel, erected by master tradesmen from Europe, is crafted with ancient paving stones excavated in Montreal, dating from the city's earliest days. The chapel was consecrated in 1995 to the thirteenth-century St. Agnes of Bohemia (Ms. Antony is a native of Czechoslovakia).

To develop the vineyard, Ms. Antony retained Christian Barthomeuf, who had been making apple wines, including ice cider, since retiring in 1991 from Domaine des Côtes d'Ardoise, the winery at Dunham where modern Québec viticulture began in 1980. Under his direction, one graveled hectare was sculpted around a man-made pond into 16 terraces with a sun-drenched 30-degree southern slope. On these terraces, he planted five thousand closed-spaced vines, including Riesling, Gewürztraminer, Vidal and one of the Geisenheim crosses. Because the design of the vineyard would make it difficult to cover the vines with earth for winter protection, every vine is wrapped individually in insulating fabric each fall.

John Antony, the antique dealer's son, became so enchanted with the site that, at age 43, he began taking courses at the University of Guelph, equipping himself to manage the vineyard and make the wines. The winery plans to limit itself to producing icewine, straw wine and late harvest wine, with the wines stored in a perfect cellar replicating one built in Ms. Antony's native land by the Knights Templar in 1228.

This family winery, founded in 1978, is now grandly housed in a chateau that broadcasts how well owner Paul M. Bosc has rebuilt his career in wine after being driven from Algeria during the revolution. Trained at the University of Burgundy in Dijon, Bosc came to Canada in the mid-1960s and opened his own winery after working at Château-Gai, a commercial Ontario winery since absorbed by Vincor International Inc.

Being French, Bosc and his sons, Paul-André and Pierre-Jean, approached icewine skeptically, producing only two hundred half bottles of Riesling in 1988. But once they grasped that icewine would burnish their growing reputation for table and sparkling wines, they became among Canada's largest producers. In 1998 Château des Charmes produced about 140,000 half bottles, three-quarters Vidal and the remainder Riesling. The winery scaled back slightly since then to match production with demand — which, because of aggressive marketing in Asia as well as North America, remains brisk.

The winery's picturesque chateau has enhanced the sales of the icewine. Opened in 1994, its sweeping driveways and regal doorway leading to a circular stairway are sought out for wedding photographs and by the endless stream of tourists en route to Niagara Falls that stop at the winery's grand tasting room.

In style, the winery makes icewines with impeccable balance. The 1997 Paul Bosc Estate Riesling Icewine, gold in color with apricot and citrus flavors, is the match of a top German Eiswein. The plump, mango-flavored 1998 Vidal Icewine and the freshly piquant 1999 Vidal Icewine, with spice and pineapple flavors, reflect two contrasting vintages.

Cilento Wines 672 Chrislea Road, Woodbridge, ON L4L 8K9

Managing director Grace Locilento and her husband Angelo opened this winery in 1997 in a suburb of Toronto with

grapes grown in a Niagara-area vineyard, some 90 minutes away by an often congested highway. While table wine grapes arrive by truck, the icewine grapes are pressed at the vineyard as both regulation and common sense require. Ultimately, Italian-born Locilento intends to establish a winery and a retail shop in the vineyard.

The winery, which produces a total of about 25,000 cases of wine annually, made icewine in its first crush in 1995 and, since that time, only has skipped the 2000 vintage because it had adequate quantities from earlier years.

"Icewine is the one product that a reputable Ontario winery cannot do without," winemaker Terence Van Rooyen believes. "It is the cherry on the cake."

A South African with a master's degree in enology from the University of Stellenbosch, he was not deterred by his inexperience with icewine when he took over in 1999 from Ann Sperling, the consultant who had handled previous Cilento crushes. "I approached making icewine as I would noble late harvest wine: you have the same sort of brix and the same sort of acidity," he said.

He also has begun aging Vidal icewine in oak to give it added complexity. "It adds aromas that are more aromatic," he believes. Indeed, the sweet spice in the bouquet of the Cilento 1999 Vidal icewine contrasts with the lush tropical fruit of the 1998. The winery also makes icewine with Gewürztraminer and Riesling, packaging the latter in some vintages in a delicate hand-blown gold leaf bottle.

Winemaker Carlo Negri believes that the icewines he makes at Colio are among the "driest" in Canada. There is a distinctive lean grace to his icewines, which are fermented as high as twelve per cent, two or three per cent more alcohol than many of his peers aim for. The object is to have such a fine balance of sugar, acid and alcohol that the wines come off svelte rather than plump.

The style is in harmony with the wine palate Negri developed growing up in Trentino. Italians like their wines dry. Negri confesses that he prefers his own late harvest wines over his icewines, but only because he finds icewines overly sweet for his taste. In 1988, when he made Colio's first special dessert wine, it was modeled on the comparatively dry Italian Vin Santo style. Negri made his first icewine — two hundred liters of Vidal — in 1989 when Colio observed how well its peers were doing with the wine.

The other mark of a Negri icewine is volatile acidity so low that there is no detectable vinegary aroma. He achieves this by promoting a vigorous fermentation that gives wild yeast no chance to produce off-aromas. Negri carefully prepares a starter with yeast and a small quantity of icewine juice, feeding this every day or two with more juice until he has a strongly fermenting wine that is five per cent of the volume of the total quantity of icewine juice. Only then is this hardy starter put to work in the main volume of juice, yielding a rapid and problem-free fermentation.

Colio was established in 1980, a joint venture of Italian investors and Italian-Canadian business people who recruited Negri, a self-effacing winemaker still in the habit of wearing a formal white laboratory smock in the sprawling winery. With an ever-growing storage capacity of two million liters, Colio is producing about 200,000 cases of wine a year. Colio has increased its icewine production to about eight thousand liters a year, with both Vidal and Riesling grapes employed.

"With Vidal, we get a perfect icewine," Negri maintains. "From Riesling, we get something a little bit more. It is because Riesling is vinifera and vinifera is vinifera, no matter what."

Creekside Estate Winery 2170 Fourth Avenue, Jordan Station, ON L0R 1S0

Owners Peter Jensen and Laura McCain became enraptured with wine while honeymooning in California's Napa Valley. They now have a burgeoning wine empire, with Habitant and Pereau Vineyards in Nova Scotia's Annapolis Valley and Creekside which they acquired in 1998, expanding it quickly to 33,000 cases a year from 5,000 cases. Paragon Estate Winery, their newest winery, has been established near St. Davids, based on a 16.5-hectare vineyard in the Niagara-on-the-Lake appellation.

In the 1998 vintage, consulting winemaker Ann Sperling made 8,400 half bottles of unctuous, silken-textured Vidal icewine. Marcus Ansems, a young Australian, arrived in early 1999 just as Sperling's vintage was completing fermentation. He finished that wine and, in the 1999 vintage, made his first icewine, two thousand liters of Vidal that is light and delicate. "It's tough," he says of icewine making. "It's a labor of love. But I think it's an amazing wine. The intensity you get out of it is unlike anything you get elsewhere in the world." With an adequate inventory of icewine, Ansems in 2000 made a late harvest Vidal of a concentration approaching that of icewine.

Crown Bench Estates Winery 3850 Aberdeen Road, Beamsville, ON L0R 1B7

Livia Sipos and her spouse, Peter Kocsis, who opened this winery in 2000, have pushed the boundaries of icewine by creating new beverages incorporating it. The most unusual is called Hot Ice, made by steeping organically grown chili peppers in icewine, yielding an apéritif neither sharp nor too sweet. Equally creative is the winery's Ambrosia, icewine with the flavor of white chocolate. "We wanted to have a complete dessert in a glass," says Livia, who declines to give away the secret recipe.

However, it is difficult to imagine a dessert more complete than the 1998 Vidal icewine made by Peter, a thick, concentrated confection with notes of burnt sugar and toffee. The wine is so plump because of his practice of pressing the icewine grapes twice. In 1998, the light first pressing resulted in intensely sweet juice of about 45° Brix. The second pressing gave juice measuring 38° Brix. While this certainly is adequate for icewine, Kocsis fermented it separately to create a lighter, more delicate dessert wine called Winter Harvest, selling for two-thirds the price of icewine. That is excellent value since Kocsis already prices the icewine about 25 per cent lower than most of his peers. He produced about a thousand liters each of icewine and Winter Harvest in 1998.

In subsequent vintages, Crown Bench also has made Riesling and Cabernet Franc icewines. Crown Bench — with a production target of 5,000 cases a year of table wines — is the latest venture in Kocsis's colorful career. A member of a prominent agricultural family that fled Hungary during the 1956 revolution (his father was deputy minister of agriculture), Kocsis has a master's degree in political science. He has been both a teacher and a successful chicken farmer. He tried to retire in his mid-forties but was so restless after nine months that he purchased the ten-hectare vineyard on which Crown Bench is based. He sold grapes to other winemakers for several years and, after seeing prizewinning wines made from his grapes, he established Crown Bench where he now is setting out to make his own winning wines.

D'Angelo Estate Winery 5141 Concession 5, RR #4, Amherstburg, ON N9V 2Y9

I n 1989, the year he made his first commercial crush, Salvatore D'Angelo timidly set aside just one row of Vidal vines for icewine, carefully protected with netting that cost $150. When the grapes were being picked, he noticed his mother disentangling the net and keeping it whole while frozen grapes were dropping to the ground. D'Angelo sharply reminded her that the grapes were worth more than the net. Thus assured, she scythed the net away with shears to salvage the grapes.

Starting with juice that was 32° Brix, D'Angelo produced about 15 cases of icewine in his first year. He soon recognized that, at that sweetness, the wine lacked concentration. Since then, he starts with 38° to 40° Brix. He has become so adept at making icewine that his 1996 vintage won a double gold medal at competition, which means the judges thought it a perfect wine.

It was a significant achievement for D'Angelo, an electrician and school teacher by training and a winemaker in his blood. "I'm Italian," he explains. He learned winemaking from his father, who brought the family to Canada in 1955 when Salvatore was three. By the time the son was in his teens, he was the more technically proficient of the two. In 1979 Sal D'Angelo began looking for land for his own vineyard, finally buying a farm east of Amherstburg on which he planted 17 hectares of vines with the guidance of Carlo Negri, the manager of the nearby Colio winery, and still the purchaser of most of D'Angelo's Vidal.

Because this farm has proven better for hardy hybrid varieties, D'Angelo has developed a second vineyard for five hectares of vinifera at Colchester, at what is the most southern vineyard on the Canadian mainland. In 2001, he was looking at vineyard property in British Columbia.

VQA • Niagara Peninsula • VQA

Vidal

Icewine

1998

White Wine
Vin Blanc

12.0 % alc/vol.   375 ml

PRODUCT OF CANADA
• DESOUSA WINE CELLARS CORP. •
PRODUIT DU CANADA

De Sousa Wine Cellars 3753 Quarry Road, Beamsville ON L0R 1B0

John De Sousa replies with brutal honesty when asked if he enjoys making icewine. "Not at all! It is too painstaking. I'd rather do the Ports." Which is hardly surprising, given that his father, also John, came to Canada in 1961 from Portugal, succeeding as jeweler while pining to get back into the wine business.

The elder De Sousa, who died in 1997, acquired a vineyard in 1979, replacing the labrusca grapes with premium hybrids and vinifera, including Touriga Nacional, one of the main grapes in Port. This wine is as painstaking as icewine since the tender variety must be buried to protect the vines over winter. De Sousa makes about 1,800 liters of Port a year. The winery's bread and butter is a full-bodied red sold in four-liter jugs under the brand name Dois Amigos.

The two friends were the winemakers who steered the winery in its initial vintages, one Portuguese and the other German-born Dieter Guttler, then working in Ontario. He made the first De Sousa icewine in 1993. Why icewine? "We are also a Canadian winery," John De Sousa says. "We are not just hermits burying our heads in the sand." Every year, the winery produces about two hundred liters each of Vidal and Riesling icewine.

Vignoble Dietrich-Jooss 407, Grande-Ligne, Iberville, QC J2X 4J2

Winemaker Victor Dietrich was the younger of two brothers in a family winery near Ingersheim at Alsace that was too small for all the families it needed to support. In 1986 he and Christiane Jooss, his spouse, bought a dairy farm southeast of Montreal near the community of Iberville and joined the growing band of hardy winegrowers in Québec. Their six-hectare vineyard yields between 30,000 and 40,000 bottles of wine each year. Dietrich-Jooss made its first Vin de Glace in 1993. "We had only one hundred half bottles," says Stéphanie Dietrich, their daughter and a winemaking graduate from Montpellier in France.

Production seldom is higher than five hundred bottles because viticulture in Québec is unusually challenging. At Dietrich-Jooss, as at many other establishments, the low-trained vines are buried with earth in November as a protection against hard winter frost and are not uncovered until early May. But the vines set aside for icewine, which cannot be covered, are netted before harvest as a defence against birds and tented after harvest with tough fabric sheets onto which a covering of earth is shoveled.

In most winters, the vineyard also is covered with an insulating blanket of snow, shown on the label of the winery's icewine, called Sélection Impériale. "Here in Québec, we don't need to harvest by night, the winter being colder than in other provinces," Stéphanie says. The grapes are picked at temperatures as low as -20°C but pressed between -10°C and -12°C. A blend of grape varieties is employed, including Cayuga White, Vidal and Geisenheim 318, a white hybrid. "Our icewine is not too sweet but it has a good acidity and aroma," Stéphanie says. In a charming touch, the wine is named Cuvée Stéphanie.

Domaine Combret 32057 #13 Road, Oliver, BC V0H 1T0

Before opening one of British Columbia's most efficiently designed wineries in 1994, the Combret family made wine in the south of France for 10 generations. They transplanted such traditions as producing fine dry rosé but also adapted to Canadian traditions. Olivier Combret, the winemaker, made the family's first icewine in 1995, a Riesling with exotic apple notes that recalled Calvados. He produced a Pinot Noir icewine in 1999 and a Chardonnay icewine in 2000. He chooses different varieties to avoid putting too much stress on the vines. "It's very exhausting on the vines," he believes. "We do a rotation." He seldom produces more than two thousand liters of icewine in a vintage.

Vignoble Domaine des Côtes d'Ardoise 879 rue Bruce, R.R. #2, Dunham, QC J0E 1M0

One of Québec's original vineyards, it was begun in 1981 in the townships southeast of Montreal by Christian Barthomeuf, the son of a wine salesman. In 1974 Barthomeuf emigrated from France and, after buying the farm in Dunham three years later, concluded it was the "perfect" microclimate for grapes, warmer than Champagne. The slate on the slopes inspired the name, Côtes d'Ardoise.

Barthomeuf's neighbors, as he admitted later, thought he was "the town crazy" for planting vines and he may have wondered the same thing one early winter when his young vines were subjected to temperatures as bitterly cold as -37°C. It was trial and error in the vineyard; he planted such vinifera as Gamay, Chardonnay and Pinot Noir but the varieties that proved themselves over the years have been hardy hybrids like De Chaunac, Seyval Blanc and Maréchal Foch. Barthomeuf squeezed out a mere 38 bottles in 1982. In the following year, when he made one thousand bottles of wine, he was greatly encouraged when everything was sold within five hours.

Barthomeuf remained as winemaker until 1991 but the winery, which had slipped into financial difficulty, was acquired in 1984 by Dr. Jacques Papillon, a Montreal plastic surgeon with the resources to expand it to an annual production of 2,500 cases.

The winery made one modest stab at icewine early in the 1990s but the systematic production began in 1998 when Vera Klokocka and John Fletcher, winemakers formerly from British Columbia, were retained to make the wines at Côtes d'Ardoise. The Czech-born Klokocka previously owned Hillside Cellars, a farm winery that opened in 1990, and after she sold it in 1996, Fletcher managed it for several years. Klokocka began making Riesling icewine at Hillside in 1992. Fletcher had gained experience during several icewine vintages at the Jackson-Triggs winery near Oliver, where he worked before joining Hillside, where he expanded the icewine program.

In Québec, Fletcher has had to adapt his experience to a different viticultural reality. "The toughest part here in Québec is that you should not grow grapes," he says, only partly in jest. The season is short. Frost is possible as early as mid-October and winter will keep its grip in the vineyards until mid-April; it also is possible to have frost in May, with growers protecting their crops by pruning only lightly at first. Productivity in the seven and a half hectare vineyard is notoriously low because the 30,000 vines grow very close to the ground and the fruit is thinned brutally in an effort to achieve maturity. In early November 2000 the Vidal and Riesling blocks reserved for icewine had ripened only to 20° Brix when the fruit was picked.

The practice at Côtes d'Ardoise is to place the grapes on trays inside a greenhouse, allowing them to dehydrate until about mid-December. The grapes then freeze naturally, to be pressed somewhere between -14°C and -20°C. In this manner, the winemakers achieve a must concentrated to more than 40° Brix. Fletcher does not believe he has the option of leaving the fruit to hang in the vineyard. "We leave them as long as we dare but we still have to harden the vines off," he says. To keep them from being killed by the severe cold, the vines need to be dormant before being covered with earth in mid to late November. Under these challenging conditions, they make about two thousand half bottles of icewine a year.

Domaine de Grand Pré 11611 Highway 1, Grand Pré, NS B0P 1M0

This was the pioneering Nova Scotia winery and struggled accordingly. The founder in 1977 was Roger Dial, a wine-loving political science professor. He developed a vineyard based on hardy Russian grapes whose unpronounceable names made it difficult to market the sturdy wines. Grand Pré went into receivership in 1988 and again a second time five years later, before being acquired by Hanspeter Stutz, a Swiss banker. He dispatched his son, Jürg, to study winemaking in Switzerland. Meanwhile the vineyards were replanted with more conventional grapes and the gracious nineteenth-century structures were redeveloped to include a restaurant and an art gallery.

The winery reopened in 2000 with wines from the 1999 vintage, including about 2,400 half bottles of 1999 Vidal icewine. "The juice for this wine came from the Warner Vineyards in Lakeville," Jürg says, referring to a grower who also has supplied icewine grapes to Jost Vineyards, Nova Scotia's other icewine producer. In the 2000 vintage, Stutz used Warner grapes to make both Vidal and New York Muscat icewines. When the Vidal vines in Grand Pré's own vineyard are in their fifth year in 2001, they are expected to begin providing icewine grapes.

205

EastDell Estates 4041 Locust Lane, Beamsville ON L0R 1B2

M ichael East and partner Susan O'Dell left the corporate fast lane in 1996 by buying a small vineyard near Beamsville in 1996. Three years later they geared up the pace of their lives again by purchasing the nearby Walters Estates, a new winery that had been struggling. Now renamed EastDell, the winery has become a destination, both for its wines and for the stunning views across Lake Ontario from the new bistro.

East and O'Dell took over inventory, which included a 1995 Vidal icewine and several iced fruit wines. In 1999, 750 liters of Vidal icewine and 100 liters of Riesling icewine were made by EastDell's new winemaker, Tatjana Cuk. A native of the former Yugoslavia, she graduated from a Serbian winemaking school before coming to Canada in 1995. She says that this, her first experience with making icewine, posed no particular difficulty, perhaps because the icewine juice was purchased from a grower, saving her from the usual icewine initiation of picking frozen grapes at night.

Gehringer Brothers Estate Winery Road 8, RR1, S23, C4, Oliver, BC V0H 1T0

T he sons of a wine-loving immigrant from Germany, Walter and Gordon Gehringer made this winery's first icewines in 1991, five years after it opened. An unexpectedly early sharp cold settled across the Okanagan at the end of October, just as the vintage for table wines was finishing, freezing some unpicked grapes. The Gehringers, who had already planned a Riesling icewine, seized the chance to buy Ehrenfelser for a second icewine and Chancellor, a red variety, for the year's third icewine.

Riesling and Ehrenfelser remain the backbone of Gehringer

icewines, with Cabernet Franc being employed for smaller volumes of red icewine. Early icewine harvests suit the style — fresh and clean with piquant acidity — that the German-trained Gehringers prefer in icewines. Nature does not always provide an early icewine harvest for the Gehringers, who set aside more than three hectares of vineyard just for icewine. The required freezing temperatures were suitably early on December 11 in 2000 and in mid-December in 1998. But in 1999, the Gehringers, along with all their peers, struggled with an unseasonably mild winter and were unable to pick until late January in 2000.

Grape Tree Estate Wines Inc. 308 Mersea Road 3, Leamington, ON N8H 3V5

For Steven Brook, the road-to-Damascus experience came in the early 1980s at a Deinhard tasting. "I didn't realize I liked wine until 1979 or 1980," says Brook, who was born in 1963 and grew up in an ordinary household in Windsor. At the tasting, he was "instantly struck" by the intensity and elegance of the sweet wines.

In 1983 he went to Germany on what he still remembers as an "Auslese rampage" through leading wineries, returning to Canada just as the Pelee Island winery made its first icewine. Seduced by sweet wine, Brook formed an amateur winemaking club, launched a televised wine show, became a product consultant for the Liquor Control Board of Ontario and a keen volunteer picker of icewine grapes. "I've been involved in helping people to make icewine for 15 years," he said in 2001, shortly after opening the Grape Tree estate winery.

Because he already owned vineyards, Brook began making small quantities of Vidal and Riesling icewine in 1995. Today, Grape Tree produces between 800 and 1,000 cases of icewine annually, about a fifth of its total production in 2000. Brook marvels that his winery, located in Canada's southernmost wine region, makes the frost-inspired wine.

"Here we are, south of the whole country of France," he points out. "How can we possibly make icewine? We are Rioja in latitude."

The answer is that the continental winter is cold enough to freeze shallow expanses of nearby Lake Erie. However, the hot, humid summers produce grapes high in sugar, low in acidity. Deliberately, Brook has planted vines intended for icewine in an east-to-west direction so that the grapes on the northern side of the row are shaded from the baking sun. He also tends to overcrop those vines. "Acidity is something we value hugely in our icewines," he says. These techniques enable Brook to make well-balanced icewines that are rich, with complex flavors of apricot, orange peel and toffee.

Gray Monk Estate Winery 1055 Camp Road, Okanagan Center, BC V2V 2H4

F amily-operated Gray Monk, which opened in 1982, has been a pioneer grower of vinifera grapes in British Columbia. Austrian-born George Heiss and his German-born wife, Trudy, were successful hairdressers who changed careers in 1972 to grow grapes and make wine. Ardent students of viticulture, they were among the first to import vines directly from Alsace, including Auxerrois, Pinot Gris and Gewürztraminer, and played a role in proving that European grape varieties could thrive in Canada.

Ehrenfelser is the variety of choice for icewine by George Heiss, Jr., one of their sons and the winemaker. A graduate of Weinsberg in Germany, Heiss Jr. apprenticed at Weingut Louis Guntrum but made his first icewine at his family's winery in 1994. He chose Ehrenfelser from a vineyard block near the gleaming white winery because the variety remains healthy on the vine late into the year and because its fruity flavors suit icewine. Heiss Jr. made subsequent icewines in 1998, 1999 and 2000, limiting production to around four thousand half bottles each year.

Hainle Vineyards Estate Winery 5355 Trepanier Bench Road, Peachland, BC V0H 1X0

The first commercially available icewines from a Canadian vineyard came from this small British Columbia winery which was developed by Walter Hainle, his winemaker son Tilman, and their families. The elder Hainle, who died in 1995 at the age of 80, was a German businessman from Württemberg who emigrated to Canada in 1970. With grape-growing friends in the Okanagan, he began to make wine for personal consumption.

Neither trained as a winemaker nor especially versed in Eisweine, Walter Hainle "came at the whole subject of wine from an amateur enthusiast's point of view," according to Tilman. When an unexpected freeze caught the grapes in his friend's vineyard in 1973, Walter Hainle did what so many others before him had done in similar circumstances: he made icewine. No tasting notes remain but it was successful enough that he began making it deliberately. In 1977 the vineyard owner demanded the grapes be picked early. Walter complied and placed them in a commercial freezer before pressing them. That was the last time the Hainles tried to help Mother Nature. The wine, Tilman found, had little fruit and a frosty taste.

In 1978 the Hainles began harvesting icewine grapes in their own mountainside vineyard and this vintage, along with 1982, 1983 and 1987, were among those that went on sale after the winery opened its doors in 1988. The early vintages were made with a white variety called Okanagan Riesling, a local labrusca hybrid, while those since 1982 have been made with Johannisberg Riesling.

The wine list of the Sooke Harbour House, a Vancouver Island restaurant with a vast cellar, includes 10 vintages of Hainle icewine, starting with the all but vanished 1978. "The Hainle icewines made from Okanagan Riesling are atypical and present sweet sherry-like tonalities," a tasting note reports.

Tilman Hainle, who graduated from the Weinsberg winemaking school in Germany, always makes icewine in small volumes. "To mass produce an icewine is an oxymoron," he argues.

In 1997, when peach grower Fraser Mowat turned 40, he decided there was a better future in grapes. Vines soon began replacing fruit trees on his property and the winery opened in August 2000. The Mowat family's attractive farm occupies a bench overlooking Jordan Harbour and is a site of quiet pastoral beauty. Mowat plans to build a boardwalk along the harbor, shaded walking trails among the groves of trees and an elegant winery with commanding views over the water. "We want it to be a destination here," he says.

While the winery is focused on table wines with Bordeaux red varieties, Harbour Estates produced more than 20,000 half bottles of icewine in 1999, from Vidal, Riesling and Cabernet Franc. Stylistically, the icewines emphasize fresh, clean fruit flavors with good, but not obtrusive, acidity. To match its icewine production to its sales, the winery scaled back in the 2000 vintage, making about 12,000 half bottles of Vidal and Riesling.

Hawthorne Mountain Vineyards Green Lake Road, Box 480, Okanagan Falls, BC V0H 1R0

With a cool site high on the side of a mountain, Hawthorne Mountain is among British Columbia's top producers of Gewürztraminer table wines and one of the first in the Okanagan to make an icewine from the same variety.

The winery has since moved to varieties with better acidity at maturity, notably Ehrenfelser and Pinot Blanc. The winery's 1995 Pinot Blanc turned out to be a syrupy icewine because the grapes were picked at -18°C and, because the cold weather persisted, the frozen grapes remained in the press for two weeks, oozing juice exceeding 50° Brix, not far off the sweetness of honey. In 1996, when cool weather resulted in immature grapes, the winery salvaged highly acidic Oraniensteiner, a German-created cross, by turning it into a tart icewine.

"You can't make icewine from unripe grapes because every-thing, including acidity, is amplified," says Bruce Ewert, Hawthorne Mountain's winemaker since 1997.

Ewert likes Ehrenfelser for icewine because this grape, with its distinctive tropical fruit profile, ripens to high sugars while retain-ing balancing acidity. He made his first Ehrenfelser icewine in 1993 at the Andrés winery near Vancouver (it also was the first icewine made at that winery). At Hawthorne Mountain, he made about three thousand half bottles of Ehrenfelser icewine in each of 1997 and 1998 but turned the fruit into late harvest in the warm winter of 1999, after waiting vainly until February 14, 2000, for an icewine freeze.

Ewert made up for a missed icewine vintage with the 2000 har-vest. The winery left 10 tons of Ehrenfelser on the vines. With the luck of an early December cold snap, Ewert pressed enough juice from the grapes for 2,700 liters of icewine.

Henry of Pelham Family Estate 1469 Pelham Road, RR # 1, St. Catharines, ON L2R 6P7

After the American Revolution of 1776, American colonists loyal to Britain moved north to Canada where they were called United Empire Loyalists. Among them was Nicholas Smith, who was granted Crown land not far from Niagara Falls. Henry Smith, one of his sons, built an inn and a tollgate in 1842 on what was called Pelham Road and began to sign himself Henry of Pelham. Almost a century and half later, three young brothers named Speck, direct descendants of the Smith family, appropriated that historic name for the winery they located in restored heritage buildings.

Henry of Pelham began making icewine in 1989, the winery's second vintage, almost always with Riesling (nearly 15,000 half bottles in 1998). Paul Speck, the winery's president, prefers Riesling for icewine but makes Vidal, which he acknowledges is preferred by some consumers. "Vidal drinks nicer when young," he says. "It has a lot more peach, a lot more apricot — it is a lot more front-end loaded. Riesling is more delicate and over the long term, it makes a finer wine." The winery's reputation has been built with its Chardonnay and Riesling table wines but winemaker Ron Giesbrecht is equally meticulous with icewine.

"For us at Henry of Pelham, the icewine is the *top* wine," Speck insists. "If we are going to be purists with any wine we make, we want to be especially pure about this." In style, the Pelham icewines mirror the classic German Eisweine, with relatively low alcohols, for a Canadian icewine, between 9 and 10.5 per cent. That is deliberate. "We have found it makes the best icewine," Speck believes.

Hernder Estate Wines 1607 8th Avenue, St. Catharines, ON L2R 6P7

F red Hernder is one of Canada's largest independent grape growers, with about 243 hectares in Ontario. These vineyards support an array of businesses, from the export of grape juice to the United States to the production of wine kits. The centerpiece is this 40,000-case winery which operates from a splendidly restored old barn that it is a popular wedding venue.

Ray Cornell, the winemaker, began making icewine here with Vidal and Riesling in 1993, two years after the winery opened. With the Riesling, of which 2,000 liters was made, Hernder won a trophy for the best dessert wine at the 1995 All-Canada Wine Competition. Since then, Cornell has added icewines from Cabernet Franc and Pinot Gris, in a style notable for soft acidity and a candied intensity of aromas and flavors.

As well, he has developed several iced fruit wines, using cranberries, cherries, strawberries, raspberries, pears and peaches. They are less sweet than icewines but, with Cornell's sure touch, express the fresh fruit flavors. Both icewines and iced fruit wines remain a modest, if important, part of Hernder's extensive range of wines.

Named for a creek that flows past the property, this winery relies on a vineyard with the south Okanagan's oldest vinifera vines, including Pinot Blanc. This variety is a great favorite of Frank Supernak, the winemaker here since 1996, and he has made icewine with the variety every vintage since then. It is a durable variety for icewine, with thick-skinned berries that "hang forever."

The quantity produced is never large: in the 2000 vintage, for example, he made less than 5,000 half bottles.

Some is barrel-fermented to enhance the caramel notes that Supernak prefers. When the grapes have been pressed for icewine, Supernak lets the skins thaw partially for a second pressing, to yield between seven hundred and eight hundred liters of clean juice he uses to add a balancing touch of residual sugar to the estate-bottled Pinot Blanc table wine. "I can't understand why anybody would throw the skins out after the first pressing," he says.

In 1999 Hester Creek made its first red icewine, about 1,700 bottles of Cabernet Franc. That was followed in 2000 with about an equal quantity of barrel-fermented Merlot icewine.

"Personally, I prefer the Merlot icewine to the Cabernet Franc," he says. "It has more of the prune and blackberry flavors that I want."

Merlot is not an ideal red for icewine because the berries are thin-skinned and the stalks holding the bunches on the vine are weak. Hester Creek succeeded with a Merlot icewine in 2000 because there was a deep early December freeze before there was a significant loss of fruit.

This winery was established in 1979 by Joseph Pohorly, a history buff who called it Newark Wines, after the original name of Niagara-on-the-Lake. The name was changed for obvious reasons by Scholl & Hillebrand, the German wine and spirits group that acquired control in 1983. In that year Hillebrand was one of the two Ontario wineries that made icewine commercially the first time. Under the ownership now of Andrés Wines, Hillebrand has been acclaimed for the wines made by Jean-Laurent (J.L.) Groulx, the French winemaker who joined Hillebrand in 1989.

Hillebrand has made icewine every year since 1983, even in years like 1988 when an unseasonably warm winter led to a February 1989 harvest of grapes so dehydrated — "totally figged" is how Groulx describes them — that the juice yield was a mere 39 liters for each tonne, compared to more normal yields of 100 to 150 liters.

Since 1989 Hillebrand has been aging its Trius brand icewine in French oak barrels for at least four months; in 1996 Groulx also began fermenting some of his icewines in barrel. "The world is our inspiration," he explains. "Château d'Yquem spends three and a half years in barrel." Groulx believes that barrel treatment gives the wines a smoother finish, a conclusion borne out in tastings in which Hillebrand icewines have been described as having a "genteel, lush texture." Because Vidal is so intensely aromatic, the oak flavors do not dominate. Hillebrand primarily makes its icewine with Vidal, with a modest quantity of Riesling. The production in 1998 for Hillebrand and for the associated Peller Estates label in Ontario was 80,000 liters.

Hillside Estate Winery 1350 Naramata Road, Penticton, BC V2A 8T6

Hillside, which began in 1990 as a small producer selling most of its wines from a cramped farm-house storefront, has grown into a multi-storied winery with a restaurant, meeting facil-

ities and a cheerful tasting room. The icewine program is modest, about three thousand bottles each of Vidal and Riesling icewine in most vintages. "In the future, we'll move away from Vidal," Ken Lauzon, the general manager, says. "We only want to produce one icewine and Riesling is superior." The winery, whose flagship white is dry Muscat Ottonel, also is increasing its production of late harvest wines, including one from the Muscat variety.

House of Rose 2270 Garner Road, Kelowna, BC V1P 1E2

Retired school teacher Vern Rose turned his three-hectare farm into a vineyard after attending a New Zealand seminar on cool-climate viticulture in 1988. Ironically, he was attending a similar seminar in Australia in January 2000 when the appropriate icewine frost hit his vineyard. Very few of his peers in the Okanagan had been able to harvest any icewine grapes from the 1999 vintage because of the persistently warm winter. On January 11, Gary Strachan, a consulting winemaker, arrived for duties at the House of Rose at about nine o'clock in the morning and was astounded to find the vineyard temperature was -10.5°C, while much of the rest of the Okanagan was only a few degrees below freezing.

"Oh, well, that it was it and it was missed," Strachan thought. But he knew that the House of Rose site is one of the coolest in the Okanagan and he knew the weather was not expected to change for several days. He had Russell Rose, Vern's son, alert the pickers for that night. "Bingo!" Strachan exulted. "It was -10 by eight at night and -12 the next morning." House of Rose, due to its unique climate, was able to produce 1,500 liters of icewine when other wineries were still awaiting the proper conditions.

Inniskillin Wines RR #1, Niagara Parkway at Line 3, Niagara-on-the-Lake, ON L0S 1J0

See chapter 8.

Jackson-Triggs 2145 Niagara Stone Road, Niagara-on-the-Lake, ON L05 1J0

This is the name under which Vincor International Ltd., Canada's largest winery, produces wines at several facilities. Vincor also owns Inniskillin and the combined volume of the wineries makes the Vincor group the world's largest icewine producer.

The main varieties employed are Vidal (primarily in Ontario) and Riesling (primarily in British Columbia). At the Niagara Falls winery, Polish-born Mira Ananicz, who has been with Jackson-Triggs and predecessor wineries for about three decades, has made icewines in collaboration with Inniskillin's Karl Kaiser.

In the quest of red icewines, Ananicz employed Cabernet Franc and experimented with Villard Noir. "It was strictly an internal experiment," says Bruce Walker, the executive vice-president at Jackson-Triggs. Villard Noir is a red-fleshed French hybrid grape that never was widely planted in Ontario and now has been largely replaced by vinifera vines, preventing Jackson-Triggs from pursuing Villard Noir seriously for icewine. "It was a spectacular dark red icewine with a very velvety texture," Walker recalls. Inniskillin also has done trials with Dornfelder, another red-fleshed grape. Its low acidity limits this variety to the role of teinturier.

In the 2000 vintage the Jackson-Triggs icewines in Ontario were made for the first time at a new winery just outside Niagara-on-the-Lake by winemaker Tom Seaver. A California native with a degree from the University of California at Fresno, Seaver's winemaking career has been largely in Canada.

The new Jackson-Triggs winery, with a capacity of 105,000 cases, is among the best-equipped in North America, designed for gentle handling of the must. In the 2000 vintage, the winery crushed about 100 tonnes of icewine grapes, using four vertical basket presses with a capacity of about 350 kilos in each basket. The yield was 1,400 liters of Cabernet Franc, 2,100 liters of Gewürztraminer, 2,000 liters of Riesling, and 4,000 liters of Vidal.

"The plan is for this facility to do a lot of icewine," Seaver says. "We have a lot of small tanks and the flexibility to do different batches." In style, the Jackson-Triggs icewines, which are not barrel-fermented, are intentionally different from those made at Inniskillin. "I would find theirs a heavier style, bolder on the fruit," Seaver suggests. "We are leaning to a more delicate style."

At the Jackson-Triggs winery in British Columbia's Okanagan Valley, the icewines are made by Bruce Nicholson. His Riesling icewines in 1997 and again in 1998 were wines of power and finesse that amassed gold medals both in domestic and in international competition. At London's International Wine and Spirit Competition in October 2000, Nicholson and his Riesling icewines earned trophies as the best Canadian producer and for the best Canadian icewine for the second consecutive year.

Nicholson is a chemical engineer who went to work in 1986 in the laboratory at Chateau-Gai, one of the predecessors to Jackson-Triggs. His mentor there was Mira Ananicz. Nicholson was transferred to British Columbia in 1987 where he has refined his award-winning technique, producing as much as five thousand liters of icewine a year.

"I ferment it as low as I can get it," he says. His icewines ferment perhaps as long as five months at approximately 12°C, achieving an alcohol level of about nine per cent. Nicholson has an additional trick up his sleeve that enlivens the fruitiness of the winery's Grand Reserve, or premium, icewine. He reserves fresh icewine juice, adding about five per cent by volume to the wine just days before fermentation is ended.

Joseph Pohorly, the owner of this winery, maintains that he produced Canada's first commercially successful icewine from Vidal grapes in 1983. He was then one of the owners of Newark Wines Inc. which he established in 1979.

The encouragement to make icewine came from Bernhard Breuer, now a well-regarded German winery owner and formerly a consultant. Pohorly in 1982 had sold controlling interest of Newark to Scholl and Hillebrand of Rüdesheim on the Rhine. The new owners sent Breuer, who urged Pohorly to make icewine.

Pohorly had made a trial lot in 1982. He and Peter Gamble, then his winemaker, left Vidal on the vines into December, without nets, until the losses to birds became unacceptable. They salvaged the remaining grapes and stored them until it was cold enough to take them outside and let them freeze naturally. This was not forbidden at the time because there were no rules at all in Canada then for making icewine. "It was not done in a freezer," Pohorly says. "Mother Nature did everything." The following year he deployed nets over the vines.

That Pohorly was among the first Canadians to produce icewines reflects his entrepreneurial character. A civil engineer and former school teacher, he was 49 when he started Hillebrand. He sold the winery in 1986 to build and operate a large, comfortable hotel in Niagara-on-the-Lake. But he missed the wine business so, in 1992, he acquired an eight-hectare farm down the road from Hillebrand and launched Joseph's, which opened in 1996. The winery immediately included Vidal icewine in its range.

Joseph's has made icewine every year since it opened and now produces about 10,000 liters a year. Pohorly also makes iced fruit wines from apple, peach and pear. In his spare time, he is working on a doctorate in engineering, with a thesis on the extraction of grapeseed oil.

Jost Vineyards Malagash, Wallace, NS B0K 1E0

The late Hans Jost, who emigrated in 1970 from the Rhine Valley to Nova Scotia, made the first icewine in Atlantic Canada — and one of the earliest Canadian icewines — in 1985. Riesling, Kerner and Bacchus grapes were picked at -10°C early on the morning of December 7. In the charming tradition no longer permitted in Germany, he honored the saint's feastday by calling this St. Nicolaus Icewine.

Jost died three years after making that wine and the winery passed to the control of his son, Hans Christian, a graduate of Geisenheim, who has continued to make icewine with great success. The Jost Vidal Icewine 1999 was declared the wine of the year at a recent All-Canadian Wine Championship competition.

The winery also makes Muscat icewine as well as what it calls Pomme Glacé, an apple beverage in the icewine style. With nearly 30 hectares of vineyards in Nova Scotia, Jost is Atlantic Canada's largest winery, with a complete range of table wines.

Kettle Valley Winery 2988 Hayman Road, Naramata, BC V0H 1N0

Kettle Valley was into its third vintage in 1995 when owners Tim Watts and Bob Ferguson, one-time amateur winemakers who have become skilled professionals, made icewine for the first time, from Chardonnay.

They also planned to make a red icewine from Pinot Noir but were frustrated when the grapes warmed to -6°C. The resulting wine fermented naturally to 18 per cent alcohol when it developed what Ferguson called a "nutty Sherry flavor." The wine was released under the proprietary name, DeRailer. Since the winery is named for the nearby abandoned Kettle Valley Railroad, the name is as much a play on railroading as on the "derailing" of the winery's plans. Because the wine sold well, Kettle Valley made a similar DeRailer in 1999 from frozen grapes which yielded a must of 38° Brix, sweet enough for icewine.

I n 1991 John Hall, after a decade or two of dealing in winery amalgamations, returned to his winemaking roots by investing in the Rieder Distillery, which Otto Reider, a Swiss eau-de-vie maker, had founded in 1971. Hall added a winery license and took immediate advantage of the two licenses to make a Vidal icewine from the 1991 vintage and Canada's first icewine grappa from the skins and juice not used for icewine. His very first icewine won a gold medal at a major Italian competition and he has since won more than 40 international awards for his icewines.

In 1993, he blended seven-year-old brandy with icewine to come up with Icewine & Brandy, a 17 per cent alcohol beverage with a fruity aroma and flavors of orange, mango and chocolate. "Today, it remains one of our flagship products," he says proudly of his creation.

Now one of Ontario's largest wineries with a production of about 200,000 (nine-liter) cases a year, Kittling Ridge makes between 13,000 and 18,000 liters annually of icewine. Through the 1990s, Hall employed only Vidal; in the 2000 vintage he also made a red icewine with Cabernet Franc.

The winery owns no vineyards, buying instead from growers. For icewine grapes, Kittling Ridge takes control of the designated vines in October, assuming the risk and managing the vineyards. The piquant style of Hall's icewines results from his determination to preserve as much acidity as possible. "A lot of people think our icewines are drier than other icewines," he says.

Often, customers lingering over a glass of wine in Kittling Ridge's tasting room ask how the winery got its name. On an early warm day in March 1992, just after he acquired control of the distillery, Hall took his lunch to a nearby hilltop park favored by birders observing the migrating hawks and eagles. Here he discovered that "kittling" is jargon for birds floating languidly on the air currents. "I thought that is a wonderful name for a winery," he recalls. Ridge refers to the nearby Niagara escarpment.

Konzelmann Estate Winery 1096 Lakeshore Road, Niagara-on-the-Lake, ON L0S 1J0

Already pursuing a career as a winemaker in Germany, Herbert Konzelmann discovered the attraction of Canada during a hunting trip. After an intensive search for vineyard property, he purchased a site not far from the southwestern shore of Lake Ontario and planted 30,000 vines. The winery opened in 1986 and made its first icewine, from Vidal, in 1987.

A medium-sized producer by Canadian standards, Konzelmann made about 45,000 half bottles of Vidal icewine in 2000. Bruno Reis, the winery's sales director, acknowledges that Riesling is the "king" of grapes in Germany but Vidal is "Canada's special grape."

The winery's style is expressed in the 1998 Vidal icewine, an aromatic, plump-textured wine with flavors of peaches and tropical fruits. The winery also made several vintages of Riesling icewine and, in most vintages since 1991, an aromatic and spicy icewine from a vinifera cross it calls Riesling Traminer. Konzelmann also made that rarity, a Gewürztraminer icewine, in 1992, a cool vintage that preserved the acidity in this variety.

Lake Breeze Vineyards 930 Sammet Road, Naramata, BC V0H 1N0

This neat white stucco winery opened in 1996, the creation of Paul and Verena Moser. Although born in Switzerland, they spent a quarter century in business in South Africa before moving to Canada where they replicated a Cape winery in the Okanagan Valley. Moser even planted some Pinotage grapes and hired Garron

Elmes, a young South African winemaker who immediately rose to the challenge of icewine, making about 150 liters in 1996 and again in 1997, using Ehrenfelser grapes.

The winery changed hands in October 1998 after most of the vintage was complete but while some grapes, this time Pinot Blanc, remained for icewine. For Wayne and Joanne Finn, the new owners, it was a baptism of fire because Elmes had already returned to South Africa for Christmas when cold weather gripped the vineyard. The Finns, who previously had run a helicopter business, relied on detailed instructions left behind by their winemaker and successfully produced five hundred liters of icewine. "It was an interesting adventure," Wayne Finn says. "We didn't finish pressing the grapes until three in the morning."

Lakeview Cellars Estate Winery 4037 Cherry Avenue, RR #1, Vineland, ON L0R 2C0

Lakeview, which now produces about 12,000 cases a year, was opened in 1991 by grower Eddy Gurinskas and his wife, Lorraine. A talented winemaker, Gurinskas accumulated awards, including prizes for Vidal icewine, while still an amateur winemaker.

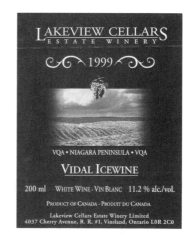

Big bold reds from Bordeaux varieties as well as Zweigelt and Baco Noir are his specialty. When Gurinskas turned professional, Vidal remained an icewine staple. He has won awards with every vintage of icewine made since 1991. In the 2000 vintage, he also made a Riesling icewine and planned one from Gewürztraminer until deer got into the vineyard and ate the grapes. Lakeview also makes Apple Delight, an apple wine in the icewine style.

Lang Vineyards 2493 Gammon Road, RR # 1, S11, C55, Naramata, BC V0H 1N0

Günther Lang and his wife Kristina almost depopulated a village near Stuttgart when they emigrated to Canada's Okanagan Valley in 1980 because they soon were followed by both their families. Lang and his brother Hans both purchased vineyards.

Günther established a superbly equipped winery in 1990, with Riesling as the flagship varietal. A one-time manager at Daimler-Benz in Stuttgart, Lang is a creative marketer who began packaging his icewine in bottles tinted in the brilliant blue of a polar sky. He found he could even sell empty bottles!

Lang began making icewine in 1992, producing about five hundred liters of Riesling. He also supplied frozen grapes to the Mission Hill winery that year for its icewine. Now Lang Vineyards produces between two and three thousand liters of icewine annually, primarily Riesling. A Merlot icewine was made in 1998, proving so successful with the winery's customers in Asia that Lang tries to make about two thousand liters when the vintage favors this rarely made red icewine.

In 1997, Petra Koeller, a young German winemaker, was hired, leaving Lang to concern himself, as he puts it, with "new ideas." One such idea is a line of wines flavored with pure Canadian maple syrup. "The idea came from icewine," Günther says. "I asked myself how we would service the Asian markets in years when we could not make icewine." The answer was to employ the quintessential Canadian confection, which is made by tapping the sap of maple trees each spring and concentrating it by boiling. The syrup is blended with either red or white wines to produce what Lang calls The Original Canadian Maple Wine. The white, based on Auxerrois, is almost as sweet as icewine, while the red, made with a cuvée of reds, has the sweetness of a late harvest wine.

Lang also uses maple syrup as a dosage for several bottle-fermented sparkling wines, selling as The Original Canadian Maple Brut. "It is tasty," he says reassuringly.

I t is Lyse LeBlanc's tradition to thank her icewine pickers by listing their names on the back label of each bottle of icewine. The 1998 Vidal Icewine, for example, memorializes the 24 who turned out on a cold night on December 22 that year. In the early morning, when the picking was done, they also stayed for another tradition, a feast of hearty Québec Christmas fare (tourtière, pork hock stew, baked beans) prepared in advance by Lyse, who has turned icewine making into a harvest-ending festival. "What a great sensation when you're done!" she says. "It's like having written your last final exam."

This small, well-regarded winery came about almost by chance. Pierre and Lyse LeBlanc, both real estate agents, took time away from business to plant a vineyard (now seven hectares) on property then owned by Pierre's parents.

"It was not our intention to be a winery," she says. But after several years of selling juice — the vineyard was planted entirely in white varieties including Vidal — she found she had all the basic equipment. She also had surplus juice that needed to be vinified. Pierre made the first wine but Lyse, who now runs the entire operation, soon took over. "I had more affinity for the details," she found.

Lyse even made two trial lots of icewine before making the commitment to a commercial production in 1992, vinifying about a thousand liters of Vidal icewine, along with a small quantity of table wines from unsold juice. It was her intention to produce icewine exclusively but, once the winery opened in 1993, she realized that a broader range of wines was needed to sustain traffic to the wine shop. Now she makes both red and white table wines as well. The volume of icewine made here has ranged from 300 liters to 1,500 liters a year. The style shows a polished elegance and a balance achieved by targeting juice no sweeter than 38° Brix. "After that," she maintains, "the wine becomes cloying."

Daniel Lenko Estate Winery 5216 Regional Road 81, Beamsville, ON L0R 1B3

I n 1960 Bill Lenko, Daniel's father, was one of the first independent growers to plant Chardonnay in Canada. His Beamsville property became legendary for the quality of its grapes, with which many other winemakers made award-winning wines. Predictably, Daniel Lenko's 1999 Chardonnay — the first vintage to be released from the new winery when it opened in late 2000 — garnered awards as soon as Lenko began competing.

Soon after Daniel, born in 1967, took over the family farm from his father, he developed the winery to wrest more value from his father's superior grapes. The 30 acres of vineyards gave him the potential to produce between 10,000 and 12,000 cases of wine a year. Currently, the winery produces about a third of that volume; Lenko has no difficulty selling the rest of his grapes to other wineries.

With help from Jim Warren, a veteran consulting winemaker, Lenko produces premium wines. He began making icewine in 1999, producing one thousand liters of 1999 barrel-fermented Vidal in a style that is vibrantly fresh. After the 2000 vintage, when Vidal icewine again was made, Lenko removed those vines from his vineyard to make room for other varieties. He intends that his future icewines will be made with Riesling and the quantities limited to about five hundred liters, just enough for his regular customers and the visitors to the winery.

Magnotta Winery Corporation 271 Chrislea Road, Vaughan, ON L4L 8N6

" I cewine does not have to be $50 to be world class," Gabriel Magnotta begins, uttering one of those opinions that have made him and his wife, Rossana, controversial within the Canadian wine industry but highly successful with consumers.

His competitors bristle when Magnotta dispenses his calculations on how much it costs to make a bottle of icewine. He believes it is nowhere near the general retail price demanded by others.

Magnotta's icewine seldom sells for more than $30 and sometimes for less.

In September 1998 Magnotta proclaimed an "icewine celebration" and offered his Vidal icewine at $19.95 for 375 ml bottles and $13 for 200 ml bottles. The winery sold 18,000 bottles of icewine in two weeks while the competitors fumed at the discounting some later had to match. "The name of the game is affordable excellence," he maintains. "We have 30 million people in Canada. Most of them have not tried icewine." The varietal icewines from this winery include Gewürztraminer, Vidal, Riesling and Cabernet Franc.

The Italian-born Magnottas grew up in Canada with a deeply ingrained wine heritage. "Everybody in Italy grows up with grapes," Gabriel Magnotta observes. "Wine is an everyday occurrence. It is like bread." They built a business supplying grapes and juice to home winemakers and, when their clients began to ask for finished wines, they decided in 1989 to open a winery.

When he learned it would take two years to get a winery license, Magnotta outflanked the bureaucrats by purchasing a failing Ontario winery, transferring the license to his business in a suburb of Toronto. His winery was open in less than a year and icewine, now Magnotta's flagship among a comprehensive list of wines, spirits and beers, was launched in 1991.

From the beginning, Magnotta has priced its icewines (and most of its other wines) below that of competitors. However, the winery has

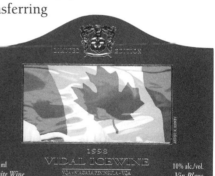

an impressive array of awards to show that low prices need not mean low quality. Indeed, Magnotta is quick to take legal action against any critic who would suggest otherwise. In 1999 he launched an audacious lawsuit claiming damages of $8 million against the Liquor Control Board of Ontario, North America's largest state-owned retailer of wine and spirits, claiming that LCBO employees routinely were slandering Magnotta icewines and other products. (It was settled out of court.)

Besides selling some of Canada's most affordable icewines, Magnotta has been a leader in creating beverages based on icewine. The winery spent two years developing what is claimed to be the first VQA sparkling Vidal icewine made in Canada, made by a proprietary technique that Magnotta keeps to himself. The winery's Sparkling Ice Cuvée de Prestige Vidal has a powerful aroma of strawberries and tropical fruits, lifted by the bubbles. There also is a sparkling Cabernet Franc with the distinctive aroma and taste of toffee.

(In the final years of the 1990s, inspired by the Millennium's demand for Champagne, other producers in Germany and Canada also made sparkling icewines. Summerhill in British Columbia and Peller Estates in Ontario have used icewine as a sweetening dosage in classically made, bottle-fermented sparkling wines. In October 1999 Inniskillin in Ontario unveiled its own VQA sparkling Vidal icewine, produced from 1998 vintage grapes that were picked during the first two weeks of January 1999 and then turned into bubbly by the Méthode Cuve Close. This involves fermenting the wine in a pressure vessel, allowing the winemaker to arrest fermentation at the desired point. The wine, naturally carbonated, is bottled from this vessel. Artificial carbonation of sparkling icewine is not permitted for wines bearing the VQA seal of Canada's Vintners Quality Alliance.)

Because Magnotta also operates a distillery, it has produced what it calls Ice Grappa, another claimed Magnotta first. It is a good idea, if not entirely original. Many German wineries make a similar product, called Trester, by using the spent skins of Eiswein and other late harvest wines.

"We thought the skins were going to waste," Gabriel Magnotta explains. Thus, when the first pressing of grapes for icewine is completed, the skins of the grapes that others discard are fermented, reaching about eight per cent alcohol, and this wine is then double distilled, much as Cognac is.

The winery has used its most stunning packaging for Ice Grappa, putting the clear liquid into delicately slender, clear bottles, each one of which has cluster of tiny crystalline grapes sparkling amid the grappa.

"Layers of floral perfumes tantalize the nose," the winery writes in a description of Ice Grappa. "The palate feels the rustic heat of the alcohol which then blossoms into subtle caramel and butterscotch ..."

When he reflects on what the winery has done to develop the market for icewine in its first 10 years, Gabriel Magnotta seems genuinely puzzled that his peers still see him as an outsider. "I'm a little upset with the whole industry that they don't recognize our contribution," he complains.

Malivoire Wine Company 4260 King Street East, Beamsville, ON L0R 1B0

E ven before this winery opened in the fall of 1999, its 1997 Gewürztraminer icewine had won a gold medal at the 1999 International Wine and Spirit Competition in Britain. There are two reasons for this impressive début: site selection and winemaking.

It began in 1995 when Martin Malivoire, a motion picture special effects producer, and his partner Moira Saganski, looking for a weekend residence, bought a vineyard on the Niagara Peninsula's Beamsville Bench. The varieties growing in what now is called Moira's Vineyard included unusually intense Gewürztraminer. Malivoire subsequently replanted with companion varieties grown in Alsace and Burgundy while keeping Gewürztraminer alongside the Pinot Noir and Chardonnay meticulously grown in organic vineyards. He designed a new winery equipped for gentle handling of grapes and wines. British Columbia–born Ann Sperling, who made award-winning icewines in the early 1990s at the CedarCreek winery near Kelowna, makes the wines.

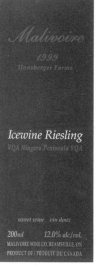

Malivoire's 1997 icewine was made from five tonnes of grapes harvested on December 31 that year, yielding juice than measured 40° Brix. The wine is plump with richly honeyed fruit on the palate. Only 900 half bottles were made. In 1998 vintage, the winery only harvested enough grapes to produce 480 bottles of Gewürztraminer icewine; to stretch the supply, Malivoire used two hundred milliliter bottles. In a sensitive touch, the back labels on the icewines list the small band of pickers.

In the 1999 vintage Sperling switched to Riesling for icewine, making 350 liters. "I was not satisfied that making an icewine from Moira's Vineyard was the best use of the fruit," she said. Besides, she added, "Riesling is the best grape for icewine." At Malivoire, icewine serves as a glittering adornment to its wines.

Maple Grove Estate Winery 4063 North Service Road, Beamsville, ON L0R 1B0

See Vinoteca Inc.

Vignoble du Marathonien 318 route 202, Havelock, QC J0S 2C0

Electrical engineer Jean Joly and his spouse, Line, opened this winery in 1990 in countryside where apples have been grown for more than a century. Joly, whose ancestors came from France in 1650, was drawn into wine gradually after becoming an amateur winemaker.

Due south of Montreal and five kilometers north of the United States border, the 1.5 hectare Marathonien vineyard was planted in 1990 in gravel soil laid down centuries ago when Lake Champlain covered the area. The winery produces primarily white wines. Beginning in 1994, the winery has made a very limited quantity (less than one thousand half bottles) of icewine from the Vidal grape. It is, they say, "the jewel of our house."

Netherlands-born John Marynissen was one of Ontario's best amateur winemakers before, at the age of 65, he opened this family winery in 1991 on a farm where he has grown grapes since 1954. His mentor was Karl Kaiser, the winemaker at nearby Inniskillin, a winery renowned for its icewine.

As amateurs will do, Marynissen explored the boundaries of winemaking, making a red icewine one year from secondary bunches of Gamay. "It makes a nice icewine but I would sooner use it for table wine," he says.

Marynissen, which produces about 10,000 cases of wine a year, is well regarded for its red table wines. However, two hectares of the farm's twenty-four-hectare vineyard is planted to Vidal for icewine, with Marynissen producing a luscious, peach-flavored style with room-filling aromas.

"If you make it in a freezer," he says, speaking with the experience of an amateur, "you don't get the nose." Marynissen limits its icewine production to about 1,500 liters a year. "We are flooded," he says bluntly of the volume of production in Ontario. "We are way *over-flooded.*"

Vignoble Mission du Vigneron 1044 Pierre Laporte, Brigham, QC
J2K 4R3

The story of this Québec winery is shot through with romance. A native of Mexico City, Alejandro Guerrero met and wooed Marie-Josée Clusiau in 1982 in Ontario; both describe themselves as lovers of wine and, in particular, of icewine. They settled near Montreal after marrying in 1984, with a dream of living in the country.

"Since I was young I wanted to have a farm," Guerrero says. "The idea of having a farm and living in the country was always alive and with the passing years, it became more and more clear that it was a vineyard we wanted." Ultimately, they purchased a 20-hectare property which they began planting in 1997.

In the first vintage in 2000, and with the help of consulting winemakers Vera Klokocka and John Fletcher, they produced 150 liters of icewine, blending Vidal and a Geisenheim hybrid. "The climate is very appropriate for icewine making, since we are assured to get very cold temperatures every year," Guerrero says.

Mission Hill Family Estate 1730 Mission Hill Road, Westbank, BC V4T 2E4

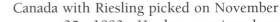

A hilltop winery dating from 1966, Mission Hill's architecture is singularly dramatic; an austere finger of a bell tower completed in 2000 capped a multi-million-dollar reconstruction of the winery. The investment includes vast computer-monitored barrel cellars that enable John Simes, the New Zealand–born winemaker, to keep improving critically acclaimed table wines.

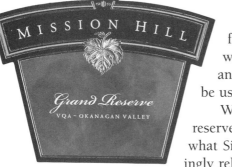

Simes made his first icewine just four months after arriving in Canada with Riesling picked on November 25, 1992. He has continued to make small quantities of icewine from Vidal and Gewürztraminer as well. The young blocks of Riesling and Pinot Noir near the winery may be used for icewine in the future.

Whether or not he asks a grower to reserve grapes for icewine depends on what Simes reads each fall in the increasingly reliable long-range weather forecasts. He did not like the forecast in the 1999 vintage (which correctly projected a mild winter) and, for the first time in many years, made no icewine. In 2000, with a deeper freeze predicted, Simes reserved some healthy Chardonnay grapes that were "the best fruit available." An early December harvest produced about 12,000 half bottles of Chardonnay icewine.

T his winery, which opened in 2001, is operated by three brothers who were born in Punjab but grew up in Canada after their father settled there in 1962. The Gidda family began growing grapes in 1976 and now owns 71 hectares of vineyards in different parts of southern British Columbia. Alan Marks, the winemaker, produced late harvest wines in the 2000 vintage but the winery plans to add Ehrenfelser icewine to its range.

Marks, a Missouri native with a doctorate in enology, has made icewine in Canada since 1994 when he joined Summerhill Estate Winery. He once tried to make a Seyval Blanc icewine when he worked previously at the Hermannhoff winery in Hermann, Missouri. The region's late-season humidity doomed the project by causing too much bunch rot among the grapes.

Norfolk Estate Winery RR #1, St. Williams, ON N0E 1P0

W hen tobacco and apple grower George Benko switched from tobacco in 1984, he committed totally to apples, including many exotic new varieties. In 1995 he and Shirley, his wife, opened Ontario's first apple winery. Among those wines is Ice Apple Wine, a gold medal winner in various competitions, and a creative companion called Ice Apple Ginseng. There is a root of ginseng in each bottle.

Ocala Orchards Fruit Winery RR #2, 971 High Point Road, Port Perry, ON L9L 1B3

D espite the name, this winery, which was opened in 1995 by Irwin and Alissa Smith, also has a four-hectare vineyard. The winery made its first small quantity of Vidal icewine from a New Year's Eve morning harvest in 1998. Port Perry is a challenging new vineyard area about an hour northeast of Toronto. All the vines are grown on low trellises and are buried each autumn for protection against severe cold.

Vignoble de L'Orpailleur 1086, rue Bruce, Dunham, QC J0E 1M0

Producing about 70,000 bottles a year, this is Québec's largest winery, operated by Charles-Henri de Coussergues, who grew up in a vineyard in the Midi. The vineyards were planted in 1982 and the winery opened three years later, with most of the wines made from the Seyval Blanc grape. That variety was chosen for its hardiness as well as for its ability to make solid table whites; the owners did trials with more than 30 varieties in search of a hardy vine. They also grow Seyval Noir for rosé and Vidal, another sturdy white. A creative winery, in 1996 it began making kosher table wines for Montreal's Jewish community. In 1997, the winery made 246 liters of Vidal icewine.

Paradise Ranch Vineyards, Paradise Ranch Road, Naramata, BC V0H 1N0

Picturesque but secluded, this 40-hectare vineyard spent most of the twentieth century as a cattle ranch on bench land overlooking British Columbia's Okanagan Lake. It was purchased in 1975 by Hu Harries, a professional economist with a love of agriculture. Vineyards began replacing beef in 1981.

The management of Paradise Ranch subsequently was taken over by Jeffrey Harries, the son of Hu and a general practitioner, who decided in the mid 1990s to produce icewine exclusively from grapes not sold to commercial wineries. "We decide that there is a niche," Jeff Harries said. "We'd be uniquely dessert wine producers and we'd be big." As early as 1990, Paradise Ranch was selling icewine grapes to other wineries.

The success that Mission Hill had with Paradise Ranch fruit

inspired Harries to get a winery license in 1998, concentrating on icewine. Anticipating the license, Paradise Ranch had plunged into icewine in the 1997 vintage. Without a winery at the time Paradise Ranch had the wines produced and marketed by nearby Red Rooster Winery. Six different varietals were made: Chardonnay, Riesling, Vidal, Pinot Blanc, Viognier and Verdelet. "My favorite then," recalls Prudence Mahrer, one of Red Rooster's owners, "was the Chardonnay, which was dark yellow and syrupy."

The 1998 icewine vintage at Paradise Ranch was huge (although it has since been eclipsed by 2000). The multiple days of cold weather in 1998 extending from just before Christmas to early January enabled the vineyard to harvest 330 tonnes of grapes for icewine. The result was eight different wines, including Merlot and Pinot Gris, and a total of 45,000 half bottles.

The 1999 vintage was blessed neither by prolonged cold nor an early freeze. When the harvest occurred from the night of January 19 to the morning of January 20, Paradise Ranch's pickers got the grapes off. However, it began to warm soon after. While bins of grapes were waiting to be pressed, the temperature rose and stayed well above the legally required -8°C for icewine. Paradise Ranch pressed nine thousand gallons of must but only twelve hundred gallons qualified as icewine. "The rest is late harvest," Harries says. "The late harvest Merlot is a pretty awesome wine."

However, the 2000 harvest was done under ideal conditions in early December, resulting in 40,000 liters or more than 100,000 half bottles. In that vintage, Paradise limited itself to three of its most successful varieties for icewine: Riesling, Chardonnay and Merlot.

Established in 1982, this winery was one of Ontario's first icewine producers, a notable achievement. While the winery itself is on the north shore of Lake Erie, the two hundred hectares of vineyards are on Pelee Island, a diked island in the lake that is closer to the Ohio shore than to the Canadian shore. The island is on a major flyway for migratory birds. In 1983 when the winery first netted vines for icewine, conservation officers tore down the nets to liberate trapped birds and the winery lost significant quantities of unprotected grapes to birds. Austrian-born Walter Strehn, then the general manager, was charged with poaching but succeeded in having the charges dropped.

Pelee Island, now using tighter nets that do not entangle birds, has been able to make icewine in nearly every succeeding vintage. In 1989 the winery made Canada's first red icewine, from Lemberger; a decade later, the wine retained a brilliant hue but the flavor had taken on the character midway between a dry sherry and a ruby port.

Since 1986 the winemaker has been German-born Walter Schmoranz, now the general manager, who is assisted by Martin Janz, a winemaker from the Rheingau. Schmoranz believes that the island's location makes for unique icewine. The grapes destined for icewine hang for three to four months beyond the normal vintage in September and October. The berries dehydrate during the long fall and also go through cycles of freezing and thawing that break down the structure of the grapes and, Schmoranz believes, contributes to the singular flavors of Pelee Island icewine.

The location also presents a difficulty. The ferry linking Pelee

Island to the Canadian mainland operates, depending on Lake Erie's ice, only from mid-March to mid-December. Usually, the ferry has stopped running by the time the icewine freeze arrives. The winery then charters light aircraft to fly its pickers to Pelee Island (a 10-minute flight). The picked grapes are crushed on the island; the juice, lightly sulphured, remains there in tank until the ferry begins running in March. Then it is transported to the Pelee Island winery at Kingsville where fermentation takes place.

Annual production now averages 8,000 to 10,000 liters of Vidal icewine. In the 2000 vintage, Pelee Island made about 800 liters of Cabernet Franc (only its second red icewine) and several hundred liters of Riesling icewine. One reason for making the latter, Janz admits, is so that he and Schmoranz have a vinifera icewine to show off when they return to Germany to compare their craft with that of winemakers there.

They need hardly be apologetic about their Vidal icewines. The 1995, slightly low in acid, has plump raisin flavors, with the Rubenesque voluptuousness that often characterizes Vidal. The 1996, on the other hand, has the racy acidity that a German would appreciate. The 1998 (none could be made in the warm 1997 winter) combines the virtues of the previous two vintages: plump apricot fruit with lively acidity that makes for a lasting finish.

Peller Estates 697 South Service Road, Winona, ON L8E 5S4

The Andrés group of wineries were founded in 1961 by an entrepreneurial former brewer named Andrew Peller who reasoned that a French flair in the company's name would benefit its sales. The successful strategy had run its course by the time his grandson, John Peller, took over running what is Canada's second largest winery. Now the Peller name is used for all of the group's premium wines except for those made at **Hillebrand Estates**, its Niagara boutique. In 2001, Andrés opened a new Peller winery just outside Niagara-on-the-Lake, designed in a style harmonious with Victorian ambiance of the community.

Icewines under the Peller Estates Founder's Series label include a Vidal produced at the Winona winery from grapes purchased throughout the Niagara Peninsula. In the bountiful 1998 vintage, Peller Estates produced about 180,000 half bottles of icewine, so much that none was made from Vidal in 1999 and only a third that quantity was made in 2000.

As part of the launch of the new winery, Peller has added a premium oak-aged icewine from Riesling, making about 6,000 half bottles in 1999 and 2,400 in 2000. The label of the Riesling commemorates Andrew Peller, the company's founder. Winemaker Robert Summers likes the unctous style. The 1998 Vidal icewine, he says, begins with an intense apricot aroma, has flavors of apricot, kiwi, mango and papaya and possesses firm acidity. His tasting notes on the 1999 Riesling describe a wine with a "smooth creamy palate [which] leads the way to a lightly toasted, lingering sweet citrus finish."

Equally interesting is the Peller Estates Founder's Series Cristalle, a sparkling wine with an icewine dosage. The basic blend is Chardonnay and Pinot Noir, fermented in the bottle in the classic Champagne method. When the lees are disgorged, a dosage of Vidal icewine is added. The result is an off-dry sparkling wine with a bouquet of apricot, apples and honey and with a palate of tropical fruits. An Andrés-produced Vidal icewine also is found in export markets under the Points North label.

At the company's winery in British Columbia, the flagship icewine is Peller Estates Limited Edition Trinity, crafted of Vidal with less quantities of Ehrenfelser and Riesling in the finished blend. Winemaker David Hays makes about three thousand liters annually of this barrel-aged wine. "The Vidal brings a lot of flavor of pears and peaches," he says. "The dried fruit and raisin characters come from the Riesling and the Ehrenfelser."

N orman Beal spent two decades in the corporate fast lane as an international oil trader before, in a quality-of-life career change, he built one of Ontario's most ambitious new wineries.

Peninsula Ridge opened in 2000, with plans to grow to 30,000 cases a year. While 70 per cent of the wines are Bordeaux-variety reds, the winery made about two thousand bottles of Vidal icewine from its début vintage in 1999 and twelve thousand bottles in 2000. "For an Ontario producer, icewine is something that is expected," Beal says. "It's something we need to round out our portfolio and it is something that Canadians can do well." Peninsula Ridge demonstrated that with its first offering, an elegant and polished wine that was fermented and aged for nine months in new French oak.

Beal has one hesitation about icewine. "In a way, it is over-shadowing some of the other fine wines that are being done by the Ontario industry," he says.

Pillitteri Estates RR #2, 1696 Highway 55, Niagara-on-the-Lake, ON L0S 1J0

T wo things happened to Gary Pillitteri in 1988: he failed to win a seat in the Canadian parliament but, a keen amateur wine-maker, he did win a gold medal for his icewine. That prompted him to develop a winery which opened in 1993, the same year, ironi-cally, in which the Sicilian-born Pillitteri succeeded in being elect-ed to Parliament. The task of running the rapidly growing winery, one of Canada's large icewine producers, was turned over his son Charles and his daughter Connie.

Sue-Ann Staff, Pillitteri's winemaker, produces about 30,000 liters a year, primarily Vidal, with small quantities also made from other varieties. Staff searched the vineyards supplying the winery until she found the Gewürztraminer clone that best retains its acidity when mature, essential for icewine. "It does present challenges compared with the other varieties," she found. "Because the skins are so much thinner, it dehydrates that much quicker."

She admires Riesling for its elegance and ability to age. In 1998, she produced a Riesling Icewine that won a perfect score from all the judges at a 1999 American Wine Society competition. Since then, she has begun exploring the boundaries of icewine with, for example, a barrel-fermented Riesling, a barrel-fermented Cabernet Franc and the rarely seen Merlot icewine. "It's unique and interesting," she says of Merlot. "It has flavors of cranberries and crabapples."

The style of Pillitteri icewine largely is dictated by the harvest conditions. "If I can add my own flair, I will," Staff says. "I like to achieve nice up-front fruit. I want it elegant. I don't want a big, rich wine. I'd rather have a nice acidity to balance the sweetness and to keep it light on the palate. It has to be consumable."

Poplar Grove RR #1, 1060 Poplar Grove Road, Penticton, BC V2A 8T6

Ian Sutherland and his wife Gitta, a nurse turned vineyardist, scored an immediate triumph by winning a gold medal for their first Cabernet Franc table wine at the 1998 Okanagan Wine Festival. This tiny winery makes consistently fine Bordeaux reds.

Sutherland, a pipefitter by trade, honed his skills as a self-taught winemaker in New Zealand. Always eager for a winemaking challenge, Sutherland in the 1999 vintage made his first icewine, five hundred liters of Gewürztraminer. The wine turned out well but, because the grapes could not be picked until early 2000, he found that the subsequent productivity of the vines suffered. Sutherland decided that Poplar Grove's next icewine will be made from Riesling.

Quails' Gate Vineyards 3303 Boucherie Road, Westbank, BC V1Z 2H3

This northern Okanagan winery, which opened in 1989, made its first icewine in 1993. Tony Stewart, one of the owners, recalls picking the Riesling grapes at 4:30 A.M., with the temperature at -16°C. "This temperature is the reason why we are making an icewine that is so concentrated," Stewart says. "It set the precedent that we wait until we get temperatures below -10°C."

Quails' Gate, also known for its botrytized Optima dessert wines, has increased icewine production until, in 1998, nine thousand liters of Riesling icewine were produced. The run of typically deep Canadian temperatures was interrupted by the unusually warm 1999 winter. Quails' Gate did not have the required minimum freeze until January 19, 2000, and the cold did not persist long enough for the winery to pick and process all the grapes. Three hundred liters of juice technically qualified as icewine but was not as rich as Quails' Gate desired. The winery blended it into forty-five hundred liters of late harvest Riesling. "Thus, for 1999 we have only a Special Select Late Harvest Riesling," Stewart said. It was another story in 2000 when winter bit the Okanagan on December 11. Quails' Gate had reserved 25 tons of Riesling grapes, which were picked at -14°C to yield an intensely sweet must measuring 50.8° Brix.

For much of its history Quails' Gate has employed Australian winemakers, none of whom ever had confronted the challenge of icewine before. "Nothing in Australia prepared me for this kind of crazy winemaking," said Ashley Hooper, who had just joined the Canadian winery in early 2000. "It's kind of a festive way to finish up a great harvest."

Reif Estate Winery 15608 Niagara Parkway, Niagara-on-the-Lake, ON L0S 1J0

In the late 1990s, winemaker Klaus Reif turned down an order from a Moscow wine buyer who wanted an entire shipping container of icewine. Firstly, he did not have enough wine that to fill the container and secondly, he doubted that the prospective client had $300,000 for the wine.

The anecdote highlights the apparent market for icewines compared with the difficulty that Reif (and other Canadian wineries) had selling the wines a dozen years earlier when the style was not widely known. Until Robert M. Parker, Jr., the influential American wine critic, rated a 1987 Reif icewine among the best wines he had tasted in 1989, Reif struggled to sell his icewines at a reasonable price. The Reif Estate made as little as two hundred liters of icewine a year in the 1980s, with the 1,387 liters made in 1987 being the high point for the decade. After the Parker review, demand and production surged. By 1998, the winery was producing as much as 20,000 liters of icewine annually. In 2000, Reif made his first red icewine, some 220 liters with Cabernet Sauvignon.

Born in 1963, the son of a German winery owner, Reif came to Canada in 1987 to work at and later take over the winery started by his uncle, Ewald. Klaus had made icewine while apprenticing in Germany. In Ontario, he was astonished at how much more ripe and concentrated the icewine juice was compared with that in Germany. He has developed a style of making some of Ontario's biggest icewines, both with Vidal and with Riesling. "I just believe in a heavy icewine," he says. "I love German Eiswein. It is very elegant and a very pleasant wine to drink. But you drink a Canadian icewine and you say WOW! It is like a powerhouse."

In 1990 Reif, pushing the limits of winemaking, set out to ferment Riesling juice that had 51° Brix — perhaps 20° higher than typical German icewine must. It took 18 months and several injections of fresh yeast before fermentation completed. Such a lengthy fermentation poses risks that the wine will develop volatile acidity (a vinegar aroma) or oxidize.

Reif moderated his approach somewhat and now works with must weights in the mid-40s. His enthusiasm for icewine is such, he says, that "I can't even sleep the night before we pick because I am so excited." But where he once rose from his bed hourly and went outside to read the thermometer, Reif now has installed a thermometer with an exterior sensor and a digital display in his bedroom so that he can monitor the temperature from the warmth of his bed.

Royal DeMaria Wines Co. 4551 Cherry Avenue, Vineland, ON L0R 1B1

Joseph DeMaria proclaims his winery, established in 1997, to be "Canada's icewine specialist" because it produces only icewine. Unlike Paradise Ranch, the icewine specialist in British Columbia, DeMaria has no intention of making late harvest wines in those years when nature does not provide icewine conditions. It is all or nothing.

An Ontario native born in 1961 of Italian parents, DeMaria is a Toronto hairdresser who continues to operate a hair salon. His icewine epiphany occurred in 1991 when he tasted it for the first time while touring Niagara-region wineries. "It was fantastic," he remembers. Soon he began making trial lots at his home, started planning a winery and in 1997 purchased a 10-hectare vineyard near Vineland.

Initially, he sold 12,000 liters of icewine juice to other producers from the 1997 harvest. The vineyard yielded 18,000 liters in 1998 when, with a winery license in hand, he kept 5,000 liters of Vidal for his icewine début. In the 1999 vintage, he added icewines from Riesling, Gewürztraminer and Pinot Gris.

At the same time, the self-taught winemaker began entering his wine in competition, getting a confidence boost when the 1998 Vidal won silver medals at three different international competitions in 2000. In the following year, his 1999 Riesling icewine was judged the best sweet wine at Cuvée 2001, a major Ontario competition, and his Vidal icewine won a double gold at the Finger Lakes International Wine Competition. At Vinexpo in 2001, DeMaria wines won gold, silver and bronze medals.

With the wind in his sails, DeMaria closed down his merchant juice business and limited production to his own winery's needs. He made 8,000 liters for DeMaria in the 2000 vintage. He has added, or has plans for, additional varieties for icewine, including Chardonnay, Pinot Blanc, Muscat Ottonel, Cabernet Franc, Sauvignon Blanc, Merlot and Gamay.

The desired winemaking style captures the fruit of the varieties, subtly balanced with acidity. "We don't want to be a sugar factory," DeMaria says. There is an element of mystery to the style: in 1999, he says he made what he believed was a winemaking error which proved effective in expressing the varietal fruit.

"The flavors were pushed forward and the sugars were pushed back," he describes the outcome, which he repeated in subsequent vintages. "It's high risk but it does work." It is a technique he is not yet prepared to divulge.

DeMaria's strategy includes aggressive pricing that sets him apart from competitors which have begun to apply commodity pricing when producing icewines in volume. He believes his Merlot and Gamay icewines, which can be produced only in small volume and perhaps twice in a decade, can fetch several hundred dollars a half bottle from select clientele and restaurants. "It's not going to be for the average consumer," he says, observing that "people who have money like to spend money." He also is examining methods of selling icewine futures.

His icewine-only approach begins in the vineyard. The vines are cropped more heavily than would be the case if he were making table wines. The harvested grapes are pressed in small Italian basket presses and the juice is handled gently.

DeMaria sets high standards for himself, to the point in 1999 when he dumped a five-hundred-liter tank of icewine juice whose aroma and taste displeased him. "People called me a mad man," he admits. "The reason I did it was because we are doing only quality."

Slamka Cellars 2815 Ourtoland Road, Kelowna, BC V1Z 2H5

An unusually early November 15 freeze in 1994 enabled Peter Slamka to make the first icewine for this family-owned winery, which had opened two years later. The wine was a cuvée Riesling with about 15 per cent Auxerrois. In succeeding vintages, he reversed the ratio, with the Riesling there chiefly to increase the wine's acidity. He makes about a thousand bottles a year.

The Slamka family (Peter's father was born in Czechoslovakia) has grown grapes in the north Okanagan since 1970, in cool hillside vineyards with a southeastern exposure. The Auxerrois, from one of the oldest plantings in British Columbia, yields icewine with toffee, butterscotch and peach flavors.

In the 2000 vintage, Slamka also made icewine for the first time from Seyval Blanc after buying a neighboring vineyard growing the variety. Because Seyval Blanc has good acidity and hangs well on the vine, Slamka thinks it may take over Riesling's role in his icewines.

Southbrook Farms Winery 1061 Major MacKenzie Dr., Maple, ON
L4C 4X9

Formerly home to Canada's largest Jersey dairy herd, Southbrook opened its winery in 1992 in its century-old barn and now produces about 7,000 cases a year, including well-regarded fruit wines.

Wine is a logical extension of the agricultural products sold from the farm to a clientele of more than 130,000 a year from nearby Toronto. Wine also reflects the passion of winemaker (and former farm manager) Derek Barnett and owner (and wine enthusiast) Bill Redelmeier. "We have 75 years of drinking experience between us," Barnett quips. He made a trial lot of icewine in 1994 and has been making commercial quantities since 1995, primarily with Vidal but occasionally with Gewürztraminer and Riesling — but never with red varieties. "Why waste good Cabernet Franc on icewine?" Redelmeier asks. Southbrook, which buys its grapes from Niagara area vineyards, produces about 1,500 liters of icewine a year, although Barnett did make five thousand liters in 1998, a large vintage for almost every Ontario producer.

He aims to make Vidal icewine with fresh acidity. His 1998 Vidal, while harvested at 45° Brix, shows good balance, with intense tropical fruit flavors and a rich texture set against good acidity. "I find a lot of icewines a little too sticky," he says. "I like to use them as food." When Southbrook has winemaker dinners, Barnett likes to serve icewine between courses, as palate refreshers.

St. Hubertus Estate Winery 5225 Lakeshore Road, Kelowna, BC
V1W 4J1

Two years after this winery opened, Swiss-born brothers Leo and Andy Gebert made the first St. Hubertus icewine in 1993, using Bacchus, an aromatic grape seldom employed for icewine, perhaps because it ripens early with modest acidity.

When Bacchus was next used for icewine in the 2000 vintage, it was married with Pinot Blanc, benefiting from the latter's better structure and acidity.

In the intervening vintages, both Riesling and Pinot Blanc icewines have been produced at St. Hubertus. The first red icewine, from Pinot Noir, was made in 2000. The volumes are small (typical was 756 liters of Pinot Blanc icewine in 1999).

The winery describes icewine as "the ultimate dessert in a bottle." It is the ornamental crown of this small winery's table wines, which, in a reflection of the Swiss heritage of the owners, includes one of the few Chasselas wines made in Canada.

Leo Gebert grew up in the Swiss wine community of Rapperswil, trained as a banker but really wanted to be a farmer. Switzerland's exorbitant land prices drove him to the Okanagan in 1984 where he found a 22.25-hectare vineyard set in a mountain landscape to remind him of home. His younger brother Andy, a plumber by training, followed five years later and became a partner in St. Hubertus.

St. Lazlo Vineyards RR #1, S95, L8, Keremeos, BC V0X 1N0

Fiercely independent, Joe Ritlop marches to his own drum at St. Lazlo. "I grow my own grapes and I make my own wine and I mind my own business," he once told a journalist.

A native of Slovenia where his family grew grapes, Ritlop established his vineyard in 1974 in the sun-drenched Similkameen Valley in southern British Columbia. He began making icewine in 1982, maintaining a dessert wine focus (he also makes a wine he calls Tokai Aszu).

His style is rustic and natural: no chemicals in the vineyard, no preservatives in the wine cellar where the grapes ferment entirely with wild yeast.

Stonechurch Vineyards 1242 Irvine Road, Niagara-on-the-Lake, ON L0S 1J0

F ran Hunse has learned that, as she puts it, "you have to live your whole life around the icewine harvest." Canadians mark Thanksgiving early in October but the Hunse family does not eat its Thanksgiving dinner until the icewine harvest is complete, sometimes not before February.

Stonechurch was opened in 1990, based on vineyards farmed by Lambert and Grace Hunse, who came to Canada from Holland in the 1950s. Their son Rick and Fran, his wife, took over Stonechurch in 1995 and have grown it to producing 30,000 cases a year, including a rare Morio Muscat table wine.

The winery began making icewine in 1991 and keeps some wines back so that collectors can acquire verticals. The 1991 Vidal icewine still available a decade later — a gold medal winner at Vinitaly in 1994 — had become languorously peachy with caramel overtones. The style remains consistent: the 1997 Vidal icewine shows intensely spicy fruit with toffee notes, while the 1999 has aromas of fresh peaches and flavors of light caramel and peaches.

Fran Hunse recalls the 1999 harvest vividly. Stonechurch, which relies on "friends and anybody who owes us a favor" for pickers, harvested some of the grapes on the night of December 30. Even though it was cold again the following evening, she and her husband went to a party welcoming in the new century. She fretted that they had made a mistake when, on the way home, they saw pickers at work in neighboring vineyards. It was another two weeks before it was cold enough again to finish the picking.

Stoney Ridge Cellars 3201 King Street, Vineland, ON L0R 2C0

T his winery was started in 1985 by Jim Warren, a gifted amateur with a boundless curiosity as a winemaker. As the winery grew, he made as many as 50 different wines, both from fruits and from grapes. The winery has produced icewines with Vidal,

Traminer, Gewürztraminer and apples, cranberries and blueberries. The 1997 barrel-fermented Gewürztraminer won the trophy for the top dessert wine at Vinexpo in 1999. Its 1997 Iced Apple-Best won a gold medal at the 1998 Toronto Wine and Cheese Show. Stoney Ridge was acquired in 1998 by a group headed by Ottawa businessman John Belanger. Warren now consults for other wineries and for many of Canada's fruit wine producers.

Strewn Estate Winery 1339 Lakeshore Road, Niagara-on-the-Lake ON L0S 1J0

Winemaker Joe Will, who opened this winery in 1997 in partnership with Newman Smith, was introduced to icewines by British Columbia's Hainle family. An Alberta native and a home winemaker, Will in 1989 left a career in journalism and public relations to make wine. He persuaded Tilman Hainle to employ him after he pruned the Hainle vineyard without pay.

After a year, Will, who has a chemistry degree, went to Roseworthy College in Australia for a graduate diploma in winemaking. (One of his projects there was the production of an icewine-style wine with artificially frozen Chenin Blanc grapes.) When he returned to Canada in 1992, he became the first winemaker at the Pillitteri winery near Niagara-on-the-Lake where, under an agreement with his employer, he also made two vintages for the planned Strewn winery, including its first icewine in 1994.

The winery (which includes a cooking school run by Jane Langdon, Will's spouse) is in a sprawling former fruit cannery tastefully restored to its 1930s style. Will, who made the first icewines for Pillitteri, immediately included icewine in Strewn's portfolio. "Icewine is part of the Canadian image," he says. "It is what we are and what we can do. It is probably our signature wine as a wine region."

In 1998, the winery's biggest icewine vintage, Strewn made 26,000 liters — mostly Vidal plus a bit of barrel-fermented Riesling icewine. With inventory from several other vintages, Will scaled back to 3,500 liters in 2000. "It is easier to make than to sell," he says. His icewine has won critical acclaim, including a grand gold medal at Vinitaly for the 1997 Vidal. "I'm looking to making a full-flavored, full-bodied wine with lots of weight, lots of texture for the Vidal," he says. "It is the intensity and complexity of flavor that is the hallmark of icewine."

Sumac Ridge Estate Winery 17403 Highway 97, Box 307, Summerland, BC V0H 1Z0

Established in 1980, Sumac Ridge makes polished table wines and bottle-fermented sparkling wines. For icewine, the winery has focused on Pinot Blanc, a variety that, because of its moderate acidity but good sugars, yields plump and sweet icewines. One of the shrewdest marketers in the Canadian wine industry, Sumac Ridge was among the first to package icewine in single-service 50-milliliter bottles. About eight thousand bottles of these tiny bottles, all filled and labeled by hand, are made at Sumac Ridge in most vintages. The affordably priced samples, now an industry trend, have introduced thousands to the taste of icewine. Sumac Ridge, which only makes the total equivalent of six thousand half bottles of icewine annually, also packages it in conventional bottles.

Summerhill Estate Winery 4870 Chute Lake Road, Kelowna, BC V1W 4M3

A flamboyant winery opened in 1992 by Stephen Cipes, a flamboyant New Yorker who believes in aging the wines under a pyramid, Summerhill has made Riesling icewine since 1992. (That first icewine went to market with a label reading "Eis Wein.")

While that variety remains the mainstay of a

total annual icewine production of about 10,000 liters, the winery's Pinot Noir icewine has the notoriety of having been Canada's most expensive wine. Made since the mid-1990s, it has sold for just over $100 for a 375 ml bottle. The thin-skinned Pinot Noir grape is not used too often for icewine because it is susceptible to rot. Alan Marks, the consulting winemaker at Summerhill, says the winery is able to keep its icewine Pinot Noir on the vines successfully because there is little rot during the Okanagan's dry and cool autumn nights.

In the 2000 vintage, Josh Scott, Summerhill's new winemaker, made just over 15,000 half bottles of Pinot Noir icewine and 14,500 half bottles of Riesling icewine. New to Summerhill, he also made 3,600 bottles of Merlot icewine. "Our Pinot Noir is popular," he says. "We wanted to experiment with more red icewines."

Sunnybrook Farm Estate Winery 1425 Lakeshore Road, Niagara-on-the-Lake, ON L0S 1J0

Orchardists Gerald Goertz and his spouse Vivien opened Sunnybrook Farm, one of Canada's first fruit wineries, in 1993. It was not easy being a pioneer.

Several established grape wineries objected to Sunnybrook Farm calling itself an estate winery; one winery owner objected when Goertz made a wine from a fruit whose varietal name was the same as that owner's surname. The Wine Council of Ontario refused his membership until he made one hundred cases of grape wine.

When he began making iced wines in 1995, he was prevented for several years from calling them iced (which is why one of his products still is called Winter Pear).

Subsequently, the fruit wineries established a national association, along with a quality assurance program, allaying industry fears that low-quality iced fruit wines would damage the reputation of icewine.

"I do not make plonk," Gerald insists. He overcame his detractors by producing natural wines expressing clean and focused tastes and aromas. Vintage-dated wines, ranging from dry to icewine style, are produced from fruits and berries including apples, pears, peaches, plums, nectarines, cherries, raspberries, strawberries and blueberries.

The iced wines — Iced Peach, Iced Cherry and Winter Pear — are made by freezing fruit and pressing it "the same as you would icewine grapes," Gerald says, adding that "we do not try and make our fruit wines taste and feel like grape wines." Even so, the Iced Peach tastes remarkably like a Vidal icewine.

Thirty Bench Wines 4281 Mountainview Road, Beamsville, ON LOR 1B0

This tiny winery is operated by Dr. Thomas Muckle, one of the most passionate of "amateurs" in Canadian wine in the noblest sense of that word. Born in England in 1931, he came to Canada in 1970 to teach at the McMaster University Medical School in Hamilton. He was living near Ontario wine country but, finding that the products then available tasted like "strawberries and glue," he took a winemaking course and began to make his own.

After his white 1977 Seyval Blanc swept amateur competitions, Muckle gathered partners to develop a vineyard and a winery. He was a founding partner in 1986 of Cave Spring Cellars and, after selling his interest there, established Thirty Bench in 1994 with new partners.

The partners divide the winemaking duties, with Austrian-born Frank Zeritsch, a Hamilton businessman and another accomplished amateur, making the icewines. Why icewine? "Just because it was a challenge," says Muckle, an admirer of Riesling both for table wines and for icewine. "It is a pity to drink them young. They become very luscious in old age."

The Thirty Bench icewines show bracing, but not ripping, acidity when young, with fresh and clean fruit that integrates within a few years, showing rich apricot flavors and often a distinctive hint of truffles in the aroma.

Thomas & Vaughan Winemakers 4245 King Street, Beamsville, ON L0R 1B1

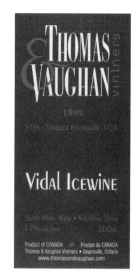

T he winery takes its name from owners Thomas Kocsis and Barbara Vaughan. A second-generation grower with 40 hectares of vineyard, Kocsis opened the winery in 1999 after observing that his grapes were producing award-winning wines elsewhere.

The focus here is on red wines, including an Old Vines Foch and the Bordeaux varietals. The first Vidal icewine was made in 1997. The winery skipped 1998 but produced about 3,000 liters in 1999 and nearly as much in 2000. Under the direction of consulting winemaker Barry Pogue, the winery's 1999 is elegantly balanced with fresh peach and mango flavors.

Tinhorn Creek Vineyards 32830 Tinhorn Creek Road, RR #1, S58, C10, Oliver, BC V0H 1T0

T his cream-colored chateau, grandly overlooking the south Okanagan Valley, was established in 1995. Sandra Oldfield, the California-born winemaker, found that the property included an existing small planting of Kerner, not a variety that figured in her table wine plans. Prior to the 2000 vintage, half of the grapes were sold and the remainder, because of its good acidity and luscious fruit, became award-winning icewine. While Tinhorn Creek is a substantial producer, Oldfield believes in keeping icewine volumes in check, making between four thousand and six thousand half bottles a year (see chapter 9).

Vineland Estates Winery RR #1, 3620 Moyer Road, Vineland, ON L0R 2C0

This winery is based on a demonstration vineyard that was planted in 1979 just outside the village of Vineland by a nurseryman and winemaker from the Mosel, Hermann Weis. He was demonstrating that the Riesling vines he was trying to sell in Canada would thrive in spite of the legendary Canadian winters. By the time Weis sold the winery in 1992 to a Canadian businessman, the brilliantly made Rieslings from Vineland Estates, not to mention the Chardonnay, had dispelled all doubt.

The winery is managed by brothers Allan and Brian Schmidt who grew up in British Columbia. The first icewine, a few hundred liters, was made at Vineland in 1988 from Vidal, backed by what Allan Schmidt remembers as the "unbridled enthusiasm" of Hermann Weis. Since 1989 the Vidal icewines from Vineland often have contained between 10 and 15 per cent Riesling in the blend. The Schmidt brothers have found this gives a backbone of acidity to the plump and fruity Vidal.

Vineland produced 14,000 liters of icewine in 1998, the peak for the decade. As much as half of the production is sold to Asia. "Icewine is an entry point," Allan Schmidt says. "It has given us access to markets where we would not otherwise have been able to prove ourselves. We are now selling our Cabernet Sauvignon [table wine] in Asia."

In the 1999 vintage, the winery also made its first Cabernet Franc icewine, fermenting half in acacia barrels to give an exotic lift to the wine's strawberry flavors. Vineland's 1999 Riesling icewine was made from an early picking, yielding clean, racy fruit. Brian Schmidt, who now handles winemaking, would rather have the grapes on the vines longer, picking up flavors as they weather.

"It's a beautiful wine, quite elegant, but I'd like to see a little more definition," he says of his 1999 Riesling icewine. He was more pleased with the 2000 Riesling icewine, made from a later picking. "It has those caramelized aromas I prefer."

Vinoteca Inc 527 Jevlan Drive, Woodbridge, ON L4L 8W1

One of the turning points for Canadian icewine was the 1993 Vinitaly wine fair in Italy at which several Canadian winemakers won medals. "We Canadians became the wonder of the show," says Vinoteca's Giovanni Follegot. The silver medal won there for his 1991 Vidal, only his second icewine, hangs proudly in the winery which he and his wife Rosanna opened in 1989 in this suburb north of Toronto.

Born in Italy's Veneto wine region, Follegot entered the wine business only after a long career with automobiles. He came to North America in the 1960s to race cars and motorcycles. He settled in Canada after a race meet at Mosport, the original venue for the Canadian Grand Prix, becoming a dealer in Ferrari and other classic European marques. Two immaculate Ferrari cars from his personal collection were in storage in the winery early in 2001. "It's a strange combination, cars and wine, but what are you going to do," Follegot laughs.

The well-equipped winery operates with ideas borrowed from Italy, including its brisk trade in wines in 18-liter containers. While he picked up some winemaking knowledge from his family in Italy, Follegot's mentor in Canada was Klaus Reif, a master at making icewine. "I didn't even know what icewine was," Follegot says. Experience now has given him definite views on the style of Vinoteca icewines. "I try to stay away from syrupy-style wines," he says. "I'll even allow a little oxidation to rub off the sweetness." Follegot also owns tiny Maple Grove Estate Winery near Beamsville and also makes a small quantity of icewine here.

Willow Heights Estate Winery 3751 King St., Vineland, ON L0R 2C0

Nicole Speranzini, this winery's sales and marketing vice-president, remembers the Christmas when her father, Ronald, gave her a ski suit. "I said, 'I don't ski, Dad.' He said it was for icewine picking." Her father is so passionate about making wine that even before he made the first vintage for Willow Heights in 1992, he volunteered to pick icewine grapes for other producers, warding off the cold with fortifying draughts of Sambuca.

Speranzini spent three decades as a steel industry quality assurance manager before giving his full time to Willow Heights. The winery was conceived after he spent 22 years as an amateur winemaker, so accomplished that his peers (now his competitors) encouraged him to become professional. A methodical man, Speranzini first took an extension course in winemaking from the University of California "to get my chemistry up."

Willow Heights opened in a small, rustic building in 1994, moving four years later to an attractive Mediterranean style winery on the wine route just outside Vineland. The flagship wines are Chardonnay and Pinot Noir, but every year Speranzini produces between 300 and 500 cases of Vidal icewine. Stylistically, he strives for clean fruit flavors lifted by piquant acidity. One of his best has been the gold medal–winning 1997 Vidal icewine when the cool growing season yielded a wine that, three years later, still showed youthful freshness, peach flavors and a zesty finish.

12

The Americans

hâteau Grand Traverse, Michigan's first icewine producer, owes its existence to founder Edward O'Keefe's decades-old infatuation with Riesling, a love affair successfully passed on to his two sons. Sean O'Keefe, the younger son, resisted the passion at first, majoring in literature in college, including medieval German writers. Consequently, he learned enough German to enroll in winemaking studies at Geisenheim, equipping himself to work in the family winery under the tutelage of the more experienced Bernd Croissant, the winery's German-trained wine-maker and the author of its recent icewines.

Young O'Keefe proved himself a quick study. In the 1998 vintage, when Château Grand Traverse made Riesling wines in half a dozen styles, Sean came of age by making an elegantly dry Riesling table wine with juice pressed from whole clusters. "We're Riesling nuts," Sean O'Keefe confesses. "I don't think of any other white wine grape with which you can have so much play with different styles and different flavors. And when you can make an icewine, it is the crème de la crème."

Across the United States, other producers are joining the community of wineries that make icewine or, with the help of commercial freezers, dessert wines in the icewine style. Lightly regulated, the American wine industry enjoys a flexibility on icewine production that is not available to most Europeans or Canadians (and, for that matter, not needed in the wintry north). Only a labeling constraint is imposed by the Bureau of Alcohol, Tobacco and Firearms, the American federal regulator that concerns itself with wine. The BATF encourages the use of "ice wine" (American usage breaks it into two words) only for wines made with naturally frozen grapes. When the wine is made from commercially frozen grapes — the process is called cryo-extraction — the producer is expected to come up with a different name, a challenge met easily by most winemakers. The examples run from the simple elegance of *Eis* at Bedell Cellars on New York's Long Island and *Eisrébe* at Joseph Phelps Vineyards in California; to the obscure Latin *Glaciovinum* at Lakewood Vineyards in New York's Finger Lakes; to *Vin de Glacière,* or wine of the ice box, from Randall Grahm, whose Bonny Doon Vineyard in Santa Cruz is the largest producer of icewine-style wines in America.

To take nothing away from the quality of its wines, the success of Bonny Doon has always owed a good deal to Grahm's creative and funny labels, replete with bookish allusions that appeal to English lit graduates like Sean O'Keefe. However, O'Keefe needs no literary devices for the labels at Château Grand Traverse where the icewine is made with naturally frozen grapes. It is among the small number of American wineries within reach of the cold finger of the Canadian winter at the appropriate time almost every year.

Château Grand Traverse was the first winery (and is now one of five or six) on the Old Mission Peninsula, a 40-kilometer-long finger of fertile land extending northwards into Lake Michigan's Grand Traverse Bay. Once given over primarily to cherry and peach orchards, the peninsula in recent times has suffered the encroachment of grand country homes built by individuals escaping the grim industrial landscape of southern Michigan and neighboring states. Edward O'Keefe, who also made his fortune as an industrialist in Detroit and Philadelphia, placed a covenant on his carefully contoured forty-hectare site to protect its future as a producing vineyard and winery.

When he decided to establish a vineyard in 1974, the pioneering O'Keefe had no background in wine or any other alcoholic beverage. Leon Adams, the doyen of American wine writers, incorrectly wrote that O'Keefe was related to a Canadian brewing family of that name. "I have no idea where that came from," O'Keefe says.

There is nothing complicated about his journey to wine; when he began drinking table wines, he was particularly drawn to German wines until he aspired to make wines of comparable quality in Michigan.

O'Keefe's ambition struck his peers as foolhardy, given the mediocrity of Michigan wines at the time. Grapes have been grown in the state (primarily in the southwest corner along Lake Michigan) since the late nineteenth century, in vineyards dominated then, and surprisingly even now, by native labrusca varieties like Concord (now sold for the juice trade). Winemaking was curtailed by Prohibition and, after repeal in 1933, wineries resumed making wines with labrusca and hybrid grapes. They had a market because low state taxes on Michigan wines kept the prices under those of competing wines. "But until very lately," Leon Adams wrote in the 1985 edition of *The Wines of America,* "few of the Michigan wineries tried to produce anything fine."[1]

O'Keefe could see no reason why that should continue even if the agriculturists all told him that the vinifera grapes he so admired would not flourish in Michigan. Common sense told him that vinifera vines are no more tender than the cherries which had grown for decades on the Old Mission Peninsula. "When he planted vinifera here, it wasn't a lark," Sean O'Keefe says. The elder O'Keefe consulted such experts as Dr. Helmut Becker, the renowned grape breeder at Geisenheim. Becker, backed by the University of California at Davis, agreed that Riesling and other vinifera would survive on the peninsula.

Many of the vines at Château Grand Traverse now are 25 years old and producing at their prime. All of the other wineries on the peninsula also grow only vinifera, including Chateau Chantal, the other icewine producer here with vineyards a few kilometers further north, on the highest windblown slopes of this finger of land. The deep bays on either side of the peninsula moderate the climate, causing a late spring bud break but a long autumn when the grapes mature slowly, developing flavor without losing acidity. This is ideal for growing piquant Rieslings.

Winters are bitter, cold enough that in some years ice forms on Lake Michigan. Ice on West Traverse Bay becomes a bridge used by deer to cross the bay, forage on the peninsula and nibble at the grape plants. Violent November winds across the bay often strip late harvest grape bunches from the vines. However, the vines are protected from frost when storms spawned over the Great Lakes dump snow on the vineyards. In 1995, Château Grand Traverse had just began picking icewine grapes on December 8 when an immense storm left only the vine tops exposed. The O'Keefes and employees at the winery resumed picking on December 13 by shoveling snow away from the remaining bunches of grapes.

There was a lot of shoveling to do because the 1995 vintage had been large and the winery, after making all its other Rieslings, had set aside slightly more than half a hectare of the vineyard for icewine. "We made about three thousand half bottles," remembers Sean O'Keefe, who, home from Germany for Christmas, added his broad back to the shovel brigade.

Like the German wineries much admired by the O'Keefes, Château Grand Traverse makes icewine only in those years when the quality of the grapes is judged adequate. None was made in 1998 because the Riesling matured in a hot, dry season and failed to retain enough acidity.

In style, the elegantly balanced icewines at Château Grand Traverse owe much to the German influence that has held sway here almost from the start, including several German-trained wine-makers, among them Mark Johnson, who made the 1992 icewine at the O'Keefe winery and who later became the winemaker at Chateau Chantal up the road. The latter winery, which opened in 1993, regularly makes small quantities of hand-crafted icewines which serve as a talking point for their other Michigan wines.

"It is mostly a novelty, a feather in our cap," Chateau Chantal's Elizabeth Berger says. "California can't do an icewine, so it gives us a lead [with consumers] into why some varieties do better in a cool climate." With Sean O'Keefe, the icewine and the winery's other fine Rieslings are his calling card during his frequent trips to other wine regions. The quality allows him to confront the issue of the reputation of the state's wines. "I'm so used to being from Michigan and always having a chip on my shoulder," he admits.

Across the continent in Washington state where cold winters are sometimes deep enough to damage vines, a handful of wineries has produced icewine, including that state's largest producer, Stimson Lane Vineyards and Estates. The wineries under Stimson Lane are Chateau Ste. Michelle and Columbia Crest. Neither has been a frequent producer of icewine because, while Washington vineyards get cold, the freezing temperatures often occur so late in the year that there is too much risk for growers.

"Cryo-extraction is an option but we have chosen to do it naturally," Bob Betz, Stimson Lane's vice-president for enology research, said in 1999. "In thirty-two vintages at Chateau Ste. Michelle, we made two icewines and in fourteen vintages at Columbia Crest, we made three." Two of those at Columbia Crest were made in the same year: the 1997 vintage was picked and vinified in January 1998 and the 1998 vintage was processed in December that year. "It was one of those freaky things," he laughs.

In those rare years when nature cooperates, the wineries will make perhaps 24,000 bottles of Riesling icewine in total, quite enough that Betz still was offering tastings of the 1995s from both wineries at the end of the decade. The style is comparable to German Eisweine, although with higher alcohol levels because Washington vineyards have no trouble ripening Riesling. "My thinking," Betz says, "is that an icewine needs to show really clean fruit."

In between the producers that make entirely natural icewines and those that employ the nearest commercial freezer, there are those wineries that use both methods at the same time. One example is Hunt Country Vineyards, a farm winery that Art and Joyce Hunt run near Branchport on Keuka Lake, one of New York's Finger Lakes.

"It really infuriates us, the focus on how the grape is frozen," says Tim Benedict, the winemaker, who resents suggestions that Hunt Country might be cheating to produce its superb Vidal icewines. At Hunt Country, the icewine grapes stay on the vines well beyond the end of the normal vintage to develop honeyed flavors during the early winter cycles of freezing and thawing. In late November or in December, when Benedict judges the hang time to be sufficient and when the grapes are frozen, they are picked and kept in cold storage at the correct icewine temperature until there is a lull in the vintage and the winemaker has time to deal with icewine. The key to a good icewine, he insists, is the hang time. "In the end, to me it is irrelevant how it is frozen."

A glance at a map explains why the Finger Lakes are called by that name. Slender water-filled scars carved by retreating glaciers, they modify the continental climate enough to permit viticulture. Some of the first vineyards were planted near Hammondsport at the south end of Keuka Lake early in the nineteenth century. The settlers that arrived as the century progressed included the Hunt family who developed the 70-hectare farm on which the Hunt Country winery has been built.

Art Hunt, who turned 50 in 1999, is the sixth generation of his family to run the farm. The winery was developed to support a young family and offer an opportunity to keep the property in the Hunt family for the seventh generation. In 1973, soon after graduating from college, Hunt and his wife, Joyce, took over the farm — then devoted to general agriculture — and began planting red wine grapes, primarily labrusca, for the Taylor wine company. By the time the vineyard was producing, consumer tastes had shifted abruptly to white wines, while Coca-Cola Ltd. took over Taylor and began moving it to California.

"There went the market for wine grapes," Hunt recalls. "So a few of us decided we would have to start our own small wineries." He and others replaced some of the labrusca grapes with better wine grapes, both hybrids and vinifera. He opened the doors at Hunt Country in 1982 with wines from the 1981 vintage and has created a winery with the capacity to make 50,000 gallons (almost 200,000 liters) a year.

"Now, 20 years later, we have re-invented the New York wine industry as a premium world-class wine industry making some extremely nice cold climate wines," says Hunt, now one of perhaps 50 Finger Lakes wineries.

The production of icewine is comparatively recent and is limited to a handful of the wineries, many of which are content to make late harvest wines from varieties like Riesling and Vignoles. The latter, sometimes still called Ravat Blanc, a variation of the original name assigned to it by its French creator, has carved a niche for off-dry wines because the grape has unusually high acidity even when mature and because the tight bunches are readily infected with botrytis.

Compared with naturally made icewine, late harvest dessert wines are less risky and, arguably, equally profitable. The first icewines in the Finger Lakes, recounts Art Hunt, were produced in the early 1980s at the experimental cellars at the Great Western winery in Hammondsport. Once a leading producer of sparkling wines, Great Western passed through a succession of owners in the 1980s. The icewine trials were a casualty of this instability but not before Hunt was inspired to make icewine.

"One time in November, I was out in the [Great Western] vineyard," Hunt recalls. "It was a very cold day and there were grapes left on the vine. I tasted them and they were like the most wonderful sorbet and I realized these were the Vidal icewine grapes. A few years later, when we had some Vidal producing, we decided to make it." That first icewine, only a few hundred cases, was made in 1987. "It turned out wonderfully and we won all kinds of awards ... and it happened year after year. We realize that we are just fortunate to be in an ideal climate right here on Keuka Lake for getting very intense fruit flavors in our icewine grapes. We are now considered one of the best producers in the United States."

Hunt Country has sought to make icewine every year since, with the exception of 1996, a season that was so hot that the overripe Vidal lacked the necessary acidity. In 1997 a severe windstorm in early November blew most of the grapes off the vines and only three hundred cases (twelve half bottles in each case) of wine was salvaged. Hunt Country recovered in the bounteous 1998 harvest to produce about fifteen hundred cases, also making the winery one of the largest icewine producers in the eastern United States. At the urging of its agents, Hunt Country has begun to explore exports to Asia and the Caribbean.

The grapes meant for icewine typically remain on the vine into early December, by which time the freeze-thaw cycles have begun to brown the skins of the Vidal and to create the plum and raisin flavors that Hunt believes are desirable for icewine. The grapes are picked frozen and are placed in a walk-in freezer. "We can't press more than one ton at a time," Hunt explains. "And we can get the temperature to an ideal degree to get the maximum quality of flavor." By leaving the grapes hanging until December without any protective netting, Hunt Country accepts the losses from winds and birds that other American producers prevent by picking earlier and letting freezers do nature's work.

"We get the quality that you just don't quite get picking them at normal harvest, say mid-October, and freezing them," Hunt says. "That makes a very nice, clean, sweet, intense wine but it does not have quite as much complexity. That comes as those grapes freeze and thaw during the Indian summers. The freezing seems to be what loosens the flavors from the skins."

While Art Hunt drew his inspiration from munching frozen Vidal in the Great Western vineyard, Bill Wagner at Wagner Vineyards got his from California's Randall Grahm. The Californian, who had already begun making acclaimed dessert wines in 1986 with commercially frozen grapes, visited the Finger Lakes in 1988 to purchase labrusca grapes for brandy production. John Herbert, one of the two veteran winemakers at Wagner Vineyards, remembers Grahm describing his technique.

"Bill thought that was very interesting," Herbert says. "That fall, we sent a few tons of grapes to a freezer plant." Since then, a similar approach has been adopted by other Finger Lakes producers that make icewine-style wines. "It takes a long time to get cold here," Herbert says. The necessary freeze for naturally made icewines seldom occurs before late December and by then, most growers would have suffered substantial losses to birds, wind and other hazards. With no rules to the contrary, it is more sensible to pick the ripe grapes into 40-pound plastic boxes and truck them 160 kilometers to the commercial freezers maintained on Lake Erie by the big vegetable processors. They are brought back when Herbert and Ann Raffetto, the other winemaker at Wagner, have time to deal with them. Since Wagner now produces about one hundred thousand gallons a year in a vintage that begins in early September, the winemakers have much to contend with besides making icewine. A recent list of wines available at the winery ran to 32 selections.

Bill Wagner is one of the great entrepreneurs of New York wine. A native of the Finger Lakes region, he was among those who were struggling to make a living as grape growers until the state in 1976 allowed farm wineries. Anticipating that, Wagner began building his winery in 1975, an optimistically large octagonal facility overlooking his vineyards near Lodi on the east side of Seneca Lake. His optimism was not misplaced. With Wagner Vineyards as a volume leader, there now are 21 wineries in the Seneca Lake Winery Association, while a number of others operate independently of the association. In the meantime, the Wagner family has acquired one hundred hectares of vineyard, opened a small craft brewery and turned the winery's former sandwich parlor into one of the best restaurants in the Finger Lakes.

The grapes sent to the freezer after Wagner's 1988 conversation with Grahm were Vidal and Vignoles. "Icewine is a perfect use for Vignoles," Raffetto says. A California native with a degree in fermentation science, she shares the winemaking in a seamless partnership with Herbert, a Philadelphian whose experience is entirely hands on. (He was part of Bill Wagner's construction crew in 1975.) They once tried to make a dry table wine from Vignoles and concluded it cannot be done because Vignoles retains aggressive acidity even as it becomes lusciously sweet in maturity. But as a dessert wine, Vignoles delivers a rush of exotically tropical flavors made more complex by the grape's affinity to attract botrytis.

"It always ends up being our sweetest icewine," Raffetto says. It is a favorite in the tasting room and one of Wagner's most potent entries in wine competitions, bringing home 21 gold or double gold medals by 1998. Wagner also began making small lots of Riesling icewine in 1989, scoring gold medals as well.

With so much else happening in the winery, Wagner has chosen to limit its icewine output and, in some years, not making any at all if the tasting room still has enough of the previous vintage. In 1998, the production was 850 bottles of Riesling, 770 bottles of Vignoles and 650 of Vidal. The winery discontinued icewine from the pungently flavored Delaware grape, a native American variety, after trial lots in 1995 and 1997. "It just seemed redundant," Raffetto says. "The grapes themselves are so concentrated."

13

A Parade of American Producers

While wine is grown in almost every state in the United States, few of the vineyards are far enough north to get the deep early winter cold needed for classical icewine. This has not prevented many producers from making wines in the icewine style with the aid of commercial freezers. Unlike Europe and Canada, simulated icewine is not prohibited. However, the regulators ask that the term "Ice Wine" be used only on labels of naturally made icewine. The others are marketed under a host of creative proprietary names, such as Eis or Glaciovinum. While the distinction is not always enforced, the arrangement generally ensures that consumers understand what they are buying.

In any event, the pricing sends a clear signal, with simulated icewines typically selling for half the price of natural icewines. Arguably, the simulated icewines are excellent value. Icewine is appealing because the aromas and flavors are fresh, clean and full of exotic fruit. Logically, a wine made from healthy grapes frozen at the peak of maturity should deliver all of these qualities. Those who defend natural icewines contend that grapes need to remain on the vines late into the year, even suffering some desiccation, to produce icewines whose character and complexity rises above the clean simplicity of simulated icewines.

This debate primarily concerns wine critics, justifying countless comparative icewine tastings. The average American consumer, however, understands that he has the best of both worlds: a vast selection of good value wines in the icewine style as well as a selection of naturally made icewines whose quality rivals the best in the world.

Apex See Washington Hills, p. 291

Bedell Cellars: Main Road (Rt. 25), Cutchoque, NY, 11935

O ne of 20 Long Island wineries, this one was founded in 1980 by Kip and Susan Bedell and has since garnered accolades for its vinifera table wines — notably Merlot — grown on 12 hectares on this long finger of New York State that jabs into Long Island Sound.

The Bedells began making what they call *Eis* in 1992 and, within five years, achieved the recognition to have it served at a $25,000-a-person presidential fundraising dinner in 1998. The non-vintage dessert wine is made with Riesling grapes with five per cent Gewürztraminer in the blend. Given Long Island's maritime climate, the freezer at a local shellfish wholesaler stands in for nature. Kip Bedell produces about 1,800 half bottles a year. The wine's several gold medals include one from the International Eastern Wine Competition in 1997.

Bonny Doon Vineyard PO Box 8376, Santa Cruz, CA, 95061

B onny Doon's Randall Grahm is one of California's wittiest winemakers, whether it comes to labels or to wine. Born in Los Angeles in 1953, his first tour at university as a "permanent" liberal arts major equipped him to sweep floors at a Beverly Hills wine shop. After what he calls the exceptional good fortune of tasting "a goodly number of great French wines," the now focused Grahm earned a viticulture degree at the University of California in Davis in 1979. Two years later he bought a vineyard property in the Santa Cruz Mountains, opening the Bonny Doon winery in 1983.

After a brief infatuation with Pinot Noir, Grahm became, as he puts it, "ideologically committed" to Rhone varieties such as Grenache and Syrah. When Grahm released his first "Rhone" red in 1986, he called it *Le Cigare Volant*. That means Flying Cigar, inspired by a pompous civic ordinance made in the Châteauneuf-du-Pape region in 1954 prohibiting the landing of flying saucers.

Among Grahm's other inventions is an icewine that he calls *Vin de Glacière*, or wine of the ice box. "After a couple of years of experimentation with different techniques of concentrating grape must," Grahm says, "we began producing this product in 1986 by post-harvest freezing of grapes." The grapes are picked at a normal maturity of about 23° Brix, flash frozen and pressed while still frozen. The concentrated juice is fermented very slowly, the winery having determined that a cool, languid ferment yields a creamier texture to the wine. Grahm confessed, in one of the winery's cheeky newsletters, that "this was discovered by accident as we tried in vain to induce greater vigor to our putatively wimped out, Marcel Proust-like yeastie population."[2]

The grape variety used initially was Muscat Canelli. Grahm first called it *Vin de Glace*. When the regulators objected — "over my protestations that this simply meant 'wine of ice cream'" — he renamed it in 1988. Never one to consider that there can be too much of a good thing, Grahm made wine of the ice box not only from Muscat Canelli but also from Malvasia Bianca, Orange Muscat, Gewürztraminer, Riesling, Sémillon and Grenache.

Finally in 1995 he recognized that he had a confusing plethora of icewines and focused on what came to be called Muscat Vin de Glacière. The blend was half Muscat Canelli and 25 per cent each of Orange Muscat and Malvasia Bianca. For the 1998 version, the blend was 70 per cent Muscat Canelli, 23 per cent Orange Muscat and 7 per cent Malvasia. The wine was permitted to ferment to almost 13 per cent alcohol.

"The paradigm is definitely more *sauternais* than Teutonic Ice," Grahm wrote in a quite typical tasting note. "Again, all of the usual suspects: intense pear and extremely patriotic apple-pie in the nose; more discreet suggestions of apricot and pineapple with a healthy scoop of butterscotch topping. This wine is reminiscent of the dessert tray that is brought to you in those multi-*étoiled* French restaurants where you are encouraged to make yourself one with everything." The annual production of this thespian dessert wine, so reflecting its creator, is about 170,000 half bottles and the wine retails for about US$15.

Casa Larga Vineyards Inc. 2287 Turk Hill Rd., Fairport, NY 14450

Italian-born Andrew Colaruotolo — his colleagues simply call him Mr. C — arrived in the United States in 1950 and became a successful home builder before planting a two-hectare vineyard in 1974 near Fairport, in New York's Finger Lakes district. The vineyard and the subsequent winery were named Casa Larga after the vineyard in Italy that his grandparents had owned and where he learned viticulture.

The table wines and the sparkling wines are made primarily with vinifera grapes. In 1995 when Casa Larga decided to make icewine for the first time, it chose to employ Vidal. Typically, the grapes are harvested in mid-January, frozen on the vine, and the wine spends six months in stainless steel before being bottled. Annual production is about 2,400 half bottles.

In obeisance to his roots, Mr. C has given the icewine a poetic

Italian name, *Fiori Delle Stelle,* or Flower of the Stars. The recommended food pairing is Brie en Croute. The wine has earned Mr. C a fistful of medals at wine competitions across the country.

Chateau Benoit 6580 NE Mineral Springs Road, Carlton, OR 97111

F red and Mary Benoit, who started this Oregon winery in 1972, memorialized two granddaughters with Chateau Benoit's icewine-style dessert wines. The new owners who took over in 1999 from the retiring Benoit family have continued the charming tradition. Sweet Sophia, made with Riesling, was introduced in 1993, soon to be followed by Sweet Marie, a blend of Riesling and Gewürztraminer. Both are made by freezing mature grapes at harvest, with particular attention paid to achieving the correct balancing acidity. "We sense that too many dessert wines are overblown, with too much sweetness and added acidity," the winery says in a cellar note on Sweet Sophia. The two wines are made when sales require them. The winery made 3,300 half bottles of Sweet Sophia in 1998, skipped a year; made it again in 2000 while skipping Sweet Marie.

Chateau Chantal 15900 Rue du Vin, Old Mission Peninsula, Traverse City, MI 49686

O pened in 1993, this Michigan winery is on a 26-hectare estate at a high point on the Old Mission Peninsula, a 40-km-long finger of land on the 45th parallel. The winery made 264 half bottles of Riesling icewine in 1993, picking on the day before Christmas when the temperature was a brisk -13°C.

"We usually have warm summer afternoons and cool evenings, which allow the grapes to ripen nicely without losing their acidity," says Elizabeth Berger, one of the owners. "Rieslings especially like our climate and appellation."

Chateau Chantal next made 930 half bottles of icewine in 1995 (another Christmas Eve harvest) and 683 half bottles in 1997 (a New Year's Eve harvest). The wines all are powerful and concentrated. For example, the 1997 icewine, while properly sweet and fruity, also has 13 per cent alcohol.

The winery, whose total production is 10,000 cases a year, makes icewine whenever the weather cooperates. Chateau Chantal's location on the spine of the peninsula, while affording great views from the bed and breakfast suites, does pose challenges. The plastic sheets used to protect the winter harvest grapes from rain only are moderately effective against birds and raccoons. One year a November gale sweeping across the Great Lakes blew the entire icewine crop from the vines.

Château Grand Traverse: 12239 Center Road, Traverse City, MI 49686

Based on 40 hectares of vineyards on the Old Mission Peninsula, this winery, now producing 36,000 cases a year, was northern Michigan's first when it was established in 1974 by Edward O'Keefe, Jr. It was also the first commercial planting of European varieties in an area where the winter temperatures can plunge well below freezing. With encouragement from the late Dr. Helmut Becker, then the head of plant breeding at Geisenheim in Germany, O'Keefe pressed ahead. He reasoned, correctly, that the deep waters of Grand Traverse Bay on both sides of the narrow peninsula would moderate the winters as well as ensure a long, cool growing season. The winery began making Riesling icewine almost as soon as the vines were producing fruit, making it one of America's most experienced producers.

N ow one of the largest wineries in Washington, Chateau Ste. Michelle has been making wines since 1967 but is a rare producer of icewine because nature does not always provide the required freezing temperature. "Cryo-extraction is not a bad option but we have chosen to do it naturally," says Bob Betz, who is the vice-president of enology research at Stimson Lane Vineyards & Estates, the parent of Chateau Ste. Michelle. The winery's 1995 White Riesling Icewine Reserve, of which about 10,000 half bottles were made, was the first vintage since 1978 when less than 5,000 half bottles were made.

"It was the product of a very cold winter," Betz remembers of the 1978 icewine. The grapes were picked in early November after a brutal cold front snapped across eastern Washington. "I think we had left Riesling hanging," says Betz, struggling to remember that long-ago vintage. "But I can't recall if we just got darned lucky."

In 1995 winemaker Mike Januik was paying careful attention to the weather trends as the vintage came to a close. When the long-range forecast predicted cold temperatures, about two hectares of Riesling were left for icewine in its 800-hectare Patterson vineyard in the Columbia Valley, a vineyard on the east side of the Cascade Mountains which the winery shares with Columbia Crest, another of the Stimson Lane producers. The dry climate in this region promotes healthy grapes, important for making icewines with clean, bright fruit. Chateau Ste. Michelle further ensured itself of pristine icewine fruit by selecting any botrytized grapes for its regular late harvest Riesling.

"As luck would have it," Januik explains in a tasting note on the 1995 wine, "a cold front hit the area on November 2." The grapes were picked at -10°C and below, with the harvest beginning at midnight and finishing by dawn. (Stimson Lane wineries routinely pick all wine grapes at night so that cool, unoxidized fruit reaches the wineries.) The icewine was fermented in stainless steel and bottle-aged for a full year before being released, giving the wine time to become smoothly integrated. Januik's description: "Sweet aromas of summer fruits — apricots and peaches — swirl together with honey and a hint of fresh flowers. On the palate luscious flavors of peaches and apricots repeat ..."

Columbia Crest, which has been producing wines since 1984, made its first icewine in 1995 from Patterson vineyard grapes that were slightly botrytized. The outcome is a significantly different, if equally satisfying, wine. The juice for the Columbia Crest icewine was 31.5° Brix compared to Chateau Ste. Michelle's 36.6° Brix. As a result, the light and easy Columbia Crest wine is less concentrated but, with the botrytis, resembles a late harvest Riesling. In 1998 Columbia Crest produced two "vintages" of icewine — one from a January harvest of 1997 Sémillon and another from a December harvest of 1998 Riesling. "It was one of those freaky things," Bob Betz laughs. Curiously, Columbia Crest gave the Sémillon a 1998 vintage date.

Claar Cellars 1081 Glenwood Road, Mathews Corner, Pasco, WA 99301

The Claar family, which has farmed in this corner of Washington state since irrigation became available in 1950, planted a vineyard in 1980, with the primary variety being Riesling. The winemakers buying the grapes so often complimented the quality of the fruit that Crista Claar (the name rhymes with air) and husband Bob Whitelatch, both former U.S. Navy officers, established an estate winery in 1997 with 32 hectares of vineyard.

In that vintage, they learned just how flavor-packed their Riesling was when they produced their first icewine, a botrytized Riesling harvested on November 12, 1997. It is rare anywhere in the world to find an icewine with botrytis but nowhere more so than southeast Washington where the dessert dryness seldom promotes botrytis. That year the Claar vineyard, facing south toward the Columbia River, benefited from enough mist that the grapes were touched with noble rot. Claar produced about 7,200 half bottles. The wine was among the top 25 icewines in a "Best of Riesling" competition organized by Germany in 2000 — and was the only icewine in that group not from either Germany or Austria.

In each succeeding vintage through 2000, grapes were left for icewine but the necessary freeze never occurred. As it happened, Thomas DiBello, who made Claar's 1997 icewine, became the winemaker at CedarCreek in British Columbia in 2000, where he expects to have the right conditions for icewine every vintage.

Covey Run Winery 1500 Vintage Road, Zillah, WA, 98953

N amed for the coveys of quail on its property, this winery was formed in 1982 by a group of growers unable to sell their grapes at a reasonable price because of surplus. The wines, however, sold very well and Covey Run has become one of Washington's leading producers.

Icewine has been made in the 1995 and 1997 vintages from Riesling grapes grown in the winery's Whiskey Canyon vineyard. (The name of the vineyard is said to date from the American Prohibition era when smugglers buried contraband spirits here.) Kerry Norton, Covey Run's winemaker, gets some of his best reds from this vineyard, while the versatile Riesling vines are employed in all styles from bone-dry to the ultimate of late harvest wines.

In its tasting notes Covey Run observes that the "world of wine is full of examples of adversity being turned into greatness. Icewine is when perfectly good grapes are frozen on the vine by an early frost ... until there is just a tiny drop of sweet nectar left in each berry."

The wines are classic examples: apricot and honey aromas signal the luscious sweetness which is balanced by bright acidity. Covey Run made 2,100 half bottles in 1995 and nearly 9,500 in 1997.

Duck Pond Cellars 23145 Highway 99 W., Dundee, OR 97115

This small winery established in Oregon's Willamette Valley in 1989 by the Fries family has made its mark with table wines.

In 1997 Greg Fries, the winemaker, decided to make an icewine, as much to satisfy his winemaking curiosity as anything else. The winery grows Sémillon at a vineyard it owns in eastern Washington and, during the regular picking, Fries left one row of vines, 305 meters long. Those were picked some weeks later and placed in cold storage, to be pressed after the hectic regular vintage was over. That row of Sémillon yielded 315 liters. All the wine was packed in half bottles with the label etched directly onto the glass.

Elk Cove Vineyards 27751 NW Olson Road, Gaston, OR 97119

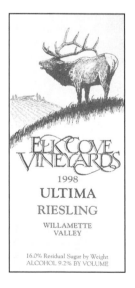

ELK COVE
VINEYARDS
1998
ULTIMA
RIESLING
WILLAMETTE
VALLEY
16.0% Residual Sugar by Weight
ALCOHOL 9.2% BY VOLUME

The seventh-oldest winery in Oregon, Elk Cove was founded in 1973 by Joe Campbell, an emergency-room physician, and his wife, Pat. In the 1800s, her great-grandparents, immigrants from Switzerland, grew grapes and made wine near the Oregon community of Helvetia. The Campbells rekindled a passion for wine while he was studying medicine at California's Stanford University.

Joe Campbell has applied a motto from medicine, "First Do No Harm," to the gentle and careful handling of grapes in the winery. Since 1989 under the name Ultima, Elk Cove has been making wines in the icewine style primarily from Riesling and occasionally from Gewürztraminer, with the help of a commercial freezer since this part of Oregon,

Yamhill County southwest of Portland, is unlikely to have natural icewine temperatures.

The 1989 Ultima Riesling won an accolade and 90 points from Robert Parker, the influential wine critic. All of the four subsequent vintages (1992, 1994, 1996 and 1998) have received similar or higher scores from various critics.

The 1998 Riesling Ultima, of which 9,600 half bottles were made, was finished with 16 per cent residual sugar and 9.2 per cent alcohol; the tasting notes describe it as having "aromas of honeydew melon and apricot [with] broad flavors of peach pie." Elk Cove only makes the wine whenever it needs more to satisfy a cult following.

Eola Hills Wine Cellars 501 South Pacific Highway, Rickreal, OR 97371

Established in 1986 and now the fourth largest winery in Oregon, Eola Hills already had a reputation for its Pinot Noir and Chardonnay before adding icewine-style wines to its range in 1992. The winery picks grapes late in the season, often with some botrytis, and places them in a freezer for pressing in December.

The first of these wines, called *Vin d'Epice,* was produced with Gewürztraminer, with about five per cent of Muscat to underline the spiciness. The tasting notes describe this wine as "unctuous, honeyed and spicy ... a magnificent dessert wine with intense varietal character."

In 1995 Eola Hills added *Vin d'Or,* a comparable wine made with Sauvignon Blanc barrel-fermented in new French oak. This is said to have aromas of vanilla, honey and pineapple with "perhaps just a touch of ginger" in the taste. Annual production of each now is between eight hundred and nine hundred cases (a dozen half bottles in a case). The wines retail at the winery for about US$16. "Once they taste it, they buy it," marketing manager Scott Gunderson says.

Now the flagship among the wineries owned by Paramount Distillers of Cleveland, Firelands began making Vidal icewine by the natural method in 1995. Firelands has eight hectares of vineyards on North Bass Island, a small, flat island in Lake Erie where grapes have grown for more than 150 years. Closer to the Canadian shore of the lake than to Sandusky on the American side, it is one of a string of islands that includes nearby Pelee Island where a Canadian winery of that name has its major vineyards.

North Bass Island, once given over to native American varieties, now grows vinifera almost exclusively (Vidal is the exception) which, in the hands Claudio Salvador, the Italian-born winemaker at Firelands, yield some of Ohio's best wines.

Ed Boas, the president of Firelands, maintains that North Bass Island, with 202 frost-free days and low rainfall, has an excellent climate and the soils for growing grapes, "except," he laments, "that it is on an island." Because no commercial ferry serves the island, where only six families are year-round residents, Firelands owns an old fishing boat to transport the grapes to its winery in Sandusky. There can be no assurance that the icewine grapes will be ready to pick before the lake begins to freeze. In the 1998 harvest, which took place just before Christmas, Boas chartered a light aircraft to airlift, if necessary, the ton of frozen Vidal grapes to the winery (at least three flights would have been needed). "But the ice held off," he says.

Icewine production at Firelands has ranged from one thousand to two thousand bottles a year but the wine, polished and not overly sweet, has been received so well that Boas would like to make more. "It's a good door opener for our market and our salespeople," he says.

See Vinifera Wine Cellars

Heritage Wine Cellars Inc. 12162 East Main Road, North East, PA 16428

F ounded in 1977, this winery on Pennsylvania's Erie shore began producing Vidal icewine in 1995 by natural methods when Robert Bostwick, the owner, recognized the rising popularity of icewine. Initially, he was buying the fruit to make 1,500 liters a year from local growers willing to take a risk on a harvest that can occur any time between late November and late December if wind storms do not blow the grapes off the vines. Subsequently, he has had to plant two acres of Vidal on his own property. "It is getting too difficult to find growers who are willing to let it hang," he says.

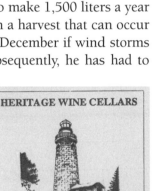

Bostwick produces a vast range of wines, including berry wines, and all can be sampled in the Heritage tasting room, even the icewine. There is one exception, a white varietal called Gladwin 113 with flavors somewhat similar to Riesling.

"It has the distinction of being the rarest wine in America," Bostwick says. The variety was created in the 1920s by a plant scientist at Cornell University named Gladwin and, somehow, Bostwick's grandfather got some plants. Today, Bostwick nurtures five hundred vines in his vineyard and sells every bottle of Gladwin 113 he makes for $25, almost as much as he gets for his icewine.

Hinman Vineyards/Silvan Ridge 27012 Briggs Hill Road, Eugene, OR 97405

E stablished in 1979, Hinman Ridge releases its premium and specialty wines under the Silvan Ridge label. That includes a cryo-extracted icewine, made since the early 1990s. The early Silvan Ridge icewines were made with Huxelrebe, a German cross which ripens to succulent sweetness. But Silvan Ridge has such a small quantity of this grape that it switched to Gewürztraminer for icewines in 1997 and again in 1999. In the latter vintage Bryan Wilson, the winemaker, made about 2,400 bottles. He skipped the 2000 vintage to make a Port-style wine but planned another icewine in 2001.

Wilson sources the grapes from a warm site in Oregon's Umpqua Valley which delivers lusciously ripe fruit. "The Gewürztraminer is just gorgeous," he says. "The icewine, when it is young, is packed with spicy, clove-like flavours." For Hinman Vineyards, which makes 25,000 cases of wine a year, the Silvan Ridge icewine is what Wilson calls "the punctuation mark" in its range.

Huber Orchard Winery, 19816 Huber Road, Starlight, IN 47106

T he Huber family can trace its wine heritage at least as far back as ancestor Simon Huber, who left Baden Baden in Germany in 1843 to come to the United States. The farming Hubers have prospered by serving the market in nearby Louisville with products ranging from Christmas trees to apples and peaches. A winery was added in 1978.

Seventh-generation Ted Huber, who now is the winemaker, has 15 hectares of grapes, almost exclusively French hybrids or North American varieties such as Niagara and Catawba. He also produces well-regarded strawberry and raspberry wines. "We're trying to make a real Midwestern wine, good wines that people can't get elsewhere," he says. The icewine is called *Indiana Autumn Frost.* Since deep natural frosts almost never occur, the fruit for this wine is placed in a commercial freezer. Tasting notes describe the wine as having "a clear straw color, with a subtle honey-and-orange-blossom aroma and an intensely sweet, fruity flavor that almost overwhelms an underlying structure of acidity."

Hunt Country Vineyards 4021 Italian Hill Road, Branchport, NY 14418

The Hunt family were pioneer farmers at Keuka Lake, in the Finger Lakes region of New York, in the early 1880s. The winery was established in 1982 on the family farm by Arthur and Joyce Hunt, the sixth generation of the family to run the farm.

Art Hunt's interest in icewine was fired when he tasted some intensely sweet and slightly frozen Vidal grapes in a nearby vineyard. When the Vidal vines that he planted began producing, he and his winemaker, Tim Benedict, began making icewine in 1987. The Hunt Country wine has been so successful that the annual production now is about fifteen hundred half-bottle cases a year, making this one of the largest icewine producers in New York state.

Hunt and Benedict, a former jazz drummer who grew up in nearby Penn Yan, believe that the grapes need to go through several cycles of freezing and thawing to develop the honeyed and raisined flavors in the wine. The grapes usually are picked in December and are brought to the desired degree of freezing by being placed in a walk-in freezer before being pressed. "In the end, how it's frozen is irrelevant," Benedict believes. "It is really the condition of the grape when it is frozen that is the key to the flavor."

Leland and Lynda Hyatt planted their Washington vineyards in 1983 and made the first vintage in 1987. The winery now produces about 35,000 cases a year, focusing on mainstream varietal reds and whites.

For classically made icewine, however, Hyatt employs the Black Muscat grape in those years when nature gives the vineyard the necessary hard frost. In 1998 Hyatt was able to make about 2,800 half bottles of a wine which showed aromas of pineapples and strawberries, with honey and mango flavors.

Frederick S. Johnson Vineyards West Main Road, Westfield, NY 14787

This boutique winery, established in 1961 on western New York's Lake Erie shore, notes proudly that the grapes it processes all are grown within 3,000 feet of the winery. This is in the best tradition of careful estate winemaking.

"Grapes start to deteriorate the moment they are picked," the winery explains, "and the further they must be transported and the longer the time until they are crushed, the greater this problem becomes."

For its icewine, Johnson vinifies naturally frozen Vidal grapes which, because they are near to the winery, can be pressed soon after being picked without the risk of warming a few undesirable degrees.

The winery also is known for another dessert wine that it calls Liebeströpfchen, or "love's little drops." Made with Delaware, a native American grape, it an intensely fruity sweet wine with overtones of botrytis. The flavors are so concentrated that the winery suggests it can even be served with ice.

Joseph Phelps Vineyards PO Box 1031, 200 Taplin Rd., St. Helena, CA 94574

R enowned now for its red table wines, Joseph Phelps Vineyards has an icewine because the original winemaker, Walter Schug, was from Germany and influenced the winery's initial dedication to Riesling and other whites when it was founded in 1973. The wines were well-made even if the varietals were not optimum for the Napa Valley.

One of the varietals planted in the winery's Spring Valley vineyards just outside St. Helena was Scheurebe, a full-flavored wine grape developed in Germany in 1916 and occasionally used in powerful Eisweine there and in Austria. Late harvest wines have been made at Phelps with Scheurebe since 1978; the 1983 Special Select Late Harvest was claimed to be "the first Trockenbeerenauslese-style Scheurebe" made in the United States.

In 1994, Craig Jones, the winemaker who succeeded Schug, put some of the grapes into a commercial freezer and the winery since has been producing about 12,000 half bottles annually of what it cleverly calls *Eisrébe*. His notes on the 1997 vintage described it as a medium-bodied dessert wine. With only 7.5 per cent alcohol but residual sugar of 17 per cent, the wine has citrus, pear and spice flavors.

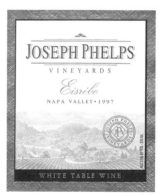

Sadly, the Scheurebe vines are nearing the end of their productive life. Because the vineyard is near to the Napa River and susceptible to a grape malady called Pearce's Disease, there is a possibility that olive trees will replace grape vines and *Eisrébe* will become a memory.

Karly Wines 11076 Bell Road, Plymouth, CA 95669

T his Amador County winery is best known for its Zinfandel, Syrah, Marsanne and Sauvignon Blanc but every year since

1988 it has made about 50 cases of an icewine-style Orange Muscat wine, available only at the winery's tasting room and by mail order. Orange Muscat grapes mature in August when there is no possibility of letting nature freeze the grapes, not that nature will ever deliver classic icewine temperatures in Amador County. So the grapes are picked at maturity and stored in a commercial freezer until the normal crush is completed, when they are retrieved and crushed.

"The smell in the winery is ethereal and it is a happy finale for each harvest," the winery says in a tasting note. "The wine is exotic and delicious smelling and tasting of apricots, pineapple, honey and oranges."

Winery owners Buck Cobb and his wife Karly (who inspired the winery's name when it was established in 1979) enjoy this wine in summer over chilled slices of fresh fruit with cream.

King Estate Winery 80854 Territorial Road, Eugene, OR 97405

One of Oregon's largest wineries (about 100,000 cases a year), King Estate first made what it calls Vin Glacé in 1998 with Pinot Gris. This is one of the two major varieties — the other being

Pinot Noir — on which King Estates is focused. For the icewine, very ripe grapes are frozen at harvest before being pressed.

In the 1999 vintage, when the winery made about 3,500 half bottles, the juice was 34° Brix and the finished Vin Glacé had 15 per cent residual sugar.

"We allow the winemakers to do something that will make them happy," quips Marion Vogler, a sales administrator. "Having this icewine also is really nice for winemakers' dinners. I haven't poured it for anyone that doesn't like it."

This Washington state winery, which makes a total of 20,000 cases of wine a year, is based on a vineyard in the Yakima Valley that was purchased as raw land in 1972 by John and Ann Williams. Since then eight other vineyards and almost as many wineries have been established in what is now called the Red Mountain area, premium Washington wine country.

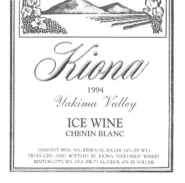

In their 16-hectare vineyard, the Williams have a low-lying one-third-hectare depression that is a frost pocket. Since 1989 this problematic section of the vineyard has been set aside in most years for modest production (about 2,300 liters in 1995) of icewine from Chenin Blanc, made in the classic fashion. Winemaker Scott Williams chose Chenin Blanc only because he has a plentiful quantity of this grape, while his Riesling is fully committed to Kiona's late harvest wines.

It was a good choice. The 1989 vintage, of which 3,000 half bottles were produced, promptly won five gold medals and one double gold in various competitions, making an instant reputation for Kiona as an icewine producer.

Lakewood Vineyards Inc. 4024 State Route #14, Watkins Glen, NY 14891

In a departure from the familiar, Lakewood winemaker Chris Stamp uses two native American grape varieties, Delaware and Concord, for icewine. The winery was established in 1987 and the first Delaware icewine was made in 1990, largely to get Stamp out of a difficult situation.

"We actually had a pretty large crop of Delaware that year," he recalls. "We didn't have a market for them and we didn't have tank space for the wine." So he made 60 gallons, or 227 liters, of icewine because, by concentrating the juice, he reduced his storage problem. The wine sold well and he has made about 1,900 liters every year since, along with another 1,100 liters of Concord icewine.

The grapes remain on the vines until the leaves fall and then are held in a freezer until Stamp has four free days to press them. "As far as quality control, it has been fantastic for us," he says of his method. The Concord icewine is sold under the label *Borealis,* and has what he calls a "cult following." Stamp's tasting notes for this light pink wine suggest that it is "explosively fruity and rich on the palate with a bright candy-like finish. An all inclusive dessert in a glass!"

The Delaware icewine is labeled *Glaciovinum,* Latin for Glacier wine. "To me, it is a little more complex," Stamp says. "It comes across as very tropical and it certainly stands out in an icewine tasting." In his tasting notes, he writes: "The incredible aromas of orange, banana, ginger and vanilla bean will sweep you away to paradise." At $9.99 a half bottle, it is a bargain journey.

Mazza Vineyards 11815 East Lake Road, North East, PA 16428

I talian-born Robert Mazza, an engineer, opened this winery in 1974 in a Spanish mission–style building which, while attractive, seems slightly misplaced on the Pennsylvania shore of Lake Erie. However, Mazza's commitment to improving the region's wines is not misplaced. In the mid-1990s he was the founding president of the Lake Erie Quality Wine Alliance.

Since 1984, when nature cooperates, Mazza Vineyards has made between four hundred and eight hundred liters of icewine annually from Vidal grapes, naturally frozen in vineyards of various growers who produce for Mazza, which relies on contract growers.

Winemaker Gary Mosier, who was mentored by a Geisenheim graduate formerly employed at Mazza, also would like to use Riesling but has not succeeded in persuading any growers to risk leaving the grapes to hang for the late icewine harvests. The 1998 picking, for example, took place on December 23.

The Mazza icewine, plump and tropical in style, occupies the rarest and most expensive niche in the winery's considerable range of wines. "It definitely helps us, sales-wise," Mosier says.

Naylor Wine Cellars Inc. 4069 Vineyard Road, Stewartstown, PA 17363

G rape growing in Pennsylvania was tried first by William Penn, who imported vines in 1683 from France and Spain. The vineyard failed, likely because the vines fell victim to phylloxera, the native North American root louse to which the European wine grapes were not (and still are not) adapted.

The next three hundred years of Pennsylvania wine-growing were plagued by other challenges, many of them rooted in Prohibitionist legislation, until the first winery opened in 1963 and paved the way for others such as Naylor Wine Cellars, which opened in 1978.

NAYLOR

1997

Intimacy

"A deeply personal after dinner wine"

The Naylor wines range from European varietals such as Pinot Gris to native Americans such as Catawba and Concord. The winery's first icewine, a mere twelve hundred half bottles, was made in 1997 with Vignoles grapes. In 1998 the winery spiked the blend with 10 per cent Vidal, accenting the tropical fruit notes.

Since Pennsylvania winters are mild, the grapes are picked in late

October at close to 30° Brix and placed in cold storage where they remain until after the American Thanksgiving in November, one of the busiest holiday weekends of the year. Then winery owner Dick Naylor and his winemaker, Ted Potter, press whole frozen bunches slowly in a German bladder press, so gently that it takes as long as seven days to extract the juice. Fermentation is done slowly.

"The resulting ice wine is just fantastic to say the least," Naylor writes in a winery newsletter. "The nose has an earthy fruitiness due to the ripeness of the fruit. On the palate there are layers of luscious fruit and a natural sweetness." The wine is called *Intimacy*. It has won numerous gold medals for Naylor and there are plans to increase the production.

Pellegrini Vineyards 23005 Main Road, Cutchoque, NY 11935

This winery on Long Island's North Fork boasts that it is located in the sunniest town in New York, with a growing season comparable to Bordeaux, not a locale conducive to naturally deep frosts. Since 1992, Pellegrini has been producing between 50 and 350 cases annually of *Winemaker's Pride Finale,* an "'off-the-vine' ice wine" using a walk-in freezer to simulate winter.

The blend consistently is Gewürztraminer (70 per cent) and Sauvignon Blanc, fermented and aged in five-hundred-liter oak barrels. The winery described its *1996 Winemaker's Pride Finale* — 345 cases were made — as "a rich and luscious jewel [with] aromas of apricot, orange peel, honey and vanilla [which] flow into wonderfully complex flavors and a long, lingering finish." It is made in the icewine style, with tangy acidity of one gram per liter and with a luscious 198 grams of residual sugar. The 1996 retailed for US$25 for a half bottle.

Ponzi Vineyards 14665 SW Winery Lane, Beaverton, OR 97007

A respected veteran of winemaking in Oregon, Dick Ponzi, the son of Italian immigrants, is a mechanical engineer who once worked in the California aerospace industry and then designed rides for the Disney Corporation. In a dramatic change of lifestyle for him and his family, Ponzi planted the estate vineyard in 1970 in the Willamette Valley, not far from Portland, and opened the winery in 1974.

Members of Ponzi's large and charming family grew up to work in the winery. His daughter, Luisa, suggested Ponzi add an icewine to a range of wines that already encompassed fine Pinot Noir, Pinot Gris and Chardonnay. The original vineyard planting included several acres of Riesling and, for many years, it was released as a dry table wine. The icewine, a light dessert wine called *Vino Gelato,* was introduced in 1994 and the winery now produces about 4,000 half bottles annually.

"The clusters are picked at the end of harvest, usually around the end of October," says Maria Ponzi, another daughter who works in the Ponzi marketing department. "They are then transported to a freezer and are frozen until January." The must, concentrated only to about 30° Brix, is fermented in stainless steel and the wine is matured four months in French oak.

Preston Wine Cellars 502 East Vineyard Drive, Pasco, WA 99301-9667

The Preston family has been making wine in Washington's Columbia Valley since 1976 but only rarely, in 1978 and again in 1986, has the production included icewine. Cathy Preston-Mouncer, the family member who handles marketing, explains on a terse information sheet: "Ice Wine ... only 'happens' about every seven to twelve years, when several conditions come together at once." Grapes often are left deliberately on the vines for late harvest wine; in those infrequent years when nature delivers an early

freeze, icewine is made rather than late harvest wine.

"The frozen grapes will have yielded approximately 40 to 50 gallons of juice per ton of grapes, whereas a normal harvest-time yield is more than 160 gallons per ton," Preston-Mouncer continues. "Just one more reason why Ice Wine is very expensive to make and buy." In 1986, when the grapes were picked on December 10, the winery made eight hundred half bottles of Riesling icewine.

SilverLake Winery 17616 15th Ave. SE, #106B, Bothel, WA 98012

With wineries in both the Seattle area and eastern Washington, SilverLake made about 2,300 liters of Riesling icewine in 1989, picking the grapes in mid-December. According to Bob Ammons, one of the winemakers, an attempt to make a classical icewine in 1997 flopped because the grapes had thawed by the time they reached the press. Ammons expects that will not happen the next time there is an opportunity to make icewine. SilverLake's recently expanded winery in eastern Washington is only 300 yards from the winery's Riesling vineyard.

Tefft Cellars 1320 Independence Road, Outlook, WA 98938

Joel Tefft, one of the proprietors, made his first icewine in 1991 from Black Muscat grapes but he gives credit for the idea to Stan Clarke, with whom he made icewine previously at Hyatt Vineyards. Clarke also was a grape grower and, as Tefft recalls, was unhappy selling his Black Muscat juice for grape juice production just because no winery wanted to make a table wine with it. He suggested turning it into the tour de force that it is as icewine.

"We produce about two hundred cases a year," Tefft says. He calls it "icewine-style" because the weather cannot be relied on to freeze the grapes on the vines. Tefft's *Black Ice*, made with the help of commercial freezing, is produced from equal portions of Black Muscat and Chenin Blanc; the Muscat brings floral aromas and the Chenin Blanc's fine acidity beings crispness. Consequently, Tefft makes an icewine that is not thick and syrupy but is refreshingly balanced and reasonably light with 13 per cent residual sugar.

In 1998, about 3,600 bottles of *Black Ice* were made and sold in a 500 ml square bottle that suggests an ice cube. The bottle size is almost as uncommon as the shape. Most icewine producers favor the 375 ml bottles, with rare exceptions like Germany's Barbara Rundquist-Müller of Zimmermann-Graeff & Müller, who argues that the half-liter size is perfect for dinner parties. American wine producers were prevented from using the larger bottle because for years the Bureau of Alcohol, Tobacco and Firearms would not allow them to use it. When it was finally permitted in 1991, the independent-minded Tefft was among the first to use it. A creative winemaker, Tefft produces several other dessert wines, including *Starboard,* a Port-style wine made from huckleberries.

Vinifera Wine Cellars 9749 Middle Road, Hammondsport, NY 14840

The faith of founder Dr. Konstantin Frank in classic European grape varieties was amply rewarded in 1997 when this winery's 1995 Johannisberg Riesling Ice Wine won the Deinhard Trophy as the best New World Riesling at the World International Wine Competition, a large annual competition held in New York.

The state's Finger Lakes district — this winery is on the shore of Keuka Lake — is thought by many to be one of the best Riesling locales in the United States. In these cool vineyards, the grape yields wines that are crisp and lively, with flavors of strawberry and apples. This winery's Riesling wines have achieved growing recognition; in 1998, it again won the Deinhard Trophy with a 1996 semi-dry Riesling table wine. The winery is a regular producer of late harvest Rieslings but rarely makes icewine because its vineyards seldom get an early hard freeze.

Dr. Frank, who was born in the Ukraine in 1899 and died in New York in 1985, was a forceful advocate for vinifera grapes at a time when the Finger Lakes region was believed suitable only for hybrids and native North American varieties.

The German-speaking Dr. Frank had taught viticulture at a Ukrainian agricultural institute before World War II. Shortly after coming to the United States in 1951, he became a laborer at the New York State Experimental Station at Geneva, whose scientists persisted in telling growers that the European varieties were marginal. This enraged Dr. Frank, an outspoken critic of the hybrid varieties and in 1953 he went to work at Gold Seal Vineyards, an early convert to vinifera. Dr. Frank then planted his own vineyard in 1962 and began marketing the wines in 1965 under the Vinifera Wine Cellars name. Dr. Frank's son Willibald and grandson Fred now run Vinifera Wine Cellars and nearby Chateau Frank, where sparkling wine is made.

Wagner Vineyards 9322 State Route 414, Lodi, NY 14860-9641

As soon as New York in 1976 passed its Farm Winery Act, grape grower Bill Wagner began developing this winery, now based on one hundred hectares of vineyard on the shores of Seneca Lake. The winery opened in 1979 and now produces 40,000 cases a year. As well, Wagner opened a micro-brewery in 1997.

Icewine production began in 1988, with Wagner's winemakers initially using two hybrids, Vidal and Ravat Blanc. A decade later, Wagner made about 10,000 half bottles of Riesling, 9,200 half bottles of Vignoles (as Ravat Blanc now is called) and 7,800 half bottles of Vidal.

The winery stores ripe grapes in a commercial freezer, pressing them at the winery at an ambient temperature that approximates natural icewine temperatures, eliminating the risk of losing the crop to birds or unfavorable weather.

Whether or not Wagner chooses to produce icewine in a particular vintage depends mostly on how much of the previous year's icewine remains unsold.

Washington Hills Cellars 111 East Lincoln Ave., Sunnyside, WA 98944

Winemaker Brian Carter, a graduate of the University of California's Davis campus and one of the partners who launched this Washington winery in 1988, made his first icewine in 1991. Because the birds got to the unprotected vines in subsequent years, his next icewine vintage was 1997. He definitely considers netting the vines now.

Carter's grape of choice is Gewürztraminer. "I've always liked it," he says. "It is an under-rated grape." He recognizes that the variety trends to drop its acidity as it matures but that deficiency is remedied easily by acidulating the must. Other than that, this is a classical icewine, harvested in 1997 on December 1 when the grapes were frozen on the vine. Only 3,400 half bottles were produced. The wine, retailing at $40, was released under the Apex label, the label that Washington Hills reserves for its premium wines.

PART IV

Icewine Elsewhere

14

The Far Corners of Icewine's World

Australia

Bloodwood Estate Griffith Road, Orange, NSW 2800

Stephen Doyle's Bloodwood Ice Riesling, made in 1994 and again in 1997, is as near to classic "on the vine" icewine as can be expected in Australia. Orange is in the highlands west of Sydney and the Bloodwood vineyards, planted in 1983 by Doyle and his wife, Rhonda, are at elevations approaching one thousand meters.

"We do have some quite cold snaps here at Orange, sometimes as low as -16°C," Doyle says. "The grapes froze and partially thawed several times on the way to the vintage."

The 1994 grapes were picked July 4 and 5 and the 1997 grapes on June 20. By comparison, the grapes for Bloodwood's Riesling table wines usually are picked in the third week of March.

Bloodwood, which produces a total of four thousand cases of wine, makes Ice Riesling infrequently because early winter rain often falls at Orange. "To make our particular style, we need bone-dry, drought conditions from late vintage to midwinter," Doyle says. "The Riesling usually has some low-level botrytis developing near harvest and this infection seems to stop and start, according to the prevailing moisture. Early light snows and sometimes severe frosts pull the infection up and defoliate the vines." That allows the winter sun to shrivel the grape bunches gradually, concentrating the sugars as high as 32° Brix, into the threshold for a light icewine.

"It is then a matter of holding our nerves and playing Russian roulette with the weather," Doyle adds. "When it holds and the snows aren't too heavy, we see some very pleasing results."

Hood Wines Denholm's Road, Cambridge, Tasmania 7170

Andrew Hood, a busy consulting winemaker and graduate of Charles Sturt University, established this small winery in 1990 with his wife, Jenny. Within a decade, he had garnered a number of awards and a nomination as winemaker of the year in Australia.

Among the wines with which Hood attracted acclaim was his Wellington Iced Riesling. From a small trial volume in 1995, he has increased the production to about 12,000 half bottles a year. "It has been an amazing success and I am trying to work out ways to increase production further," he said in early 2001. Demand in Australia, where the wine is sold for US$10 a bottle, is so strong that Hood is reluctant to export it.

"There is nowhere in Australia cold enough to produce natural icewines from grapes frozen on the vine," Hood says. By using a freezer at the winery to remove water, he concentrates Riesling juice with normal table wine maturity of 22° Brix to more than 32° Brix. This is then fermented to about 10 per cent alcohol, leaving about 40 per cent of the initial sugar still in the wine. "Because the freeze concentration process also concentrates the acids and the volatiles, the resulting wine has intense flavor with fresh, crisp balance," Hood maintains. "My strong preference is to have no botrytis influence and to rely purely on varietal fruit flavors. Hence, we often use exactly the same juice as is used in our dry table wine Riesling."

The 1997 Iced Riesling was judged the best unwooded white at the Tasmanian Wine Show in 1998, while the 1999 vintage was rated by a leading wine magazine as one of Australia's 10 best sweet wines released in 2000. Writer Huon Hooke, one of the tasters, described the wine as "refined, penetrating and intensely varietal, with pristine floral aromas." Hood believes his 2000 Iced Riesling is in the same league.

Croatia

Ljiljana i Franjo Lovrec Sv. Urban 133, 40312 Štrigova

Silver-haired Professor Franjo Lovrec and Ljiljana, his wife, are so passionate about promoting quality wines in Croatia that they run a private wine school on their small estate near the village of St. Urban. They teach, among other things, the art of growing grapes organically. By severely limiting the production of their 17,000 vines in the pursuit of quality wine, they seldom make more than 30,000 bottles of wine a year, all of it from white varieties such as Chardonnay, Pinot Gris and Graševina (the synonym for Welschriesling).

The Lovrec family claims a wine-growing tradition that is centuries old, illustrating this with a collection of antique winemaking equipment in their museum-like tasting room. So far, Lovrec has made Ledeno Vino in three vintages. In 1988 and again in 1993 the wine was made with the Graševina grape; the 1993 Ledeno Vino, of which only 80 liters was produced, was an award winner in several competitions. The most recent Ledeno Vino was made from Chardonnay that was harvested on January 1, 2000. Once again, only 80 liters were produced. The sun-bathed Lovrec vineyards, on south-facing slopes, seldom get the required conditions — three days at -7°C — for making icewine.

Czech Republic

Mikros-Vín Mikulov Nádražní 29, 69201 Mikulov, Czech Republic

This Czech wine producer evolved from a local cooperative farm when Zdenek Perina, the manager, concluded that selling grapes to larger wineries was not very profitable. It is now a premium producer, controlling 170 hectares of vineyards in the limestone-rich hills of Palava.

In the 1994 vintage, the winery made the first Ledové Víno (icewine) in the Czech Republic, one hundred liters with Ryzlink Rýnský (Rhine Riesling) grapes. "Our winemaking technique is based on the Austrian way," Perina says. "We learned from our Austrian friends." The community of Mikulov is not far from Austria's northeastern border and the Eiswein producers of Poysdorf.

"The main reason for the production of Ledové Víno was just falling in love with the product and also the idea of being the first producer of this heavenly nectar in the Czech Republic. Our first Ledové Víno on the market was an instant success and also an economical boost for our company."

The winery prices its wine at double that of Austrian Eiswein and, so far, has had no difficulty selling its limited production. Thirteen different Ledové Víno have been produced, as the winery was able to make some in each year since 1994, with Chardonnay and Ryzlink Vlašský (Welschriesling) grapes as well as Rhine Riesling. The annual volume is never large, the most abundant production having been the 1997 vintage when 865 liters was made from the three varieties combined.

The winery has created a market for others as well. "More than 20 different [icewines] were marketed in the Czech Republic in 1999," Perina observes. The reference is primarily to German and Austrian Eisweine.

Veverka Frantisek-Vinařstvi 696 15 Ccjkovice 220, Czech Republic

Čejkovice also is a short distance from northeastern Austria. History records that the Knights Templar in the thirteenth century built a fortress and wine cellars. The latter, now owned by the state, still remain in use by the local agricultural cooperative.

"Because of the favorable climatic and geographical conditions, our village has been classified as one of the best grape growing areas of southern Moravia since the beginning of the 19th century," František Veverka says proudly. Almost every house in the village has vines and a wine cellar. "This type of small wine cellar and vineyard with a few hundred grapes has been in my family for generations. Wine production was started by my grandfather and continued by my father. I learned on the job, as I was involved since my childhood."

However, wine was a sideline until 1992 when he became unemployed. That led Veverka to become a full-time winemaker, producing premium wines from a 10-hectare vineyard. In 1996, he began making Ledové Víno, both with Grüner Veltliner and Welschriesling. His icewine grapes were eaten by deer in 1997, one of the challenges that explains Veverka's modest icewine production: 50 liters in 1998, 200 liters in 1999 and 150 liters in 2000. It is difficult, he explains, to protect grapes on the vine until it is cold enough to pick them, usually in mid-December.

"The grapes are under the attack of birds, deer, weather," he says, adding indignantly, "and also thieves who steal the grapes more and more lately!"

Hungary

Château Pajzos 3950 Sárospatak, Nagy Lajos u. 12

The credit for making in 1998 what appears to have been Hungary's first icewine goes to Thomas Laszlo, a winemaker born in Canada in 1968 of parents who left Hungary during the 1956 revolution. An agriculture graduate from the University of Guelph, Laszlo spent three years, including three icewine vintages, at the Henry of Pelham winery in Ontario before going to Hungary in 1997 "to pursue my winemaking career and passion in Tokaj."

In this wine region in northeastern Hungary, he became technical director for Château Pajzos (pronounced *pie-zosh*) and Château Megyer, two properties now owned by Jean-Louis Laborde. The proprietor of Château Clinet in Pomerol, Laborde is among those investors who, beginning in the early 1990s, have been restoring the formerly state-owned wineries of Tokaj to the historic glory they enjoyed when the wines were prized in Europe's royal courts.

TOKAJI
CHATEAU PAJZOS
1998
FURMINT
HOMMAGE À
TEPLICZKY GÁBOR

Thomas Laszlo went to Hungary to make the botrytized dessert wines for which Tokaj is so renowned. He was encouraged to make icewine — *Jégbor* in Hungarian — by Tepliczky Gábor, a winemaker at Pajzos who had been trying to make icewine since 1996. His untimely death is memorialized on the labels of the 2000 bottles of 1998 Furmint icewine. Since Tokaj's appellation laws do not contemplate icewine, it cannot be labeled Jégbor but must be sold as a generic late harvest wine.

Making this style of wine in a region prone to botrytis is an enormous challenge. The large, thin-skinned Furmint grapes are prone to rot unless the vineyard is touched by a rare early frost. In

1998, the temperature dipped to -9°C early on both December 7 and December 8. Laszlo led pickers out in the dark, at four in the morning, and grapes were harvested from one hectare, enough for 400 liters of icewine. In 1999 he only had two hours of cold weather on a Saturday night, insufficient time to gather pickers, and the grapes were lost. In 2000, Pajzos again lost its icewine grapes to rain and unusually mild weather in January. "They just rotted off," Laszlo reports.

Accordingly, the winery has marketed its 1998 icewine sparingly in 200 ml bottles, often using it just to impress visiting wine writers. "It gives us a step up compared to our competitors," Laszlo finds. "Pajzos is the only company that has an icewine."

The icewine's flavors are as different as "night and day" from Tokaji Aszú. The latter, made with selected botrytized berries and matured two to three years in barrel, is gold-colored and viscous like Sauternes. The 1998 icewine was fermented cool in stainless steel tanks and bottled in April 1999, capturing fresh apple and pear fruit flavors lifted by what Laszlo calls "lightning acidity."

The residual sugar, at 174 grams per liter, puts Laszlo's Jégbor on a par with the top grade Tokaji Aszú and just six grams under the minimum required for Eszencia. Made entirely (and very rarely) from selected single berries, Eszencia is the most intense of Hungarian dessert wines and a remarkable benchmark for icewine.

Luxembourg

Charles Decker 7, Route de Mondorf, L-5441 Remerschen

C harles Decker produces only 30,000 bottles of wine a year in total but the range is exceptional for a small producer, extending from sparkling wines through dry table wines and even to a *vin de paille* or straw wine, an unusual and award-winning specialty.

Decker's first Eiswein, a mere 10 liters of Riesling, was made in

1994. In the next year, he made another 10 liters of Riesling Eiswein and 15 with Pinot Noir. Having mastered the art, Decker in 1996 made 60 liters of Riesling Eiswein with which he won the Grande Médaille d'Or at the 1999 Concours Mondial Bruxelles. Weather conditions did not permit an Eiswein in 1997 but a sharp November freeze enabled Decker to make 300 liters in 1998. The volume made in 1999, when the harvest date was December 22, was slightly lower.

"But the concentration — 172° Oechsle — was fantastic," Decker said. "Usually, we take Riesling for our Eiswein as it brings the best relationship between sugar and acidity. Harmony is the most important criterion for me."

Domaine Mme Aly Duhr 9, rue Aly Duhr, L-5401 Ahn

Established in 1872, this winery, with an annual production of 70,000 bottles, now is in the hands of brothers Léon and Abi Duhr. They are leaders in the Luxembourg wine industry, playing a key role in 1988 in gathering the country's top producers into an association called Domaine et Tradition. This association has raised the quality and the profile of the country's wines in order to compete

in spite of the high cost of Luxembourg wine production. The tiny country's vineyards cling to the steep slopes of the Moselle river, which rises here before heading north into Germany to become the Mosel. The total area under vines is perhaps 1,350 hectares and all of it is cultivated by hand.

The wines are almost exclusively white and of a high quality but the limited production means Luxembourg wine is not well known. That is even moreso for the country's icewine. Because a separate appellation had not been established for this wine style by 2000, the Duhr brothers have called theirs *Puits D'Or.* They began making it only in 1994, producing about one thousand bottles a year.

In the first two vintages, the winery used the Auxerrois grape, a variety not known for retaining acidity when it matures. Since 1996 — when the harvest occurred on December 26 — it has used the classic Riesling, achieving icewines with crisp acidity.

In the mild winter of 1997, the winery had to wait until January 28, 1998, for the necessary frost. The result was an icewine that, while lower in acidity, was fruity with a concentrated sweetness of 146° Oechsle. The 1998 vintage was, for the first time, aged nine months in new oak.

New Zealand

Chard Farm State Highway, Gibbston, Queenstown

R ob Hay, a founder and winemaker at Chard Farm, makes the claim of having produced the only natural icewine in the southern hemisphere. He gives the credit to the violent June 1991 eruption of Mount Pinatubo in the Philippines which threw an immense quantity of ash 15,000 meters into the atmosphere, obscuring the sun. Temperatures dropped measurably in the hemisphere the next year. Chard Farm is in Otago, New Zealand's most southerly — and therefore coolest — wine district.

The vineyards at Chard Farm were planted in 1987 on rolling terrain spectacularly surrounded by mountains. Hay, who had studied and worked in Germany for three years, tried to make icewine twice soon after Chard Farm was established but failed because the frost was not deep enough. It was a different matter in the 1992 vintage. Under Pinatubo's eggshell haze, he set aside an 80-meter-long row of Riesling for icewine.

"The grapes were picked on the shortest day of the year, June 22, 1992," Hay says. "Outside the temperature was -12°C. The grape temperature in the press never got above -8°C, as per the German requirements for icewine." Indeed, the juice was cold enough to crack the 20-liter glass carboy into which it was poured and only half was saved to be vinified. He opened one of his rare bottles to welcome in the new Millennium.

Lincoln Vineyards Ltd. 130 Lincoln Road, Henderson

This family-owned winery began producing Gewürztraminer icewine in 1989 from grapes grown in the Gisborne region, an appellation known for producing a rich, peppery and concentrated Gewürztraminer even for table wine. The grapes hang on the vines to achieve high sugars but are picked just before the autumn rainy season sets in and are placed in a freezer prior to being pressed for icewine. There is no other option on the north island of New Zealand where the winters are mild and wet and unsuited for icewine by natural means.

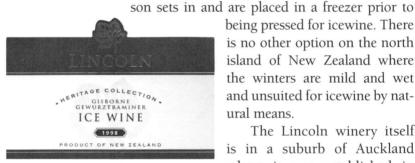

The Lincoln winery itself is in a suburb of Auckland where it was established in 1937 by Peter Fredatovich, one of many Dalmatian immigrants to settle in New Zealand, much to the benefit of winemaking there. A producer of about 45,000 cases of wines a year, Lincoln has made its reputation with Chardonnay. The winery also makes an excellent Chenin Blanc table wine but, despite this grape's versatility for late harvest wines, only uses Gewürztraminer for icewine.

Seifried Estate Redwood Road, Appleby, Box 7020, Nelson

Austrian-born Hermann Seifried, whose labels on his New Zealand wines still display the Austrian eagle, studied wine technology in Germany but never made icewine there. He arrived in New Zealand in 1971, after a few years in the South African wine industry, and opened his own winery in 1974. He was among the pioneers of winemaking in the Nelson district and persevered in the face of warnings from the "experts" in government that European grape varieties would not flourish in this cool South Island region. The winery now produces about 43,000 cases a year, primarily of well-regarded white wines.

As cool as Nelson is, it never gets cold enough to produce icewine naturally. Primarily using Riesling and Gewürztraminer, Seifried freezes the grapes before pressing them. The trick is to use very ripe fruit, as he describes in the notes for the winery's 1997 Gewürztraminer Ice Wine: "Many of the grapes had shriveled and raisined." The resulting wines are plump and richly spicy, with alcohol levels around 12 per cent. "You ask how often we make it?" Seifried says. "Just when the conditions are right. Obviously we need a hot, dry summer and autumn with absolutely no spoilage in the grapes — usually every two or three years."

Selaks Wines (Kumeu) Ltd. P.O. Box 34, Kumeu, Auckland

This small, successful winery was founded in 1934 by Marino Selak, a winemaking Croatian immigrant who soon was joined by a nephew, Mate. They were among the first to produce sparkling wines in New Zealand by the traditional Champagne method and they were one of the leaders in establishing Sauvignon Blanc as the flagship white wine for that country.

The winery now is managed by a second generation of Selaks. Winemaker Darryl Woolley has produced several vintages of what Selaks calls Traminer/Riesling Ice Wine, by freeze concentrating juice from Gewürztraminer and Riesling. The resulting wine, with 112 grams of residual sugar, is "a luscious honey-style wine" with only a short to medium-term cellaring potential.

Romania

Vie Vin Murfatlar Calea Bucuresti 19, 8764 Basarabi

ormerly a state-owned winery that was privatized in 2000, the
Murfatlar winery preserves a tradition reaching back cen-
turies, with its fine museum containing winemaking artifacts of
Greek, Roman and Dacian origin.

The winery and its vineyards are on eastern Romania's
Dobrogea Plateau, a wine-growing region not far from the Black
Sea port of Constanta. Prior to privatization, the winery controlled
two thousand hectares of vineyards, planted to classic varieties
such as Chardonnay, Pinot Gris, Muscat Ottonel, Cabernet
Sauvignon and Pinot Noir.

This winery had a brief but glorious run as an icewine produc-
er, beginning with 14,000 liters made in 1962 from Pinot Gris.
According to Cristian Din, the winery's commercial manager, this
wine had a honey-like sugar concentration of 423 grams per liter.
Perhaps not surprising for a wine that should have made the
Guinness Book of Records, samples were lodged in Romania's
National Collection of Wines. In the following year, the winery's
Traminer icewine was almost as dense at 390 grams per liter, also
enough to destine samples for the collection.

Other Murfatlar icewine vintages included a 1965
Chardonnay, both a 1968 and a 1969 Pinot Gris, a 1970 Muscat
and a 1971 Chardonnay. For reasons peculiar to a centrally
planned economy, as Romania was then, the winery stopped making icewine, there being no practical market for it at the time. The
1968 and the 1971 were included in a large London icewine tasting organized by *Wine* magazine in 1997. Both wines were judged
"too old" by the tasters.

Slovenia

The tradition of viticulture in Slovenia is so old that the wine industry has chosen as its registered symbol the image of a Roman bread mold discovered some years ago during an archeological excavation.

Currently, about 24,500 hectares are under vine, about a third of the peak when phylloxera struck in 1860. The producers range from small artisanal winemakers to large cooperatives and former state-owned wineries which have been put into the hands of private shareholders, including employees, since Slovenia gained its independence from the Yugoslav federation in 1990. Many of Slovenia's two million citizens own small private vineyards from which they produce wines for their own use and for their friends.

Slovenian winemakers work with a vast range of varietals and make the full range of styles encountered in any wine region, even including fortified wines modeled after Port. The Slovenian phrase for icewine is *Ledeno Vino*. In his 1996 book, *The Wines of Slovenia*, author Mišo Alkalaj — a mathematician in Ljubljana and a self-described passionate amateur of wine — calls Ledeno Vino "the ultimate that nature can offer."[1]

Both by regulation and by practice, grapes for icewine are picked only when the daily temperature averages a minimum of -6°C for three days. That is a degree or two warmer than the legal minimum in Germany, Austria and Canada, suggesting that Slovenian icewines can be somewhat light in style.

Slovenia (along with a sliver of Croatia on Slovenia's southeastern border) is the southernmost region for natural icewine in Europe and cannot count on the frigid temperatures further north. (Across the Adriatic in Italy, not far from Trieste, an experimental wine institute that tried to make icewine last decade was frustrated by the warm winters in the vineyards.)

Ledeno Vino is found in the country's two eastern wine regions, Posavje and Podravje. It is made by producers with vineyards on the southeastern slopes of the country's interior mountains, away from the moderating influence of the Adriatic. Podravje is the largest of

Slovenia's wine regions, sandwiched between Austria, Hungary and Croatia, and notable for moderately cold winters.

Grapes employed for Slovenian icewine include Laški Rizling. The variety is the most widely planted white grape in Slovenia and also can be found elsewhere around the Adriatic; the Austrians call it Welschriesling. Slovenian winemakers occasionally make Ledeno Vino with Renski Rizling, the local name for Rhine Riesling; with Šipon, the local name for Furmint, the grape used in Hungary for Tokaji; and with Modra Frankinja, a red variety known in Germany and North America as Lemberger.

Mišo Alkalaj recalls a 1973 Čurin Laški Rizling Ledeno Vino as the oldest Slovenian icewine in his memory as a wine taster. Technically, this cannot be called the country's oldest icewine because the Yugoslav government did not get around to defining Ledeno Vino in law until the late 1980s.

"According to my knowledge," Alkalaj adds, "icewines have been introduced to Slovenia by Archduke Johann in the mid-nineteenth century, but have always been produced in minute quantities, just for the winemakers' close friends." The reference is to a member of the thousand-year Habsburg Dynasty who, after being involved in an apparent coup, was exiled from the Vienna court to an estate he acquired in Podravje in 1822. So thorough was his transformation that he even took on a Slovenian name, Janez.

"He devoted the rest of his life to the development of viticulture in the area," Alkalaj recounts. "Archduke Janez introduced many new vines from the Rhein and Mosel valleys to the region, including Renski Rizling, Traminec, Rulandec and Modri Burgundec. Today, these are today among the most prestigious wines of Maribor area and all Podravje. He also introduced new planting schemes and training techniques, and experimented with vines brought from Hungary, Italy and even the Crimea. He founded a school of viticulture in 1832 and established a fund that granted pensions to old impoverished *vini carji* (hired vineyard workers, best described as viticultural proletariat who had worked for at least 10 years for one vineyard owner)."

However, the suggestion that the duke also introduced the production of icewine stretches credulity. Alkalaj extrapolates from the duke's knowledge of German viticulture to say "it is reasonably safe he also taught the locals how to make icewine." He adds: "I cannot give you a one hundred per cent guarantee — I have no documents to prove it."

Some of the documents in Germany, but not all, imply that Eiswein was not even discovered at this time. What *was* understood by this time, however, was the production of late harvest wines such as Hungary's Tokaji and the comparable Ausbruch wines made by Austrian winemakers at Rust. The Austrian-Hungarian empire extended into the Balkan states and dessert wines of all types were prized in the noble courts of Vienna and elsewhere. This knowledge of dessert wines was undoubtedly taught in the duke's school, setting the stage for Ledeno Vino, the ultimate late harvest wine.

Ledeno Vino only began being produced commercially in the 1980s and never in large volume. "A large producer like Vinag will produce fifteen hundred to two thousand quarter-liter bottles in a favorable year," Alkalaj says. "Small producers will go for three hundred to six hundred bottles." He contends that icewine production has waned in Slovenia in recent years because tastes and fashions have changed in international wine competitions, with judges paying more attention to dry wines than to sweet ones.

"In the 1980s a well-prepared icewine was almost certain to win a Grand Champion award," he says. "That has changed, so producers are less eager to produce these wines that were always [made] more for prestige than commercial effect."

Čurin-Prapotnik Kog 15, 2276 Kog

At the age of 71, Stanko Čurin was contemplating retirement in 2000. It would be going out on a high note, for 1999, he says, was the finest vintage in his very long experience.

Retirement will deprive Slovenia of perhaps its greatest producer of sweet wines and one who claims that he made Slovenia's first Ledeno Vino in 1985, using Renski Rizling. Fortunately for Slovenian wines, Čurin has passed on his skills to his son-in-law,

Slavko Prapotnik. As well, there is a grandson apprenticing in Čurin's compact winery (only 70,000 liters) in this village east of Ormož.

The fiercely independent Čurin was one of Slovenia's first private winegrowers, having decided in 1963 that he could make a living from vineyards. Before World War II, his family were large land owners. When most of that property was expropriated, he began making wine with the production from one and a half hectares of vineyard, gradually acquiring more until he owned the thirteen hectares he has today.

Since 1971, Čurin has been bottling his own wines and has justly earned a considerable reputation for sweet wines of all categories, from straw wine to Ledeno Vino. His claim to have made the first Ledeno Vino is challenged by the Metlika winery, whose icewine production began in 1986. It all hangs on the technicality that Ledeno Vino was not legally defined until 1986. In any event, others also claim to have made wines in this style earlier.

It is unlikely that anyone in Slovenia has made as many top flight examples as Čurin. He was inspired to make icewine after discussing and tasting some examples made by friends in Austria. The grape varieties employed include Chardonnay, Beli Pinot and, most often, Laški Rizling. In what might be Čurin's valedictorian vintage of 1999, he capped his career with a Laški Rizling with opulent fruit and concentrated sweetness superbly balanced with piquant acidity.

Franci Cvetko Kog 1, 2274 Velika Nedelja

Οne of the members of the Society of Winegrowers of the Ljutomer-Ormož Hills, Franci Cvetko specializes in dry white wines from his four hectares of vines but also has gained renown for his late harvest wines, including Ledeno Vino, from such varieties as Kerner. Some of his finest wines feature labels designed by Slovenian painters.

The 11 hectares of vineyards that Hlupič cultivates near Maribor in the region of Podravje are planted almost exclusively in white varieties. The winemaker prefers to make powerful sweet wines, including Ledeno Vino, which he has made several times since 1991.

Jeruzalem Ormož Kolodvorska 11, 2270 Ormož

A former cooperative that now is owned by both growers and employees, the winery takes its name from one of its vineyards, an area of such beauty that itinerant Crusaders are said to have called the area Jeruzalem, ending their particular Crusade there.

In modern times, it also is known for its peculiar round winery, built in 1967 into a steep hillside at the community of Ormož. The design allows for the delivery of grapes at the top, which opens onto a hilltop. The nine floors below this contain the production and storage vessels. The wine thus moves down gently by gravity to the bottling line in another building just outside the bottom level. The clever design's only flaw is that the circular design makes it difficult to replace tanks and other equipment. It is a vast facility, with more than six million liters of storage capacity, for Jeruzalem Ormož has 550 hectares of vines and 800 grower members.

The winery has made dessert wines for at least 30 years, establishing a reputation with a 1970 Šipon of Trockenbeerenauslese quality. The winery began making Ledeno Vino in the 1990s for what Danilo Šnajder, one of the two winemakers, calls "medals and reputation." His father, who was cellarmaster there for 35 years before retiring in 1990, made a Laški Rizling Ledeno Vino in 1990, a straw gold wine with an aroma of caramel and a lemony tang. Young Šnajder, an agriculture school graduate who joined the winery in 1997, made his first Ledeno Vino in 1999. He gave his father reason to be proud with one from Renski Rizling and an exceptional one from Laški Rizling, redolent with pineapple and other tropical flavors. "I just tried to make the wine by the book," Šnajder says humbly.

The other Ledeno Vino vintages of the decade — 1993, 1995 and 1996 — were made by Andreja Brglez, the other winemaker. Her most triumphant example is the 1996 Laški Rizling, a decadently luxurious wine with flavors of spice and strawberries.

Kapela Kapelski Vrh 5, 9252 Radenci

A winery with about 170 hectares of vines, Kapela is best known for its white varieties, including late harvest wines made with Chardonnay and Traminec (the local variant of Traminer). The winery makes an unusual dessert wine called *Božično Vino*. That means Christmas wine because the grapes are harvested on Christmas Day. Depending on the weather, this ranges in concentration from *jagodni izbor* — Beerenauslese — to icewine.

Kmečka Zadruga Krško Rostoharjeva 88, 8270 Krško

The Peasants' Cooperative of Krško, to translate the winery's name, produces wine from the grapes of about four hundred growers. The winery also has restored beautifully its old vaulted cellar, now one of the attractions of Krško, an otherwise plain town anchored by a nuclear power plant on the river.

The winery is the producer of a traditional Slovenian red called *Cviček*, a light dry red somewhat reminiscent of simple Chianti. For Ledeno Vino, the winery relies on grapes from the 13 hectares it owns. The first was made in 1992 from a Laški Rizling vineyard almost a century old; only one thousand half bottles were made. Over the next several years, the vineyard was out of production because it was being replanted. It was not until 1999 that a second Ledeno Vino was made, this time two thousand bottles of Sauvignon Blanc harvested on Christmas Day.

Zdravko Mastnak, the winemaker, admits that such small quantities are not commercially significant at the Peasants' Cooperative. Their role, along with the other late harvest wines made here, lies in the medals and prestige that they bring the winery. "They are very important horses in our wine cellar," Mastnak says.

Ljutomerčan Kidričeva ulica 2, 9240 Ljutomer

This winery was built in 1967 based on the same circular design of the Jeruzalem Ormož winery. Even though the wineries are only about thirty kilometers from each other, it is almost as large, with a cellar capacity of three and a half million liters. The winery has been in production much longer than that, for one of the large oak vats in the cellar was built in 1848. The winery's archives include white wines — only whites are made here — from the 1948 vintage. One of the staff maintains the cellar also contains four or five bottles of a 1965 vintage Ledeno Vino, well before the state wine laws even made provision for this style of wine.

Officially, Ljutomerčan's first Ledeno Vino was a 1991 Laški Rizling, followed by a 1993 Chardonnay. While the winery makes dessert wines each year, it was not until the 1999 vintage that the conditions again were favorable for Ledeno Vino. On December 23, with the temperature at -14°C and local accordionists providing entertainment in the winery, enough fruit was picked for fifteen hundred liters of a Chardonnay Ledeno Vino. It is a powerful wine, delivering an explosion of exotic tropical flavors. An even more opulent and richly concentrated wine was produced from a harvest on January 26, 2000, at -17°C, which yielded enough grapes for six hundred liters of Laški Rizling.

Škofija Maribor Slomškov trg 19, 2000 Maribor

A former cooperative, this winery was acquired by the Church in the late 1990s. The ecclesiastical connection is celebrated by labels which include the portrait of Anton Martin Slomšek, a recently canonized Slovenian bishop. The first Ledeno Vino, from Laški Rizling, was made in the 1996 vintage; there was no encore until the 1999 vintage when two Ledeno Vino were made, one from Laški Rizling and the other from Renski Rizling. The quantities are small, perhaps five hundred liters of each, but the intention is to crown the winery's extensive range of other wines with a prestige product.

Universsza V Mariboru Fakulteta Za Kmetijstvo Vrbanska c. 30, 2000 Maribor

This is the University of Maribor's Faculty of Agriculture. The students get practical experience managing the college's excellently sited vineyards on steep slopes overlooking Maribor. For Ledeno Vino, of which 1992 was one of the college's best vintages, the Laški Rizling variety is used most often.

Vinag Trg svobode 3, 2000 Maribor

This producer, now owned by two banks and its own shareholding employees, has 350 hectares of vines on the slopes around the university city of Maribor and a vast two-hundred-year-old cellar in two and a half kilometers of tunnels under the very center of Maribor. Almost all of its wine is white but for a minor volume of Pinot Noir. Vinag also makes fine sparkling wines.

While Vinag has a long history of making dessert wines, Ledeno Vino, typically made from Laški Rizling grapes, came into the picture primarily in the 1990s. The 1991 vintage, a December 12 harvest on two and a half hectares, is light lemon gold wine with a tang of orange peel on the palate. The 1996 vintage, from a December 28 harvest, is a luscious wine with a flavor bouquet of tropical fruits. The 1999 vintage was harvested on December 23 at a very cold -17°C, yielding a plump and intensely sweet wine with a classic apricot aroma.

The annual production of Ledeno Vino varies from five hundred to one thousand liters. Another tradition at Vinag is its annual production of 25 to 35 liters of a red vine from a Maribor-area vine that is claimed to be the world's oldest (435 years in 2000) still yielding grapes. The city's mayor gets the entire production, specially packaged in presentation bottles.

Vinarstvo Slovenske Gorice-Haloze Trstenjakova 6, 2250 Ptuj

One of Slovenia's largest producers, with four hundred hectares under management, this winery markets under the label Haloze. That is the name of the hills south of Ptuj where vineyards cling to steep slopes and along high ridges.

The winery's 750-year-old cellar in Ptuj is the oldest in Slovenia and includes a vaulted section once used by a wine-making monastery. The archive cellar here contains Slovenian wines from vintages as early as 1917. Ledeno Vino is made here from both Laški Rizling and Renski Rizling and there is a ready market to the visitors, drawn by the cellar tours and the pleasant tasting room.

Vinska Klet Metlika Cesta 15, brigade 2, 8330 Metlika

This is one of the two claimants as the first producer of Ledeno Vino in Slovenia, the rival being Čurin-Prapotnik. Metlika is a medium-sized producer in the sun-drenched Bela Krajina region of southeastern Slovenia.

The town's first wine cellar was built in 1929 but was destroyed by bombs during World War II. The facility was rebuilt in the 1950s, with the cellars in an underground tunnel and with a storage capacity of three and a half million liters. Both red and white table wines are made, with sparkling wines being added for the first time just before the new Millennium began.

The first Ledeno Vino was made here in 1986 after the winemakers had learned of such wines being made by producers elsewhere. "So we decided, why not?" says Anton Pezdirc, Metlika's manager. A modest quantity of Laški Rizling remained on the vines until December 25 when the grapes were picked at -9°C to yield three hundred liters of wine.

Because the style then was not defined under the wine laws of Yugoslavia (Slovenia still was a member of that federation), Metlika produced an extensive technical report.

It took the bureaucracy a year and a half to approve the sale of Ledeno Vino. Since then, Metlika has made this style of wine from numerous other varieties, including Renski Rizling, Sauvignon Blanc, Beli Pinot and Rumeni Muškat.

The winery's greatest success has been a double gold medal at the Vino Ljubljana competition in 2000 for its 1998 Rumeni Muškat Ledeno Vino. The grapes were harvested on December 8 at -15°C, the coldest picking temperature in Metlika's experience. The resulting wine showed exceptional flavors of pure, concentrated fruit with penetrating aromas of spice.

The winery's success has given leadership to others in Bela Krajina. At least nine other producers in the region also make Ledeno Vino, including Anton Kostelac and Jože and Anica Prus.

Vino Brežice Cesta prvih borcev 5, 8250 Brežice

Established in 1946, Vino Brežice has developed into a large and diversified beverage company producing not only wine but also fruit drinks and bottled waters and serving as Slovenia's bottler for Coca Cola and Schweppes.

The winery's cellars, some of which are still in Brežice's historic castle, have a capacity for seven million liters. The winery also is Slovenia's only producer of Port wines which, because the name now is reserved to Portugal, are marketed under the Baron Moscon label.

The Moscon family were prominent land owners in this region in the days of the Austrian empire but now are remembered only through a ruined country palace (being restored by the state) and Vino Brežice's wines. The label includes the baron's most distinguishing physical feature — six fingers on his right hand!

Formerly a bulk wine producer, Vino Brežice has been bottling varietal wines since 1983. The winemaking staff suggest that the production of dessert wines from frozen grapes may have begun around that time but were not marketed as such, if only because the market for icewines did not exist.

The winery has made a particular reputation with its red Ledeno Vino, made since 1992 from Modra Frankinja. (The variety is called Blaufränkisch in Austria and also used there for Eiswein.) White grapes used for Ledeno Vino include Chardonnay and Sauvignon Blanc.

Making this style of wine is always a challenge in the Brežice vineyards, which are in the Sava River valley in southern Slovenia. The weather almost never is cold enough before December, with some extremely late harvests. In 1997 the winery picked Chardonnay for Ledeno Vino only in early February of the following year. The result — of which only 1,300 bottles (375 ml) were made — was a fat, ripe wine tasting of honeyed peaches.

Vinogradništo Mulec Ročica 40, 2222 Jakobski Dol

H olding down at least four jobs, Roman Mulec works hard, very hard; the reward is living in one of the Maribor area's most picturesque vineyards, with a roadside chapel built by one of his ancestors and a view on a clear evening to the distant Austrian Alps.

A professional forester, Mulec is director of the state-owned forest around Maribor. From his four-hectare vineyard, the self-taught winemaker produces about 10,000 bottles of wine each year.

On that part of his mountainous farm (elevation 363 meters) too steep for vines, Mulec established a herd of domestic deer in the mid-1980s, becoming one of the first deer farmers in Slovenia. And beside the rustic winery, he completed a three-apartment guest house in 2000. His father and mother, and uncle and two sons, one a lawyer, one an agriculturist, help Mulec with all of his activities.

Mulec first made Ledeno Vino in 1992 because he likes to try something new in his winery every year. The wine, 80 liters made from Renski Rizling, was a great success, maturing into a golden wine with the acidity to balance the intense sweetness and with an aroma of dried fruits.

In the 1999 vintage, Mulec made one hundred liters each of two Ledeno Vino, harvesting in mid-December. One is Renski Rizling and is much lighter in style than the 1992. The other is a spicy Rumeni Muškat with an aroma of pears.

"Here it is very hard to produce icewine," he says. Either the birds swoop into his vineyard from the nearby forests or the necessary frost does not come early enough. Most of the Mulec dessert wines are late harvest wines from grapes picked well before the frost.

Zlati Grič Stari trg 29/a, 3210 Slovenske Konjice

This winery has established its reputation with barrel-fermented tables wines but in recent years has given sweet wines more attention. Writer Mišo Alkalaj reports that this mid-sized winery (about 76 hectares of vines) makes Ledeno Vino that is "very good."

The Zorin family has operated a tourist guest house for more than two decades. Like so many Slovenians, they produced wines from their mountainside vineyards nearby for personal consumption and for guests. The winery was established formally in 1990. While the forceful matron of the family, Anica Zorin, remained in charge of hospitality, her eldest son, Valter, switched to winemaking after studying hotel management.

As winemakers, the Zorin family consistently win awards, particularly for sweet wines. They have embraced Ledeno Vino since making their first, a spicy Laški Rizling, from a Christmas morning harvest in 1996. Two different Ledeno Vino were made in 1997; four in 1998 and six in 1999. The quantities all are between seventy and one hundred liters.

With great confidence in their quality, Anica Zorin sells these rare wines at aggressive prices. One of the finest of the Zorin Ledeno Vino is the 1998 Zurst-Belo, which simply means a cuvée of whites, in this case a blend of Laški Rizling and Renski Rizling. Spicy, even peppery, this light golden wine is fresh and tangy.

Switzerland

The small but ancient Swiss wine industry is based on 15,000 hectares of vineyards, often clinging perilously on steep slopes. Neither these sun-washed exposures nor the dominant grape varieties are conducive to Eiswein. Chasselas and Müller-Thurgau lack acidity, tough skins and the ability to hang on the vines long after the regular vintage is done. Chasselas makes many light, ephemeral white table wines but its mild acidity usually yields dessert wines that are simple and sweet.

As a consequence, only a handful of producers, primarily in German-speaking Ostschweiz (eastern Switzerland), make small quantities of Eiswein when frozen grapes can be harvested. There is little chance of seeing these wines outside that region. As the Swiss Wine Exporters' Association observes, the wines made in the 2,500 hectares of Ostschweiz vineyards are "usually drunk on the spot. Demand for wine from eastern Switzerland is now far in excess of supply."

Eiswein is rarely, if ever, made in either French-speaking western Switzerland (11,000 hectares) or warm Italian-speaking southern Switzerland. There is a wine called Vin des Glaciers produced in the Valais wine region. This has nothing to do with Eiswein. Made with an obscure white grape called Rèze, it is a sherry-like wine matured in casks in high-altitude cellars, hence the name.

In Switzerland as elsewhere, some examples of Eiswein have resulted from accidents of nature. In 1998, Erich Andrey, a winemaker near Bielersee in northwestern Switzerland, was forced by mid-October rain to suspending picking his Chasselas grapes. He simply let them hang on the off-chance that the weather would turn. Instead, the temperature dropped in mid-November. After a quick call for advice from the experts at the Wädenswil research station, he picked at four in the morning when the temperature was -8°C, earning praise as the Bielersee's first Eiswein producer, with 450 liters.

In contrast, a winemaker near Basel named Ulrich Bänninger set out quite deliberately in 1999 to make Eiswein. In the Tschäpperli vineyard near Aesch, which belongs to a family called Von Blarer, the winemaker in November selected the healthiest grapes to remain hanging for the area's first Eiswein. Three times in December the temperature came tantalizingly close to the required freeze before Bänninger led his pickers out at five in the morning on December 17.

Half of the grapes had been lost to birds, storms and rot, but he still was able to salvage 140 kg of Pinot Gris and 260 kg of Blauburgunder. The first recorded Eiswein of the Basel region, it was hailed in the *Baseler Zeitung* as evidence that Basel viticulture is "innovative."[2]

Such innovation has been challenging in recent years. "In the last several years, Eiswein has seldom been produced," says Dr. Werner Koblet, a retired director of Wädenswil. "We have had several mild winters in a row and not enough freezing days. Cellarmasters now make more straw wine. The production of both specialties remains very small [because] there is not a big demand for either type of wine."[3]

For years, the rules of making wine in Switzerland were not well defined, perhaps because, with a healthy domestic market for their wines, the Swiss have not had to pay much attention to export markets and their wine labeling demands. However, in the 1990s, an appellation system was devised. Switzerland is not yet a member of the European Union (and the majority of its citizens are opposed to joining) but the wine industry's regulations are beginning to move closer to those elsewhere in Europe. According to Dr. Koblet, there was no strict regulation for Eiswein in 2001. "This will soon change with bilateral contacts between the European Community and Switzerland," he predicts. Already, there is an effort to assure that label terminology distinguishes naturally made Eisweine from those made with the help of a freezer.

"If the [wine] control boards know of such cases, they force the producers to mention 'cryo-extraction' or something similar on the label in order to inform the consumer correctly. With the term, 'Eiswein,' the consumer knows it is really produced with cold fingers and hard work in the dark."

Weinbau Erich Andrey Hauptstrasse 29, 2514 CH-Ligerz

Regarded by his peers as one of the Bielersee region's best winemakers, Andrey made the region's first Eiswein in 1998 from Chasselas grapes that had remained on the vine for more maturity and were caught by an early frost on November 19. At 4 A.M., with the temperature at -8°C, Andrey picked two metric tonnes of fruit, producing 450 liters of Eiswein.

Peter und Reni Baur-Ammon Weinbau Hegi 26, CH-8197 Rafz

P eter Baur-Ammon and his wife, Reni, operate six hectares of vineyards. The grapes from four hectares are sold. Since 1988, when he was 20, Peter has been making wine from the remaining two, producing Müller-Thurgau, Kerner and Pinot Noir in a variety of styles. He made his first Eiswein in 1991, about 150 liters from Pinot Noir.

"It is not possible to produce it every year," his wife says. The winery makes it "because it's something special and it is possible to make a 'real' Eiswein in the northeastern part of Switzerland because of the temperatures. We are going out at four o'clock in the morning and picking the grapes at -7°C or -8°C at a minimum." Subsequent Eiswein vintages were 1992, 1993, 1995 and 1998.

Weingut Jürg Saxer im Bruppach CH-8413 Neftenbach

A t this winery near Zurich, Jürg Saxer and his winemaker, Albin Decker, made his first Eiswein in 1991, following up with four other vintages (always with Pinot Noir) through the decade when conditions were right. Harvests have been as early as November and as late as mid-January. Production averages about a thousand half bottles in each Eiswein vintage. When it is not cold enough for Eiswein, Saxer settles for late harvest wine from the grapes.

Saxer acquired the vineyard here in 1974 and added a winery

in the early 1990s. The ambitious Saxer, who also makes wines from grapes imported from Languedoc in the south of France, likes to make wines debunking the notion that Switzerland only produces top white wines. His range includes Pinot Noir, either on its own or blended with Dornfelder. He even pressed Pinot Noir into service for his first Eiswein in 1992 and for three subsequent Eisweine during the decade. The production averages about one thousand half bottles each vintage.

Gasser-Bircher Weinbau Schmalzgasse 20, CH-8215 Hallau

E rnst Gasser and his wife Esther, who have grown grapes for a generation near Hallau, one of the most northerly communities in eastern Switzerland, decided in the 1990s to create their own label. Relying on contract winemaking, they produce about 10,000 bottles a year. They added Eiswein to their selection of wines because, as their son Benjamin explains, "to sell wine, you have to do new things or have more special things that other producers don't have."

In 1999, they sent some of their late harvest Blauburgunder (Pinot Noir) grapes to their contract processor who, with the aid of artificial freezing, produced 1,060 half bottles of 1999 Hallauer "Wunderstaa" Eiswein. The grapes were picked at the beginning of November and stored for eight days in a freezer at -12°C until they were thoroughly frozen. Pressing was done a few degrees above that, extracting a juice of 172° Oechsle. "By this method the risk is not so great as with the traditional method," Ernst Gasser explains.

G eri and Beatrice Leinhard, who founded this winery in 1985 based on a small vineyard about 25 km north of Zurich, began making Eiswein in 1990 with Müller-Thurgau. "I am a type who is quite curious about new things," Geri explains. "I had heard about Eiswein." He was not too pleased with his vintages in 1990 and 1991 because the grapes were not sufficiently frozen. "For a good Eiswein, I need -9°C or -10°C to get the concentration I am looking for." That happened in 1994 when he was able to make a dense and complex Eiswein with Blauburgunder.

Teufener
Eiswein
1999

WEINGUT,
Gerilienhard
TEUFEN ZH

In the subsequent vintages of 1995, 1996 and 1999, he added about 20 per cent Gewürztraminer to the Eiswein cuvée to give the wine more complexity. His production ranges from five hundred to one thousand half bottles.

His 1999 vintage was challenging because a severe wind storm in late December ripped away the nets covering the vines, leaving the grapes exposed to birds and animals. In desperation, Leinhard and 15 of his friends picked the grapes into baskets, placing them in cool storage. Later, when the temperature dropped into Eiswein range, the baskets were placed outside. When the grapes had frozen, Leinhard pressed them to yield about a thousand half bottles of Eiswein. After that experience, he left no grapes for Eiswein in 2000 in what turned out to be a fortunate decision. The winter was unusually mild.

Emil Nüesch AG Haupstrasse 71, CH-9463 Balgach

E stablished in 1834, this winery has grown to become one of eastern Switzerland's larger producers, making about 1.5 million liters of wine a year. But when it comes to Eiswein, the volume, typical for a Swiss winery, is modest, ranging between five hundred and fifteen hundred liters in those vintages when it can be made.

Andreas Müller, the winery's manager, made his first Eiswein in 1991 with Pinot Noir grapes from a vineyard on the steep slope below Schloss Grünenstein, the small castle overlooking the village of Balgach. "It was an enological curiosity," he admits. Subsequent Eiswein vintages from this vineyard were made in 1992, 1995 and 1999. In 1994, Müller also made an Eiswein from a grower-owned vineyard at Zizers, a village south of Balgach.

Now that Eiswein has become more than a curiosity, Müller laments: "I've had years when I've left grapes hanging and it never got cold." The Eisweine, light and delicate in style, are sought out by the winery's preferred customers and specialty restaurants.

Weingut am Rosenberg Tramstrasse 23, 9442 CH-Berneck

The Schmid family has made wine here since 1866 and now owns 11 hectares, including some top Pinot Noir sites. This is the grape from which the Schmids first made Eiswein in 1976. Small quantities of Eiswein, naturally frozen, have been made in a number of subsequent vintages.

Weingut zum Sternen Rebschulweg 2, CH-5303 Würenlingen

Ths winery, which dates from 1828, now operates seven hectares of vineyard, planted primarily with mainstream varieties. However, the winery also does extensive research. Winemaker Barbara Meier made her first Eiswein in 1998 when natural frost caught grapes hanging in the experimental plot. Consequently, she says that "about 100 different varieties" comprised the Eiswein that year. It was blended in 1999 with grapes picked and frozen artificially before being pressed. Only about 100 liters of Eiswein were made from this combined vintage.

The largest wine producer in the German-speaking part of eastern Switzerland, this cooperative celebrated its centenary in 2000. It is owned by 430 growers in six cantons (Aargau, Graubünden, Schaffhausen, St. Gallen, Thurgau and Zürich).

In 1990, when a surplus of grapes taxed the winery's capacity Urs Schweingruber, the winemaker decided to solve the problem by making his first Eiswein. "The solution was to make a little wine from a lot of grapes," he laughs. He made a quick trip to Germany for advice on Eiswein prior to picking the grapes. In this and seven subsequent vintages, Schweingruber has always employed Pinot Noir from a VOLG-owned vineyard near Hallau, a village near the German border. VOLG operated a small winery there until 1997 and still has a press there for processing Eiswein grapes.

Schweingruber, who maintains he was the first winemaker in Switzerland to make Eiswein, has improved his mastery of this wine since 1990 when he made 670 liters of wine from grapes harvested at -9°C just before dawn on December 7. The fermentation proceeded unchecked until it ended naturally. Consequently, that first Eiswein, with a spicy orange-peel aroma and the flavor of plum jam, has a bold 14.4 per cent alcohol and a lean structure. Since 1996, Schweingruber has been fermenting the wine at cooler temperatures, stopping it when alcohol is around 10 per cent and the natural sweetness remains more intense.

One of his most remarkable wines of the decade is the polished 1997 Eiswein, a plump, concentrated wine with an intense cassis aroma. Because the grapes were picked very late, on February 8, 1998, only 230 liters of wine was made. The winery takes the risk of making Eiswein every vintage, at times with unfortunate results. In the 2000 vintage, the weather never was cold enough and the grapes were abandoned. Gabriela Müller, the winery's marketing director, acknowledges: "The challenge in this part of Switzerland is to have the right temperature."

The winery's Eisweine, purchased by collectors and restaurants, are offered in VOLG's catalogue for 55 Swiss francs a half bottle, a price comparable to the retail value of most Canadian icewines. That yields a good profit to justify the risk, based on Schweingruber's calculations. He determined that cost of production of the 1990 Eiswein was just over 30 Swiss francs a liter.

Weidmann Weinbau Unterburg 67, 8158 Regensberg

It is a measure of Felix Weidmann's ambition that he extracts at least two dozen different wines from this winery's four hectares of vineyard, just northwest of Zurich. The wines range from finely crafted sparkling wines to what seems improbable in Switzerland, a Port-style wine called L'Esprit du Jura.

Born in 1961, Weidmann worked in wineries in France, Spain, South Africa and Australia after he graduated from Wädenswil's winemaking program. The Weidmann winery was established in 1957 by his father and was managed for several years by Thomas Weidmann, Felix's younger brother, until Thomas emigrated to Australia. With his international experience, Felix since 1995 has transformed the winery, planting superior clones of Pinot Noir and daring to plant Sauvignon Blanc, a variety not even approved in his region until recently.

Felix and his brother made a first tentative pass at Eiswein in 1989, making a late harvest wine from grapes that were only lightly frozen. Since 1993, the winery has made a small quantity of Pinot

Noir Eiswein only in a handful of vintages when it was cold enough to do so naturally; he refuses to make cryo-extracted wine.

In 1999, Felix recalls, he had abandoned hope of making Eiswein as Christmas approached without cold weather. Then on December 23, the temperature dropped and his picking crew phoned that they would deliver frozen grapes to the winery after all. Felix was overjoyed to make his first Eiswein in three years, some 70 liters of a finely balanced wine with the aromas and flavors of a fruit compote.

Notes

Preface

1. H.W. Yoxall, *The Enjoyment of Wine* (London: Michael Joseph, 1972), p. 123.

Chapter 1

1. Richard Olney, *Yquem* (Boston: David R. Godine, Publisher, Inc., 1986).

2. Jerome Richard, "The Ice Wine Cometh," *Wine Enthusiast*, February 1994, page 34.

3. Jeffrey Benson, and Alistair Mackenzie, *Sauternes: A study of the great sweet wines of Bordeaux* (London: Sotheby's Publications, 1990) p. 30.

4. Gerhard Troost, *Handbuch de Getränketechnologie Technologie des Weines;* (Stuttgart, Verlag Eugen Ulmer, 1980), p. 35.

5. Alexander Dorozynski, and Bibiane Bell, *The Wine Book: Wines and Wine Making Around the World;* (New York, Golden Press, 1969), page 171.

6. Translation provided by Hans-Joachim Binz of Schmitt Söhne winery at Longuich in the Mosel.

7. Michael Broadbent, *The Great Vintage Wine Book* (New York, Albert A. Knopf, 1980).

8. Ibid, page 317.

9. Ibid, page 329.

10. Hugh Johnson, *Wine* (New York: Mitchell Beazley Publishers Ltd., 1966; revised 1974) p. 248.

Chapter 2

1. Hugh Johnson, *The Atlas of German Wines* (New York: Simon & Shuster, 1986) p. 69.

2. Ibid.

3. Stephen Brook, *Liquid Gold: Dessert Wines of the World,* (New York: William Morrow & Co., 1987) pp. 164–174.

4. *The Atlas of German Wines,* p. 17.
5. *Das Weinkloster Eberbach im Rheingau,* (Eltville, Verwaltung der Staatsweingüter, 1988) p. 73.

Chapter 3

1. From an historical sketch provided by Schloss Johannisberg.
2. Serena Sutcliffe, *Great Vineyards and Winemakers* (New York The Rutledge Press, 1981).
3. Stephen Brook, *Liquid Gold: Dessert Wines of the World* (New York: William Morrow & Co., 1987).

Chapter 5

1. Phillip Blom, *The Wines of Austria* (London: Faber and Faber, 2000), p. 11.
2. Ibid., p. 12.
3. Brook, p. 225

Chapter 7

1. Interview with author, February 1999.
2. Interview with author, March 2001.
3. Interview with author, March 2001.
4. Interview with author, March 2001.
5. David Coombs, *The Coombs Guide to Ontario Icewine,* 1992. Privately published.
6. Interview with Everett De Jong, Pelee Island export manager, February 2001.
7. Interview with author, February 1999.
8. Interview with author, April 2000.

Chapter 8

1. Interview with author, February 1999.

Chapter 10

1. Tony Aspler, *Wine Tidings,* October 1993, pp. 8–10.

Chapter 12

1. Leon D. Adams, *The Wines of America,* 3rd ed. (New York, McGraw-Hill Book Co.), p. 205.

Chapter 13

1. Bonny Doon Vineyard, Spring 1999, p. 6.

Chapter 14

1. Mišo Alkalaj, *Wines of Slovenia* (Ljubljana, DZS, d.d, 1996).
2. *Basler Zeitung*, May 12, 2000.
3. Interview with author, April 2001.

Bibliography

Adams, Leon D. *The Wines of America,* Third Edition, McGraw-Hill Book Co., New York.

Alkalaj, Mišo. *Wines of Slovenia,* DZS, d.d, Ljubljana, 1996.

Ambrosi, Hans. *Where the Great German Wines Grow: A Guide to the Leading Vineyards,* Hastings House Publishers Inc., New York, 1976.

————. *Wine-Atlas German and Dictionary,* Ceres-Verlag Rudolf-August Oetker KG, Bielefeld, 1976.

Aspler, Tony. *Vintage Canada,* McGraw-Hill Ryerson, Toronto, 1999.

Benson, Jeffrey and Mackenzie, Alistair. *Sauternes: A study of the great sweet wines of Bordeaux;* Sotheby's Publications, London, 1990.

Blom, Philipp. *The Wines of Austria,* Faber and Faber, London, 2000.

Borrello, Joe. *Wineries of the Great Lakes,* Spradlin & Associates, Lapeer, MI, 1995.

Bramble, Linda and Darling, Shari. *Discovering Ontario's Wine Country,* Stoddart Publishing Co., Toronto, 1992.

Broadbent, Michael: *The Great Vintage Wine Book,* Albert A. Knopf, New York, 1980.

Brook, Stephen. *Liquid Gold — dessert wines of the world,* William Morrow and Co., New York, 1987.

Cobbold, David. *les plus grands crus: The Great Wines and Vintages,* Chartwell Books Inc., Edison, NJ, 1997.

Coombs, David G. *The Coombs Guide to Ontario Icewine,* Evergold Enterprises, Toronto, 1992.

Das Weinkloster Eberbach im Rheingau, Verwaltung der Staatsweingüter, Eltville, 1988.

Diel, Armin and Payne, Joel. *German Wine Guide,* Abbeville Press Publishers, New York, 1999.

Dorozynski, Alexander and Bell, Bibiane. *The Wine Book: Wines and Wine Making Around the World;* Golden Press, New York, 1969.

Hallgarten, Fritz. *Wine Scandal,* Weidenfeld and Nicolson, London, 1986.

Johnson, Hugh. *The Atlas of German Wines,* Simon & Shuster, New York, 1986.

———. *Wine,* Mitchell Beazley Publishers Ltd., New York, 1966; revised 1974.

Laverick, Charles. *The Beverage Testing Institute's Buying Guide to Wines of North America,* Sterling Publishing Co., New York, 1999.

MacDonogh, Giles. *New Wines from the Old World: The Wines of Austria,* Österreichischer Agrarverlag, Klosterneuburg, 1997.

———. *The Wines and Food of Austria,* Mitchell Beazley Publishers, London, 1992.

Meinhard, Heinrich. *The Wines of Germany,* The International Wine and Food Society's Publishing Co., 1976.

Olney, Richard. *Yquem,* David R. Godine, Publisher, Inc., Boston, 1986.

Ray, Cyril. *The Wines of Germany,* Penguin Books, Harmondsworth, UK, 1977.

Robinson, Jancis. *The Oxford Companion to Wine,* Oxford University Press, Oxford, 1994.

Schreiner, John. *The Wineries of British Columbia,* Orca Book Publishers, Victoria, 1994.

———. *The British Columbia Wine Companion,* Orca Book Publishers, Victoria, 1996.

Sloan, John C. *The Surprising Wines of Switzerland,* Bergli Books AG, Basel, 1996.

Swiss Wine Exporters' Association. *Swiss Wines: A World of Difference,* Lausanne, 1996.

Sutcliffe, Serena. *André Simon's Wines of the World,* Second edition, McGraw-Hill Book Co., New York, 1981.

———. *Great Vineyards and Winemakers,* The Rutledge Press, New York, 1981.

Troost, Gerhard. *Handbuch de Getränketechnologie Technologie des Weines;* Verlag Eugen Ulmer, Stuttgart, 1980, page 35.

Wagner, Philip M. *Grapes Into Wine, A Guide to Winemaking in America,* Alfred A. Knopf, New York, 1976.

Yoxall, H.W. *The Enjoyment of Wine,* Michael Joseph, London, 1972.

Ziraldo, Donald J.P *Anatomy of a Winery: The Art of Wine at Inniskillin,* Key Porter, Toronto, 2000.

Index